Tracie Cantu

Running L&D Like a Business

Drive Value With Learning Operations

atd
PRESS
Alexandria, VA

© 2026 ASTD DBA the Association for Talent Development (ATD)
All rights reserved.

29 28 27 26   1 2 3 4 5

No part of this publication may be reproduced, distributed, or transmitted in any form or by any means, including photocopying, recording, information storage and retrieval systems, or other electronic or mechanical methods, without the prior written permission of the publisher, except in the case of brief quotations embodied in critical reviews and certain other noncommercial uses permitted by copyright law. For permission requests, please go to copyright.com, or contact Copyright Clearance Center (CCC), 222 Rosewood Drive, Danvers, MA 01923 (telephone: 978.750.8400; fax: 978.646.8600).

ATD Press is an internationally renowned source of insightful and practical information on talent development, training, and professional development.

ATD Press
1640 King Street
Alexandria, VA 22314 USA

Ordering information: Books published by ATD Press can be purchased by visiting ATD's website at td.org/books or by calling 800.628.2783 or 703.683.8100.

Library of Congress Control Number: 2025949259

ISBN-10: 1-96339-210-8
ISBN-13: 978-1-963392-10-4
e-ISBN: 978-1-96339-211-1

ATD Press Editorial Staff
Director: Sarah Halgas
Manager: Melissa Jones
Content Manager: Bianca Woods
Developmental Editor: Shelley Sperry
Production Editor: Katy Wiley Stewts
Text and Cover Designer: Shirley E.M. Raybuck

Text Layout: Kathleen Dyson

More Praise for *Running L&D Like a Business*

"This book meets busy L&D teams where they are and shows you exactly how to align with the business, ship great work faster, and tell a results story that leaders will believe."
—**Ryan Austin,** Founder and CEO, Cognota

"If you're stuck defending your relevance instead of driving results, this book gives you the frameworks to help your L&D team operate like the strategic business function it should be and finally prove your impact."
—**Robyn A. Defelice, PhD,** LearnOps Whisperer and Consultant, RADLearning

"This isn't just a book; it's a blueprint. If you've ever struggled to connect your L&D work to business outcomes, Tracie's approach will help you make that shift with confidence. Whether you're leading a large L&D team or flying solo, *Running L&D Like a Business* offers a clear, practical road map to move from being a training provider to a strategic business partner."
—**David Kelly,** Former Chairman and CEO, The Learning Guild

"*Running L&D Like a Business* is the playbook today's learning leaders need to connect their strategies directly to business outcomes. Tracie Cantu shows how to transform L&D from a support function into a disciplined, data-informed business partner that drives measurable performance."
—**Debbie Richards,** Chief Learning Advisor, Cognota

"*Running L&D Like a Business* will transform how you see learning and development—not as a peripheral function, but as a revenue driving business asset. If you're ready to stop training reactively and start delivering real business value, this book is your strategic road map."
—**Betty Dannewitz,** Founder, CEO, and the actual Betty of ifyouaskbetty

To Rick, Marie, and Carmen—my life is infinitely richer for having you in it.

For my parents, although you aren't entirely sure what I do for a living, I know you're proud and will always be there for me.

Contents

Introduction: The Changing Role of L&D in Business — vii

Part 1. Business Alignment
- Chapter 1. Your L&D Business Model — 1
- Chapter 2. Business-Focused Learning Needs — 29

Part 2. Scaling Learning Operations
- Chapter 3. Repeatable, Reliable, and Responsive Learning — 55
- Chapter 4. Your Learning Portfolio — 83

Part 3. Driving L&D Innovation
- Chapter 5. Emerging Technologies — 105
- Chapter 6. Modern Learning Methodologies — 127

Part 4. Navigating Agility and Change
- Chapter 7. Strategic Agility — 151
- Chapter 8. Change Management in L&D — 171

Part 5. Demonstrating Value and Continuous Improvement
- Chapter 9. The Impact of L&D — 191
- Chapter 10. A Culture of Continuous Improvement — 211

Conclusion: L&D at a Crossroads — 231

References — 245

Index — 251

About the Author — 257

About ATD — 259

Introduction
The Changing Role of L&D in Business

Expectations of what L&D can and should do have changed. Senior leaders now want learning teams to enable transformation, improve performance, and drive measurable outcomes. Upskilling and reskilling are business imperatives, not HR side projects. The speed of change and shifts in the workforce mean that learning is now, more than ever, a critical lever for business success.

But while expectations have changed, many L&D teams are still working with outdated structures and ad hoc processes that make it nearly impossible to keep up, let alone show a measurable impact. Too often, our teams are organized simply to fulfill requests, not to solve business problems. As an L&D leader, you may be producing well-designed programs, getting positive feedback, and posting solid completion rates, but your team may still be seen as a cost center instead of a strategic partner and cannot seem to prove its value to the business. When the chief financial officer (CFO) asks how your L&D work drives revenue, reduces risk, or accelerates time to performance, you might struggle to find an answer. In other words, you likely find yourself trapped between expectations and execution, without knowing how to bridge that gap.

I wrote this book to address all these challenges.

Run L&D Like a Business

If our L&D teams want a seat at the table, we must start running like a business. That means aligning tightly to strategic goals. It means managing resources and workflows with rigor. It means prioritizing initiatives based on business outcomes, not internal preferences. It also means proving our value using the same language the business already understands—the language of revenue, risk, efficiency, and performance.

Running L&D like a business isn't about turning learning into a profit center; it's about applying the same clarity, discipline, and alignment that drives every other successful business function. Finance has budgets and forecasts. Marketing has campaigns and metrics. Operations has process maps and efficiency targets. L&D needs its own blueprints that ensure every initiative is tied to a business need, delivered efficiently, and measured rigorously.

In this book, you'll find the tools to create blueprints that work for L&D functions. You'll learn how to manage learning demand like a service organization, prioritize requests based on strategic value, and use data to demonstrate impact, not just activity. You'll shift from fulfilling training requests to solving business problems. And you'll reframe your role from content creator to performance enabler.

If we want our L&D teams to be seen as indispensable partners in driving growth, transformation, and agility, this approach isn't optional. It's now a necessity.

The Case for Learning Operations

How can we bring this new approach to life? *Learning operations*—my framework for turning L&D into a high-performing business function—brings structure, discipline, and business alignment to everything L&D does. It gives teams a way to scale results without increasing headcount. It also enables us to demonstrate value clearly, consistently, and credibly.

This is your guide to building a Learning Operations Blueprint™ and a Learning Impact Reporting Blueprint™. Use this book to discover how to:

- Build a business model for L&D that defines your value and the people you serve.
- Align learning initiatives directly with customer (business) needs while delivering exceptional experiences for consumers (employees).
- Streamline operations to quickly and consistently deliver high-quality content.
- Leverage data to prove results and continuously improve.

- Stay agile, even when the business shifts and priorities change overnight.

Whether you're an L&D leader at a Fortune 500 company or a team of one at a midsize business, the principles of the Learning Operations Blueprint apply. They work because they mirror how other functions operate by focusing on value, efficiency, alignment, and performance.

A Mindset Shift

L&D can't afford to be reactive in the fast-moving world of business. Leaders don't want another request for more budget without a clear return. Companies with mature L&D capabilities are more resilient, innovative, and profitable, but this kind of maturity doesn't happen by accident. It's built through operational rigor and requires a mindset shift.

L&D must stop seeing itself only as a service provider and start acting like a business unit with customers, consumers, and a measurable value proposition. That shift begins when we understand the critical distinction between our customers and our consumers:

- **The customer is the business.** The business funds your work, expects a return on investment (ROI), and defines success in terms of performance outcomes like speed, productivity, retention, and compliance.
- **The consumers are the employees.** They engage with your work. They build skills, apply knowledge, and demonstrate whether learning sticks.

L&D must serve both, but the order matters. When L&D meets the needs of the business first, it earns the opportunity to design learning that resonates with employees. Prioritizing employee experience without a clear business case often leads to budget cuts and reduced influence. Prioritizing *only* business metrics can lead to disengaged employees and low adoption.

Our goal is not equal attention. Our goal is *sequenced attention*. Business alignment comes first; then, learning experiences can be designed to achieve those outcomes in ways that work for employees. This book will show you how to achieve this sequenced alignment and why it matters. For example:

- **If L&D prioritizes only the business,** then training becomes transactional, and engagement suffers.

- **If L&D prioritizes only the employees,** engagement may increase, but the business impact is unclear.
- **If L&D prioritizes both the business and employees—in the right sequence**—your L&D team earns credibility, funding, and influence.

Who Is This Book For?

I wrote this book for anyone responsible for or involved in the success of learning and development, regardless of team size or industry. The Learning Operations principles apply across the board, and if you want to elevate your L&D function from a reactive role to that of a strategic business partner, this book is for you.

Specifically, this book is for:

- **L&D leaders at organizations of any size.** If you lead or support a learning function, whether as part of a large team or as a team of one—you'll find practical strategies to scale your influence, align more tightly with business goals, and clearly demonstrate value. You're likely managing competing priorities, facing resource constraints, or juggling fragmented processes. This book will help you move from reactive to proactive with tools designed to run L&D like a business.
- **HR and talent leaders who oversee learning.** If you're in an HR, talent development, or employee experience department, you understand that learning is critical to engagement, retention, and performance. This book gives you a way to partner more effectively with L&D or bring structure to learning programs under your purview, especially if learning is just one part of your portfolio.
- **Executives and senior leaders who fund L&D.** If you're responsible for approving L&D budgets or evaluating the ROI of learning programs, this book will help you understand how modern learning teams can directly contribute to business growth, agility, and workforce capability. It outlines what *good* looks like and what to ask for from your learning leaders to ensure your investments in L&D are delivering measurable returns.

The bottom line? If you're tired of L&D being seen as a cost center or struggling to prove its value, this book will show you how to run L&D like a business.

Let's now walk through how the book is structured so you can find what matters most to you and your team.

What to Expect in the Chapters Ahead

We'll break down the five pillars of learning operations one by one:

- **In part 1, Business Alignment,** you'll learn how to build your L&D business model, define who your real customers are, and align every initiative to strategic business goals.
- **In part 2, Scaling Learning Operations,** you'll explore how to standardize core processes, prioritize efficiently, and manage demand with discipline, whether you have a team of two or 200.
- **In part 3, Driving L&D Innovation,** you will learn how to vet new technologies and methods through a business lens, ensuring innovation solves real problems rather than adding complexity.
- **In part 4, Navigating Agility and Change,** you will discover how to stay flexible as business needs shift. We'll cover rapid response strategies, internal consulting skills, and how to pivot without chaos.
- **In part 5, Demonstrating Value and Continuous Improvement,** you will learn how to define and measure impact, report results in business language, and build a culture of continuous improvement inside your L&D function.

A Word About Words

Throughout this book, you'll notice a few intentional word choices. I want to share the reasoning behind them up front.

I deliberately use the word *employee* instead of *learner*. While *learner* may appear more aligned with our profession, the word *employee* reinforces the reality that our primary customer is the business. Our work exists to support the organization and the people who make it run, not an idealized version of a learner.

I also use the term *data-informed* rather than *data-driven*. Data should guide decisions, not dictate them. While data is critical for insight and alignment, it does not always capture context or nuance. Human judgment still matters.

Finally, I use the terms *learning* and *training* somewhat interchangeably. I understand that for many in our field, these terms have distinct meanings, but the business doesn't make that distinction. They use both to describe any development effort, and part of our role is to speak to the language of the business. My goal is not to debate semantics. It is to connect L&D to business outcomes in terms leaders already understand. My aim is clarity, alignment, and impact, and all those goals start with clear communication.

A Final Thought Before We Begin

The gap between L&D's potential and the perception of L&D by business leaders has never been wider than it is as I write this book. But it doesn't have to stay that way. If you want to close that gap, run L&D like a business, scale your results, and secure your influence, you're in the right place.

Let's get to work.

PART 1
Business Alignment

Chapter 1
Your L&D Business Model

At a Fortune 500 healthcare company, the L&D team had been producing high-quality learning programs for years. Their learning management system (LMS) was full, their net promoter scores (NPS) were solid, and internal surveys showed employees were satisfied. However, when a new executive team asked how those programs were contributing to patient retention, reduced onboarding time, and clinic profitability, the team didn't have an answer. They had data–just not the kind the business cared about. Within 18 months, the L&D budget was cut by nearly 40 percent–not because the team lacked talent, but because they couldn't clearly connect their work to business outcomes.

This is a common situation. Many L&D teams build learning programs without a defined business model, a clear articulation of who their customers are, what problems they're solving, or how value will be measured. The result is a function that works hard but struggles to prove its worth to the rest of the organization.

How do you avoid that trap? You can start by running L&D like a business. This new approach begins with a clear business model, one that defines how the L&D function creates, delivers, and measures value in support of organizational priorities. Without a solid model, even the most well-designed programs risk being seen as disconnected from the work that matters most.

In too many organizations, the L&D department is seen as a functional necessity that fulfills training requests and ensures compliance. But beyond that limited scope, L&D has the potential for so much more, including the potential to drive significant business outcomes, enhance workforce capabilities, increase operational efficiency, and foster innovation. However, most L&D teams struggle to assert their strategic value. Instead of shaping the learning agenda, they react to business demands, delivering courses without a clear connection to business priorities. In this chapter, we will start building a blueprint to help you enhance and better communicate L&D's strategic business value so your L&D team and your organization can reach their full potential.

The Business Case for a Strategic L&D Function

Organizations with a strong learning culture are 92 percent more likely to develop innovative products and processes and 52 percent more productive than their competitors (Brassey, Christensen, and van Dam 2019). Despite this clear link between learning and business success, L&D teams often face budget cuts, leadership skepticism, and misalignment with company strategy. Why? Because many L&D teams fail to demonstrate their direct effect on business outcomes.

To change this perception, L&D needs to operate as a strategic business function that aligns its efforts with organizational priorities, optimizes efficiency, and leverages technology to deliver measurable results. You can do this by developing a structured L&D business model to address the needs of business leaders and employees while establishing L&D as a critical driver of performance and growth.

Building a New L&D Business Model

A modern L&D function must operate with the same rigor and intentionality as any other business unit, and to do that, L&D needs a structured business model that aligns learning with real business outcomes. The Learning Operations Business Model™ (which we will explore in this chapter) provides a practical framework to guide creation, delivery, and measurement of value across your organization. The model consists of four interconnected components:

- Business alignment
- Operational efficiency
- High customer value
- Positive consumer experience

We can begin exploring each of these four components by asking a framing question.

Business Alignment

As we begin to align L&D with the business, there's a question we should start with: *Are we building what the business actually needs to achieve its goals?* You must understand the business's goals, strategies, and performance gaps. This means identifying the few critical priorities leaders are most focused on—such as entering a new market, improving retention, or accelerating innovation—and unpacking the skills, behaviors, and performance outcomes needed to make those ambitions real. L&D leaders can do this by mapping the executive vision or business unit agenda, joining strategic planning sessions, and reviewing key performance indicators (KPIs), operational data, and employee feedback to spot capability gaps that hinder progress.

Once you understand those goals and gaps, they serve as a decision-making filter. Use them to determine which learning investments matter most, which can wait, and which may not be worth doing at all. With this clarity in place, business alignment is sustained when:

- Senior leaders model continuous learning.
- L&D closely partners with stakeholders to understand strategic objectives.
- Learning solutions are built to support measurable business outcomes.

Operational Efficiency

Can we deliver solutions faster, with less friction, and without sacrificing quality? This is the question that should frame our discussion of L&D's operational efficiency. Efficient operations are not about rigid process compliance. They're about building cultural habits that support consistency, adaptability, and speed to market. Operational efficiency depends on:

- Documented, repeatable, and scalable processes that reduce friction
- Clear intake, prioritization, and resourcing models
- Continuous feedback loops to improve how work gets done

High Customer Value

Can we prove how our work improves business and talent outcomes? In the case of customer value, we must start by answering this question. In the next section, we will explore why you should treat the business as your customer.

For now, just remember that customer value is about the tangible business outcomes your learning initiatives produce, including:
- Improved internal mobility or retention
- Faster speed to readiness
- Better performance or compliance outcomes

Positive Consumer Experience

The employees who participate in your learning experiences are your consumers, so the question you need to ask regarding the consumer experience is simple: *Is the learning content designed for the way people actually work and make decisions?* In the next section, we will dive further into your consumers' experiences, which help determine whether learning is actually applied. The consumer experience is shaped by:
- How learning shows up in daily work (not just in the LMS)
- Whether content is relevant, timely, and trusted
- How well learning fits within the flow of work

When you design your L&D function around these four essential components, you're not just delivering training; you're running L&D like a business.

Understanding How the Model Works: A Tale of Two L&D Teams

To understand how the Learning Operations Business Model plays out in practice, it helps to look at how different approaches show up inside real organizations. Let's consider two examples that illustrate the consequences of reactive versus strategic L&D functions, and how each shapes business perception and outcomes:

- **Company A's L&D team operates reactively.** Business leaders request training, and L&D delivers it with little business impact analysis. Courses are well-designed, but engagement is low, and no clear metrics exist to measure success. Over time, leadership questions the function's value, leading to budget reductions and diminished influence.
- **Company B's L&D team operates strategically.** They proactively engage with business leaders to understand challenges, identify

skills gaps, and design solutions that drive measurable outcomes. Training initiatives are aligned with KPIs, and success stories are regularly shared with executives. As a result, L&D is seen as a critical partner in business growth, securing greater investment and influence.

Pause to Reflect
What kind of L&D team do you want to lead and why?

These examples show us how an L&D team's approach can either limit or elevate its influence across the organization. To shift from reactive to strategic, L&D must understand the full scope of its relationships and responsibilities. Now, let's dive into the critical relationships between L&D and the business (customer) and between L&D and the consumer (employees) to understand how these connections shape priorities, expectations, and outcomes.

L&D's Customers and Consumers

There's a fundamental question all L&D leaders need to answer: *Whom does the L&D function actually serve?* The answer will define the function's priorities, structure workflows, and shape how learning content is delivered.

As I mentioned in the introduction, the Learning Operations Business Model starts with the premise that L&D serves two distinct groups: the business, which funds operations and expects measurable returns, and the employees, who engage with and apply what they learn to do their jobs better. To operate effectively, L&D must meet the needs of both groups. The way you prioritize and balance their needs will determine whether the function is seen as a cost center or a strategic driver of business success.

Often, in everyday conversation, the terms *customer* and *consumer* are used interchangeably, but in this model, the words describe distinctly different roles:

- **A customer is the decision maker who purchases a product or service, often on behalf of others.** For example, in a corporate setting, an L&D leader purchasing a learning platform for their organization is the customer; they make the decision and oversee the transaction.

- **A consumer is the end user who directly interacts with and benefits from the product or service.** In the previous example, the consumers are the employees who use the learning platform to build skills or complete required training.

The Business as L&D's Customer

The business (in the form of a board of directors or executive team) funds learning initiatives, establishes strategic objectives, and expects an ROI. The business wants assurance that training programs will improve efficiency, revenue growth, compliance, or other key business outcomes. This means L&D must present learning initiatives as both professional development opportunities and strategic solutions that drive measurable results. Table 1-1 shows some common business priorities and how L&D can support them.

Table 1-1. Common Business Priorities and How L&D Supports Them

Business Priority	L&D's Role
Increase revenue	Sales training and negotiation workshops
Improve customer satisfaction	Customer service programs and product training
Reduce compliance risks	Regulatory and safety training
Decrease employee turnover	Career development and leadership programs
Accelerate innovation	Upskilling programs in emerging technologies

First and foremost, L&D exists to support the growth and success of the business. Many organizations, however, fail to integrate learning into their core strategy. This is why it's so important for your L&D team to operate as a *business unit* within the organization, advocating for its role in achieving strategic priorities.

To do this effectively, L&D must demonstrate a clear understanding of business challenges and position learning solutions to address them. For example, suppose an organization is struggling with high turnover rates. L&D can align with HR and leadership to identify critical moments in the employee life cycle when L&D can affect retention and bench strength. If customer service ratings are declining, L&D can and should work with frontline teams to create targeted customer service programs that address and help mitigate customer complaints.

Another critical aspect of treating the business as your customer is ensuring that L&D investments are justified with data. Business leaders expect training initiatives to deliver tangible results, such as increased sales, higher productivity, or reduced risk. Therefore, L&D must implement robust measurement strategies that link learning efforts to KPIs. This includes tracking behavioral changes, performance improvements, and business outcomes, as well as participation rates, course completion, and assessment scores. Shifting traditional learning metrics (such as employee satisfaction scores, training hours delivered, and number of certifications) to business metrics (such as productivity improvements, cost savings through efficiency, revenue growth linked to training, and reductions in compliance incidents) reframes the narrative of L&D's value in terms the business is aligned on.

Employees as L&D's Consumers

While the business is funding the L&D function, its employees are determining the effectiveness of your products. Learning initiatives that fail to engage employees or align with their day-to-day responsibilities are unlikely to yield meaningful results. Employees often juggle multiple priorities, so consider these factors when designing learning experiences for employees:

- **Relevance.** Training should address real challenges and be immediately applicable in the workplace. Employees who cannot see how learning benefits them are unlikely to engage.
- **Accessibility.** Employees should be able to engage with learning on their terms, whether through mobile learning, microlearning, or on-demand resources that fit into their workflows.
- **Engagement.** Traditional e-learning modules often fail to capture attention. Interactive, scenario-based learning and social learning opportunities can enhance engagement and retention.
- **Support and reinforcement.** Learning is not a one-time event. Continuous reinforcement, coaching, and real-world application opportunities are necessary to retain and use knowledge.

Prioritizing these factors can help L&D create a learning culture that fosters individual and organizational growth.

Customer vs. Consumer: Two Approaches

Understanding the difference between the business as your customer and employees as your consumers is more than semantics. It fundamentally shapes how L&D prioritizes its work. Let's now explore two real-world examples that illustrate how different approaches to these relationships can significantly affect outcomes. These examples show how L&D's alignment or misalignment with the business and its learners can influence the function's credibility, funding, and ability to scale.

Company A: A Learner-Centric Approach Gone Wrong

A global retailer invested in a new learning experience platform with microlearning modules, gamification, and social learning features for its sales teams. The employees loved the platform, and engagement rates were sky-high.

Business leaders, however, weren't impressed. Net promoter scores (which gauge consumer satisfaction) and feedback remained stagnant, sales teams still struggled to meet sales goals, and turnover continued to rise. When executives asked about training effectiveness, the L&D team could only point to course completion rates and employee satisfaction surveys—not business outcomes. As a result, leadership cut the L&D budget the following year, shifting investment toward external consultants.

What went wrong?

The L&D team focused too much on the employee experience without aligning with business goals and demonstrating measurable results. After facing budget cuts, they began reevaluating their approach by meeting with business leaders to better understand performance gaps and identify where learning initiatives could directly support strategic priorities.

Company B: Balancing Business and Learner Needs to Maximize Value

An innovative tech company's L&D team took a different approach. Instead of focusing solely on engagement, they prioritized business outcomes across multiple sales teams, from creator and business advertisements to in-app purchases and SaaS enablement. Here are the actions the L&D team took:

- They met with senior leaders to identify top business challenges.
- They designed learning solutions that directly addressed critical skills gaps.

- They measured results beyond completion rates, tracking how training affected key metrics like sales growth and customer retention.

Accordingly, the results were crystal clear in their metrics:
- New-hire onboarding programs cut ramp-up time by 28 percent.
- Sales enablement training led to a 17 percent increase in revenue per sales rep.
- Leadership development programs increased internal promotions by 12 percent.

The key difference between Company A and Company B? The L&D team at Company B treated business leaders as their primary customers while still delivering meaningful learning experiences for employees.

Finding the Right Balance

Balancing the needs of business leaders and employees can be difficult even in the best of times and it always requires a thoughtful approach. When your L&D team leans too heavily toward business objectives, training can become transactional and employees may feel forced into programs that don't align with their needs. On the other hand, if L&D focuses only on engagement without considering business impact, it risks being perceived as a cost center rather than a strategic function.

Here are some ways to create a good balance:
- **Involve business leaders and employees in your learning design process.** Try using needs assessments, focus groups, and pilot programs that gather insights from stakeholders before scaling initiatives.
- **Leverage data to ensure programs meet business and employee needs.** Learning analytics can reveal which courses lead to measurable improvements, while employee feedback can identify gaps in content and delivery.
- **Shift from one-size-fits-all training to personalized learning experiences.** Not all employees need the same training, and businesses benefit when learning content is tailored to job roles and career paths. Adaptive learning technologies, skills assessments, and competency frameworks can help L&D align development opportunities with business priorities and employee career growth.

Pause to Reflect
What steps can you take to ensure your L&D function delivers measurable value to business leaders and employees?

L&D as a Strategic, Proactive Partner

Many L&D teams function reactively, responding to training requests without clearly supporting strategic objectives. To elevate its role, L&D must shift from being an order taker to becoming a proactive advisor by anticipating workforce challenges, aligning learning solutions to business goals, and driving measurable outcomes. A *reactive approach* results in fragmented learning initiatives that lack strategic value. By contrast, *proactive* L&D leaders engage in workforce planning, analyze financial reporting, and partner with business units to ensure learning drives performance. To achieve this, L&D must engage in strategic conversations, ensure learning objectives support business priorities, and propose solutions that address emerging needs.

A helpful way to assess L&D's current role within an organization is to consider the spectrum of roles from order taker to strategic partner. Order takers respond to requests without questioning business relevance, while strategic partners engage in problem solving and tailoring learning initiatives to broader organizational goals. If you are somewhere between these two, take stock of where you stand today and identify which behaviors, mindsets, and capabilities are holding you back. This awareness can help you chart a path toward becoming a true strategic partner. To move along the spectrum toward strategic partner, you will need to develop internal consulting skills, build credibility, and embed learning initiatives into business planning.

Developing a Consulting Mindset

Becoming a strategic partner is a journey that requires intentional change. The first and most important step is adopting a consulting mindset—moving beyond simply delivering training to solving real business problems. Instead of responding to requests with, "What training do you need?" you should ask, "What business outcome are you trying to achieve?" or "What business problem are you trying to solve?" This approach positions L&D as an enabler of performance, not a content provider, and gives you the ability to diagnose problems, understand how the business works, influence stakeholders, and say no when necessary.

An internal consultant knows how to diagnose problems. They don't just take requests at face value. They go beyond surface-level symptoms (such as "Employees don't know how to do X") to uncover the real barriers, whether they're unclear role expectations, broken processes, or a lack of leadership support. Techniques that can help validate assumptions before jumping to solutions include stakeholder interviews, data-driven analysis, Cathy Moore's Action Mapping visual design approach, and the Five Whys, which is a problem-solving method in which you repeatedly ask *why* to uncover deeper reasons for the problem each time (Moore n.d.; Serrat 2017).

An internal consultant also develops critical business acumen. L&D leaders must understand how their organizations make money, what metrics matter most to leadership, and how different functions contribute to success. They need to read corporate financial reports, attend strategy meetings, and actively listen to leaders' priorities.

Equally important, an internal consultant needs to know how to influence and manage stakeholders effectively. Being a strategic partner requires strong relationship-building skills, the ability to speak the language of the business, and the confidence to challenge ineffective solutions. Stakeholders often come to L&D with predetermined requests for training, but the best internal consultants guide the conversation toward identifying the real problem and propose alternative solutions that could drive better results. They may also have to push back when training isn't the answer, which leads us to our next critical skill.

An internal consultant learns when and how to say no. This is perhaps the most underrated and challenging skill for a strategic partner. When stakeholders request training that isn't aligned with business outcomes or won't solve the root problem, a well-prepared L&D leader should redirect the conversation toward solutions that will. For example, when a stakeholder asks, "Can you build a training course?" the L&D leader can shift the conversation by asking, "How can we solve this business challenge?" and offering scalable, just-in-time solutions instead of one-off courses.

Building Relationships With Stakeholders

Strengthening relationships with business stakeholders begins with aligning L&D initiatives to their priorities. Start by understanding their goals, challenges, and key metrics to frame L&D as a business driver, not just a support function. Engage stakeholders early, maintaining regular check-ins and demonstrating business acumen, to help position L&D as a strategic partner rather than a service provider. Among your most valuable tools in this pursuit will be clear communication, transparency, and data-driven storytelling. These tools can reinforce the value of learning investments, ensuring that L&D is seen as an enabler of business success.

Beyond aligning with stakeholders' priorities, L&D needs to deliver quick wins while also driving long-term results. *Quick wins* help solve relevant business problems, leverage technology for efficiency, and use automation to make learning more accessible. When L&D functions as a consultative partner—offering insights, anticipating needs, and demonstrating measurable results—it fosters more trust and deeper collaboration, ensuring that learning remains an integral part of the business strategy.

Use Structured Engagement

To strengthen relationships with stakeholders, L&D leaders should adopt a structured engagement approach that includes:

- Holding regular strategy meetings with business unit leaders to discuss learning needs and challenges
- Becoming involved in departmental reviews to identify skills gaps and workforce trends
- Collaborating with HR and talent management teams to integrate learning content into career pathways and succession planning
- Providing consultative reporting on a learning initiative's effectiveness and its influence on business outcomes.

One of the most effective ways to integrate L&D into your organization's business strategy is through a formalized stakeholder advisory group. This cross-functional group can provide ongoing input into learning initiatives and foster stronger relationships between L&D and the rest of the organization. Cultivating strong, continuous relationships with business stakeholders positions L&D as a strategic partner rather than a reactive service provider.

These close relationships with stakeholders also require you to adopt a data-driven approach to business alignment. That includes regularly engaging with business leaders, analyzing workforce trends, and using measurable data to guide you in prioritizing learning investments.

While this chapter introduces the foundational importance of stakeholder engagement, the next will expand on this concept by sharing a structured framework for integrating business priorities into L&D decision making, including the mechanics of effective stakeholder collaboration, methods for gathering critical data, diagnosing performance gaps rooted in business needs, and structuring learning priorities based on their potential business results.

Combating the Loss of Strategic Influence

Recent trends suggest that L&D's presence in business strategy discussions has diminished over time. Only about 40 percent of business leaders view L&D as a key strategic function (Brassey, Christensen, and van Dam 2019). Budget constraints, a lack of well-defined strategy, and an overemphasis on tactical execution have contributed to this decline. Unfortunately, when L&D is perceived as a transactional function or a cost center rather than a strategic enabler, it loses influence over many business decisions.

Without clear metrics linking learning initiatives to business outcomes, executives may deprioritize L&D in strategic planning. The rise of self-directed learning and digital learning platforms has also led some business leaders to believe that formal L&D departments are unnecessary.

To counteract this perception and loss of influence, L&D needs to take a more evidence-based approach to demonstrate its value. Using metrics such as employee performance improvement, retention rates, and business KPIs tied to learning outcomes can help L&D prove its strategic value. Learning leaders should present these insights in executive-level discussions, positioning L&D as a driver of business success.

The Need for Internal Marketing

Re-establishing L&D's strategic influence also requires internal marketing. L&D must advocate for its role by showcasing success stories, demonstrating ROI, and positioning learning initiatives as enablers to achieving company objectives. This can be accomplished by:

- Presenting learning impact reports at leadership meetings

- Showcasing case studies that illustrate how learning initiatives have solved business challenges
- Aligning learning outcomes with key corporate metrics such as revenue growth, customer satisfaction, and operational efficiency

Furthermore, L&D must cultivate executive sponsorship. Leaders who champion learning initiatives at the highest levels create organizational momentum for L&D's role in business success. Building relationships with key executives and demonstrating how your learning strategies support their priorities ensures that L&D is a key player in the decision-making process across the business.

Embedding L&D in Your Organizational Culture

A multibillion-dollar industrial distribution company recently faced a critical challenge: A quarter of employees were leaving the company after one year, with many of them citing a lack of development opportunities as the key reason for their departure. Recognizing that learning was not just a perk but a strategic necessity, the company built a highly effective learning organization that directly addressed the employees' concerns.

Company leaders launched a series of leadership development programs closely integrated with business goals, which also provided structured learning development pathways for employees, and the positive effect was measurable quickly.

Organizations that invest in a strong learning culture see measurable returns, including higher engagement, stronger retention, and sharper performance. Research from Gallup, LinkedIn, Josh Bersin, Deloitte, and McKinsey shows that employees who are offered continuous development are more engaged, more likely to stay, and part of organizations that deliver higher productivity, adapt faster to customer needs, and meet performance targets more consistently.

For your L&D function to be seen as a true strategic partner, it must become an integral part of your company and its culture. Organizations that embed learning into daily operations rather than treating it as a separate function see greater engagement, knowledge retention, and business results.

Embedding L&D successfully requires a shift from one-time training events to continuous learning experiences. Organizations can achieve this by:

- Integrating learning into employee workflows through just-in-time resources
- Encouraging leaders to act as learning champions who reinforce key development initiatives
- Establishing mentoring and coaching programs to drive experiential learning
- Creating a culture of growth and development by supporting and collaborating with talent management

Another way to embed L&D into company culture is by creating a learning ecosystem that combines formal training, peer learning, and on-the-job development. This approach encourages employees to take ownership of their growth while ensuring that learning remains aligned with business needs.

If you want to do a pulse check of your organization's learning culture, use the two scorecards in Tools 1-1 and 1-2 at the end of this chapter to get started. Here are four practical ways to use these scorecards:

- **For self-assessment.** Ask employees and leaders to score the L&D and business functions individually.
- **To compare perceptions.** Identify gaps between the employee experience and leadership expectations.
- **To prioritize action.** Focus on low-scoring areas and design initiatives to improve learning culture.
- **To reassess quarterly.** Track improvements over time and refine initiatives.

Future-Proofing L&D's Business Role

As organizations evolve, so must L&D. To remain relevant, L&D leaders need to anticipate shifts in the workforce, embrace new technologies, and continually refine their approaches to business alignment. Let's explore several ways your L&D team can future-proof itself and maintain strategic relevance:

- **Be aware of and use emerging technologies.** Learning platforms powered by artificial intelligence (AI), skills intelligence tools, and workforce analytics will redefine how organizations develop talent going forward. AI-powered recommendations can personalize learning content at scale, while skills intelligence platforms provide real-time insights into workforce capabilities.

- **Adopt a skills-based approach.** The shift toward skills-based organizations is a major trend that is reshaping L&D. Traditional job-based structures are being replaced by skills-first talent models, requiring L&D to rethink how it designs and delivers training. L&D must work cross-functionally to identify and define task and role-based skills, align learning initiatives with those frameworks, and integrate learning content into broader talent management strategies.
- **Plan strategically for the long term.** Strategic planning is essential for L&D to remain relevant. We will discuss this more in the next chapter, but be aware that a three-to-five-year road map should include three distinct phases:
    - Phase 1. Aligning learning metrics with business goals
    - Phase 2. Implementing AI and analytics-driven learning
    - Phase 3. Transitioning to a skills-based development approach

By positioning L&D as a business-critical function, L&D leaders can secure the function's role in driving long-term business growth. This requires more than keeping pace with change. It means operating strategically, supporting business priorities, and consistently delivering measurable value. This is why Learning Operations is essential. It's a blueprint that allows L&D to scale results, plan with intention, and execute with clarity without reinventing the wheel every time.

Pause to Reflect

What steps can you take in the next six months to move your L&D function closer to a strategic partner role?

Your Learning Operations Blueprint

As I mentioned, a Learning Operations Blueprint is a structured framework that ensures the L&D department works efficiently and aligns with business objectives. Your organization can use this blueprint to create consistency and effectiveness in learning functions by clearly defining processes, governance structures, and technology strategies. Establishing a blueprint also allows L&D teams to transition from ad hoc service providers to integral contributors to business success. You must focus on three key areas—people, process, and technology—to develop a fully effective Learning Operations Blueprint. We'll discuss the components here, and then in later chapters, we'll break down how each element comes to life through the tools, systems, and practices that turn L&D into a high-performing business function.

Why Learning Operations Matter

Scaling L&D isn't just about offering more training; it's about doing so with purpose and precision. Many organizations struggle because their processes are scattered, priorities are unclear, and resources aren't used effectively. The result? Learning efforts that make you feel busy but don't deliver meaningful outcomes. Research from McKinsey and BCG shows a clear difference when companies get this right: faster employee upskilling, higher retention, and significant cost savings driven by operational efficiency (Brassey, Christensen, and van Dam 2019; BCG Henderson Institute 2020).

Consider the example of a global tech company that overhauled its L&D structure with a centralized Learning Operations model. The effect wasn't subtle. It cut training costs by 40 percent, sharpened alignment with business priorities, and saw measurable growth in employee skills, leading to a 15 percent jump in workforce productivity. Centralizing its Learning Operations wasn't about adding more programs; it was about working smarter with what the organization already had.

For L&D leaders looking to create that kind of impact, three areas matter most:
- Linking learning with business goals so the value of L&D is undeniable
- Standardizing processes to support growth (without piling on additional headcount)
- Using automation, AI, and smarter tools to streamline content management and delivery

When your learning operations are set up in this way to work for the business, they will do more than support growth; they will help create it.

Structuring Your Team

For an L&D team to operate efficiently, it must have clearly defined roles and responsibilities. Instructional designers and facilitators must craft and deliver engaging content that supports the workforce development needs. Data analysts and learning technologists should track the effectiveness of learning programs and optimize technology solutions, ensuring that learning remains relevant and measurable.

A well-structured team enables an L&D function to operate proactively rather than reactively. Organizations can ensure that learning programs directly support company goals by fostering collaboration between L&D teams and other business units. This collaboration allows L&D to remain a business enabler rather than a transactional service provider.

Consider an example of this in practice at a digital freight forwarder company that adopted a federated L&D structure to balance consistency with flexibility. The central team provided shared tools and standards, while functional, dispersed teams customized learning content for their specific needs. This enabled faster deployment of relevant training programs and stronger partnerships with the business. As a result, the L&D function gained trust and credibility as a strategic business partner.

Defining Your Process

Defining clear processes for L&D ensures efficiency, scalability, and consistency across learning initiatives. For example, standardized intake mechanisms help L&D teams assess and prioritize training requests based on strategic objectives. Following a well-defined content development approach means learning materials maintain quality and relevance across various delivery methods. Ongoing evaluation and feedback mechanisms allow organizations to measure program effectiveness, adjust learning strategies, and continuously improve their L&D efforts.

An effective learning governance model establishes service-level agreements (SLAs) with business leaders to set expectations around learning delivery timelines, performance outcomes, and accountability. Establishing clear protocols for communication and alignment between L&D and functional leaders can further enhance the integration and value of learning.

Choosing Your Technology

Technology plays a crucial role in supporting learning strategies and scaling training programs. Your LMS centralizes learning delivery, tracking, and reporting. Learning experience platforms (LXPs), however, can create more personalized and interactive learning experiences. Analytics and reporting tools allow organizations to measure the effectiveness of their learning programs, identifying areas for improvement and ensuring alignment with business priorities. In addition, automation and AI can streamline administrative processes—reducing manual effort in course enrollment, employee support, and assessment tracking—and adaptive learning technologies can enhance the personalization of learning content so employees receive relevant information that supports their role or career development needs.

Choosing the right mix of tools matters. Organizations reportedly used an average of 11 learning systems in 2020, and that number is likely higher today (RedThread Research 2023). Without a clear strategy for selecting and integrating technology, L&D teams risk redundancy, inefficiency, and missed opportunities to connect learning initiatives with business outcomes.

Implementing the Blueprint

Once you have developed your Learning Operations Blueprint, successful implementation requires stakeholder alignment, effective communication, and continuous iteration. L&D must engage business leaders, HR, and functional teams so learning initiatives support broader workforce strategies. Change management efforts should focus on educating employees and leaders about the benefits of the new framework, emphasizing how structured learning strategies enhance business performance.

Pilot programs can help test new processes, gather feedback, and refine approaches before full-scale implementation. By regularly evaluating the effectiveness of learning initiatives, L&D functions can ensure their blueprint remains effective and adaptable to evolving business needs.

When I implemented the Learning Operations Blueprint at a midsize lending company, the objective was to streamline learning requests and ensure alignment with strategic goals. We initiated a pilot program in the loan servicing division, anticipating smooth adoption due to the operational nature of the work. However, we ran into unexpected resistance, not from our stakeholder, but from our own instructional designers. They were concerned that the new intake model would reduce their creative autonomy.

Recognizing the importance of their buy-in, we paused the rollout and quickly brought the team together to refine the process. This co-creation approach turned skeptics into advocates. Within two months, we had a more efficient process that provided space for creativity while introducing necessary checkpoints. The outcome was significant: a 30 percent reduction in redundant requests and an expedited deployment of priority programs. This experience highlights a vital component of the Learning Operations Blueprint: change management.

Addressing Change Management

Driving adoption of a Learning Operations Blueprint requires a structured change management approach focused on alignment, communication, and iterative improvement. You can prepare for change in many ways, but these steps are essential:

1. **Secure executive sponsorship and engage key stakeholders**—including business leaders, HR teams, and technology partners—early so they see the blueprint as a strategic enabler rather than an administrative hurdle.
2. **Establish a clear why behind the change,** linking it to business priorities like workforce agility, cost efficiency, or compliance.
3. **Use a phased rollout approach,** beginning with a pilot group to refine processes before scaling across business units.
4. **Reinforce the adoption of the blueprint through training, playbooks, and success stories,** ensuring teams understand the benefits and have practical guidance on execution.

Overcoming Roadblocks

Common roadblocks you will likely face include resistance to change, misalignment between L&D and business leaders, and technology friction. To mitigate these and ensure cross-functional collaboration, business leaders need visibility into how learning operations will drive measurable results, and your L&D team must be involved in shaping workflows.

Another frequent challenge L&D teams face is inconsistency in processes across decentralized teams. The solution is to define standardized, scalable processes while allowing for localized flexibility where needed. Consider the example of a global logistics company. It found that each regional office had its own approach to frontline training, making it difficult to track progress or maintain quality. The L&D team responded by partnering with operations to build a common training framework with required core modules, while giving regions the ability to tailor case studies and delivery formats to local needs.

Technology fragmentation is another problem that can slow your progress. At one global tech company, the learning team discovered that 57 separate tools were being used for training delivery, scheduling, and tracking. After conducting a systems audit, they were able to cut that number in half. They then unified the platforms with a custom portal and shared application programming interfaces (APIs), cutting redundant spending and improving the learner experience across all business units.

Last, a lack of data-driven decision making can hinder your efforts at sustained adoption. Consider implementing dashboards that showcase real-time results to reinforce your ongoing commitment.

By anticipating these barriers and embedding change management from the outset, organizations can successfully transition to an effective, scalable learning operation.

Gauging the Value of a Learning Operations Blueprint

A well-defined blueprint will help your L&D team work more efficiently while demonstrating tangible organizational value. Standardized processes reduce duplication of effort and streamline learning execution. Alignment with business objectives ensures that learning programs directly support workforce productivity and organizational growth. By strategically leveraging technology, organizations can scale their learning initiatives while improving employee engagement and tracking meaningful outcomes.

Furthermore, a structured blueprint fosters a culture of continuous learning by embedding development opportunities into employees' daily workflows. When learning content is designed to be accessible, personalized, and aligned with career growth, it enhances employee engagement and retention while equipping the workforce with the skills needed to drive business success.

For example, one organization used its Learning Operations Blueprint to tackle the growing demand for frontline leadership training. The L&D team previously struggled to keep pace, customizing each request and rebuilding materials, often from scratch. By applying the blueprint, they standardized their intake, design, and deployment process, making the program repeatable without sacrificing quality. Within two quarters, they doubled delivery capacity, improved learner satisfaction by 17 percent, and equipped business leaders with clear data on participation and performance outcomes. The Learning Operations Blueprint didn't just streamline execution; it gave L&D the tools to deliver consistent, measurable value at scale.

When a structured Learning Operations Blueprint is fully implemented, L&D transforms from a reactive service provider to a strategic driver of business performance. Teams operate with efficiency and agility to seamlessly deliver effective learning programs. Standardized workflows reduce redundancy, accelerating time-to-market for learning solutions while maintaining consistency across global teams. Learning technologies are integrated and optimized, providing real-time insights into employee engagement, program effectiveness, and business outcomes. Instead of struggling to prove results, L&D leaders have data-backed evidence that ties learning initiatives to measurable business results, whether it's improving workforce productivity, closing skills gaps, or driving innovation. With automation and streamlined operations, L&D can shift focus from managing chaos to enabling growth, becoming a proactive partner that fuels enterprise-wide success.

 Pause to Reflect
If your L&D team had to operate like a high-performing business unit, what processes, technologies, and metrics would need to change to drive measurable results?

The Bottom Line

L&D has the potential to be more than just a training provider. However, to achieve this, it has to operate strategically, align learning initiatives with business priorities, and deliver measurable impact. The difference between an L&D team that struggles for relevance and one that commands influence isn't talent or effort—it's approach.

By treating business leaders as customers and employees as consumers, the L&D function can balance addressing stakeholder needs and proving its value through tangible business outcomes. The key is shifting from a reactive service model to a proactive, data-driven function that demonstrates ROI, enables workforce performance, and earns executive trust.

Remember, if L&D prioritizes:
- **Only the business,** it risks producing compliance-driven training and employee disengagement
- **Only the employees,** it risks a lack of business impact, despite engaged employees
- **Both the business and the employees effectively,** its learning solutions will be strategic and meaningful

To strike the right balance:
- Conduct stakeholder mapping to align business sponsors and employee advocates.
- Use learning analytics to ensure training is effective for both groups.
- Leverage learning technologies, such as AI-driven personalization, to scale training efficiently.

How to Take Action to Establish Your L&D Business Model

After digesting the information in this chapter about L&D business models and blueprints, you may be looking for ways to take action. The good news is that you don't need a massive overhaul of your department or workflows to start making progress. Here are three things you can do now to begin implementing the ideas in this chapter:

- **Ask.** Reach out to your stakeholders and ask, "What are your top business challenges this year, and how can L&D help solve them?" The answer to this question will set the stage for better alignment and position your L&D team as problem-solvers rather than just content providers.
- **Identify.** Find one key metric you can shift from traditional learning indicators (such as course completions) to a

business-impact measure (such as increased productivity, reduced errors, or higher sales). Start tracking and reporting it to demonstrate L&D's direct contribution to business success.
- **Create.** Make a simple stakeholder matrix identifying who funds, sponsors, and benefits from L&D initiatives. This will help clarify where you should focus your engagement efforts to strengthen alignment and secure buy-in.

These small initial steps will help you lay the groundwork for repositioning L&D as a strategic business partner. The crucial next step is to ensure that L&D's learning priorities align with business needs. Without prioritization and a structured approach to needs analysis, your L&D department risks falling back into an order-taking role. The next chapter will explore how to move from reactive training delivery to a business-driven learning strategy.

Tool 1-1.
Employee Learning Experience Scorecard

Use this scorecard to evaluate how employees perceive and engage with learning in your organization.

Scoring guide:
- 1–2 = Needs significant improvement
- 3 = Some progress, but inconsistent
- 4–5 = Strong learning culture

Action plan: Identify low-scoring areas and prioritize quick wins (such as launching peer learning groups or integrating learning nudges into daily work).

Category	Indicators	Score (1–5)	Notes and Action Plan
Access to learning	Employees can easily access learning resources (e.g., the LMS, coaching, and external learning).		
Embedded learning	Learning is integrated into daily work (e.g., on-the-job coaching, microlearning, and knowledge-sharing forums).		
Personalized development	Employees can access career development plans and learning pathways tailored to their goals.		
Psychological safety	Employees feel safe to ask questions, share failures, and experiment without fear of consequences.		
Learner autonomy	Employees can influence what, when, and how they learn rather than being assigned one-size-fits-all training.		
Collaboration and knowledge sharing	There are active communities of practice, peer coaching, and informal learning networks.		
Recognition and rewards	Learning efforts are recognized and rewarded by managers and leadership.		

Tool 1-2.
Leadership and Organizational Support Scorecard

Use this scorecard to assess how leadership and business functions support and reinforce a learning culture at your organization.

Scoring guide:
- 1–2 = Needs significant improvement
- 3 = Some progress, but inconsistent
- 4–5 = Strong learning culture

Action plan: Engage leadership in discussions about low-scoring areas and embed learning into the business strategy (such as by integrating learning goals into performance reviews).

Category	Indicators	Score (1–5)	Notes and Action Plan
Executive buy-in	Leaders actively champion learning and model continuous development.		
Manager involvement	Managers regularly discuss development goals and support employees in their learning.		
Budget and investment	The organization invests in learning resources, technology, and programs.		
Alignment to business goals	Learning initiatives are clearly tied to business priorities and performance.		
Time for learning	Employees have dedicated time for learning without it conflicting with work demands.		
Feedback and continuous improvement	Learning programs are assessed for effectiveness, with input from employees.		
Innovation and experimentation	Employees are encouraged to experiment, test new ideas, and learn from failures.		

Tool 1-3.
Quick-Start Learning Operations Blueprint Checklist

Use this checklist to get started on your Learning Operations Blueprint.

Define business alignment:
- ☐ Identify key business objectives your L&D team supports.
- ☐ Clarify measurable outcomes (e.g., increased productivity and reduced compliance risks).
- ☐ Secure stakeholder alignment. (Who are your champions?)

Map your learning ecosystem:
- ☐ Document all learning technologies, tools, and platforms.
- ☐ Identify gaps and redundancies.
- ☐ Align system capabilities with business needs.

Standardize processes for scale:
- ☐ Define repeatable workflows (e.g., content development, delivery, and measurement).
- ☐ Establish governance. (Who owns what? What are the approval processes?)
- ☐ Create templates and guidelines for efficiency.

Optimize learning technology:
- ☐ Assess current tools for effectiveness and user experience.
- ☐ Automate where possible (e.g., enrollment and reporting).
- ☐ Integrate data across systems to improve insights.

Implement measurement and reporting:
- ☐ Define key metrics (e.g., efficiency, engagement, and business impact).
- ☐ Implement dashboards for real-time tracking.
- ☐ Close the loop by using data to inform future decisions.

Pilot test and iterate:
- ☐ Start with a small, high-impact initiative.
- ☐ Gather feedback, adjust, and scale.
- ☐ Continuously improve the blueprint based on business needs and employee behavior.

Chapter 2
Business-Focused Learning Needs

In a strategy meeting at a high-growth fintech firm, the head of sales stated bluntly, "Training isn't keeping up. We've launched three products this year, and my team still doesn't know how to talk about two of them."

Caught off guard, the L&D manager realized this was the first time they had heard about the new product lines. Their team had spent the past quarter rolling out a highly rated leadership series and updating compliance modules (initiatives that had checked all the boxes on engagement and completion), but none of those efforts had addressed the sales team's immediate needs. Even worse, the disconnect was only discovered after performance had suffered.

Unfortunately, this scenario is all too common—not because L&D teams lack skill or dedication, but because they are often excluded from essential conversations that determine business priorities. When learning operates in isolation from business strategy, the result is well-intentioned work that fails to move the needle.

That disconnect between business priorities and L&D initiatives is rarely deliberate, but it's a symptom of a *reactive, training-first approach*. When L&D teams are not embedded in strategic planning, they end up solving for symptoms, not root causes. And while their programs may be well-designed and well-received, they will inevitably miss the mark.

Your L&D team likely operates reactively, fielding training requests from managers, launching programs based on qualitative trends, or addressing skills gaps in isolation. Real business results don't come from checking a training box but from solving performance problems that directly affect key business outcomes.

This chapter explores how you can move your approach to L&D beyond surface-level training to discover the learning gaps hindering business success. You'll learn how to apply a business lens to needs analysis, use data to identify root causes, and engage stakeholders to ensure learning initiatives drive measurable results. By shifting from a training-first mindset to a business-driven approach, L&D can ensure its efforts are aligned with the priorities that matter most.

Needs Analysis Through a Business Lens

A traditional training needs analysis often starts with identifying skills gaps or responding to training requests from managers and employees. While this approach ensures that learning solutions address areas perceived to need development, it falls short in linking L&D initiatives to actual business value. Simply put, not all skills gaps are business problems, and not all business problems can be solved with training.

A business-driven needs analysis shifts your focus from what employees *want* to learn to what the organization *needs* people to learn to drive measurable performance improvements. Instead of asking, "What training is needed?" the more strategic question becomes, "What's preventing employees from delivering the results the business expects?" This shift means your efforts can solve root problems that hinder business success, not just address symptoms.

Many L&D teams struggle to position themselves as business drivers rather than service providers. In chapter 1, we established that L&D needs to proactively engage with business leaders and align with the organization's strategic objectives. In this chapter, we'll focus on using a *business lens* to look at your work and prioritize your learning investments based on their business value rather than responding to ad hoc requests.

Identify Learning Gaps That Affect Business Performance

One of the biggest challenges L&D faces is designing learning solutions that solve the most critical problems. Too often, training is developed based on assumptions, vague requests, or a general sense that "people need development." Real business value, however, comes from solving tangible performance gaps in which employees struggle to execute their jobs in ways that drive key business outcomes. In short, you need to move away from just providing more courses and toward diagnosing workforce challenges with the precision of a business consultant.

Start With Business Priorities

Your first task as a business consultant is identifying learning gaps and linking them directly to business priorities. Before diving into skills assessments or performance reviews, however, your L&D team's prioritization must support the organization's most pressing business challenges. You don't want to waste time on learning initiatives that are disconnected from the problems that leadership cares about.

Every business goal—whether it's increasing revenue, improving customer retention, reducing errors, or launching new products—relies on people having the right capabilities to execute it. The key question L&D should ask isn't, "What training programs do people need?" but rather, "What's preventing employees from delivering the results the business expects?"

Use Data, Not Gut Instincts

Once business priorities are clear, the next step is to diagnose where workforce capabilities are falling short in supporting them. You can't rely on asking managers what training they think their teams need because—let's be honest—you'll hear everything from "My people need better communication skills" to "More Excel training!" without any real links back to business results. Instead of relying only on managers, use multiple data sources to help identify performance gaps, including:

- **Business metrics.** Look at sales performance, productivity rates, error rates, customer satisfaction scores, and any other measure that reveals where teams are underperforming.
- **Skills and competency assessments.** Compare employees' current capabilities with what's needed to succeed in their roles.
- **Employee and manager insights.** Your gut feelings shouldn't drive training decisions, but qualitative insights from managers and employees can help validate and contextualize quantitative data.

- **Learning data.** Completion rates and course satisfaction scores don't mean much on their own, but tracking whether trained employees perform better than those who are untrained can reveal what's working.

For instance, a large tech company wanted to improve its product development speed. Initial feedback pointed to engineers needing better time management training. However, a deeper analysis showed the real issue wasn't time management but a lack of clarity in requirements and project scope. The solution wasn't training; it was improving processes and communication between product teams and stakeholders. This kind of precision in diagnosing learning gaps separates effective L&D teams from those that just check the training box.

Distinguish Between Skills Gaps and Process Problems

Not every performance issue is a training problem. A mistake many L&D teams make is assuming that every performance or skills gap requires training when many problems stem from outdated processes, unclear expectations, or a lack of resources.

Consider compliance training. If employees consistently fail compliance audits, your reflex might be to build more training programs. However, if the real issue is a confusing system or inconsistent policy enforcement, more training won't fix the problem; instead, it will frustrate employees.

This is why a root cause analysis is helpful. Simple tools like the Five Whys technique can help you drill down to reveal the underlying issue by asking why questions until you reach a helpful conclusion. For example, if a customer service agent's performance suddenly drops off, you can ask:

1. *Why?* Because they don't follow the new process
2. *Why?* Because they're not confident about using the new system
3. *Why?* Because they haven't had enough practice
4. *Why?* Because job aids are missing and managers aren't reinforcing the initial training
5. *Why?* Because the training program was a one-time event and there's no ongoing support

Suddenly, the why questions reveal that the solution to the problem involves providing better job aids, reinforcing learning through coaching, and creating practice opportunities.

Prioritize What Matters Most

In chapter 1, we discussed the fact that your L&D team serves two distinct groups—the business (your customer) and the employees (your consumers). This distinction plays a fundamental role in how you prioritize learning needs. Your customer (the business) should drive learning priorities first; then, you can meet the learning needs of your consumers (the employees).

So, how do you know if you're prioritizing the business as your primary customer? If you can answer yes to all four of these questions, you are already well on your way:

- Do you understand your company's top business priorities and align learning programs accordingly?
- Have you established KPIs that tie training outcomes to business results?
- Are you engaging regularly with business leaders to identify new challenges?
- Can you clearly articulate the ROI of L&D investments beyond course completions and engagement feedback?

If you answered no to any of these questions, use them to help you identify areas of opportunity. Make note of any learning gaps that affected your answers.

Not All Learning Gaps Are Created Equal

Once you've identified any learning gaps, you should assess whether closing a particular gap will have a measurable effect on key business metrics, including revenue growth, customer retention, or operational efficiency. After determining which metrics would be most positively affected by improved learning experiences, you can design those experiences in a way that's engaging and effective for employees.

Your L&D team has limited resources, so prioritizing needs will be critical. Use these three questions as your first step in setting priorities:

- **Does closing this learning gap directly affect a key business metric?** If the answer is no, then improving that skill won't move the needle on business revenue, efficiency, or customer satisfaction. In that case, it is not a priority.
- **Is training the best solution to this problem?** If the answer is no, the problem may stem from unclear expectations, broken systems,

or a lack of support from leadership, which means training is not the first priority. Address the source of the problem before or instead of recommending training.
- **Is there a fast path to an effective solution for the problem?** If the answer is yes, discuss options with your team and stakeholders. A brief job aid or individual coaching program might work more efficiently than a long workshop.

Learning Gaps Prompt Action

The best L&D teams operate like business consultants by identifying real problems, prioritizing effective solutions, and use learning as one of many tools to drive performance. To take action immediately, you can:
- **Meet with a business leader this month.** Discuss their biggest workforce challenges and how L&D can help solve them.
- **Run a simple skills audit for a key role.** Compare what employees already know versus what they need to know to succeed.
- **Analyze performance data to find patterns.** In which areas are employees struggling the most, and what initiatives (training or otherwise) could make the biggest difference?

By shifting from reactive training requests to proactive performance diagnostics, and taking clear action based on those diagnostics, your L&D team will no longer be just another department; it will become a critical enabler of business success. The value of learning and development is not measured in the number of courses delivered. Instead, value is measured by the real-world influence on business results.

No more checking boxes. From now on, you must use your business lens to determine and resolve the right problems with the best solutions.

 Pause to Reflect
When was the last time your L&D team challenged a training request to uncover the real problem? What lessons did you learn that you can incorporate into your processes?

Successful Stakeholder Collaboration

The most effective L&D teams don't operate in isolation. They don't build training programs based solely on assumptions, industry trends, or what other companies are doing. Instead, they integrate with others in the business, working alongside key stakeholders to determine what learning initiatives will drive measurable results.

Collaboration isn't just a nice-to-have; it's the difference between your L&D team working as a critical business driver and becoming an overlooked support function. Without stakeholder input, you risk spending your time and budget on training content that fails to solve real business challenges. When you actively engage with business partners, they can help you keep learning initiatives laser-focused on skills and capabilities that will make a big difference.

First, Identify the Right Stakeholders

Who are the key players you need to collaborate with? How should your L&D team engage with them? How can you choose the right partners and structure collaboration so learning priorities better align with business goals?

Not every leader or team should have a say in shaping L&D's priorities. Too many voices participating in shaping learning strategy can become chaotic and unfocused as competing demands pull your team in multiple directions. If too few stakeholders are engaged, training initiatives may miss the mark and fail to address the most pressing needs. You will need to identify individuals and groups with enough influence to drive change and enough insight to ensure learning investments deliver high value. These potential collaborators typically include:

- **Senior executives.** They are responsible for setting the company's strategic direction, and their insights can help L&D link learning priorities with business objectives like revenue growth, market expansion, or operational efficiency.
- **People leaders and functional heads.** They are usually managers who oversee teams and understand which skills gaps are limiting performance. These stakeholders also provide a ground-level view of workforce challenges.
- **HR and talent management partners.** They oversee hiring, workforce planning, and internal mobility, and their input

helps ensure that learning initiatives support career growth and talent retention.
- **Finance and operations leaders.** They allocate budgets and measure efficiency, and their involvement means that L&D investments are viewed as business accelerators rather than cost centers.
- **Employees and subject matter experts (SMEs).** They engage directly with learning content and apply it on the job. Without their input, L&D risks designing programs that don't translate into meaningful workplace performance improvement.

Each of these groups brings a unique perspective, and collaborating with them allows L&D to actively shape the organization's ability to compete and grow.

Use Learning Strategy to Elevate Collaboration

Too often, L&D teams approach stakeholder engagement as a one-time exercise at the start of the year or when launching a big initiative. But real collaboration requires ongoing dialogue. Business priorities shift, your workforce needs evolve, and industry trends change. If L&D isn't consistently engaging with stakeholders, learning priorities can quickly become outdated or misaligned.

A structured, proactive approach to stakeholder collaboration strengthens L&D's strategic influence in three ways:
- Ensuring that learning investments address business priorities
- Preventing misaligned or ineffective training
- Strengthening L&D's influence and credibility

Let's discuss each in more detail.

Ensure Learning Investments Address Business Priorities

One of the most common reasons L&D teams struggle to secure adequate budgets and executive buy-in is that leaders deprioritize it because they see training as too disconnected from business priorities. By engaging stakeholders early, you can position a learning initiative as a real solution to real a business challenge. In other words, instead of responding to vague requests for more leadership training or better onboarding, you can tie learning programs to specific business outcomes.

For example, a retail company struggling with customer retention might initially assume the training issue is related to frontline service skills. However, by working with stakeholders across the sales, support, and product teams, an L&D task force might discover that employees lack deep product knowledge, which then leads to inconsistent messaging and frustrated customers. This insight would shift the learning strategy from creating generic customer service training to implementing a targeted, business-critical initiative.

Prevent Misaligned or Ineffective Training

When your L&D team operates in a silo, you risk wasting time and resources on training that doesn't solve business problems. A well-intentioned program might address a perceived skills gap, but it won't move the needle if it's not grounded in actual business needs.

Imagine a clothing manufacturing company that sees a significant increase in product defects. If the L&D team rolls out more quality control training without consulting operations leaders, they risk ignoring the underlying problem: malfunctioning sewing machines. Engaging stakeholders ensures that training will be deployed only when it can have a measurable impact and that nonlearning solutions—such as repairing or replacing faulty equipment in this case—are considered first.

Strengthen L&D's Influence and Credibility

When business leaders see you as a consulting partner, the L&D function gains influence and credibility. Instead of being asked to build a training course after all planning decisions have been made, you will participate in strategic discussions early. This shift happens when stakeholders recognize that your team wants to drive results, not just deliver content. The more L&D can demonstrate an understanding of business priorities and show how learning can support them, the more likely it will be included in decision making.

Suppose a regional healthcare provider is preparing to roll out a new electronic health record (EHR) system. In the past, the L&D team would have been looped in late to deliver software tutorials. This time, L&D leadership partnered with operations and clinical leadership at the outset to identify workflow disruptions, skills gaps, and change readiness across roles. By co-designing solutions, such as live demos and ask-me-anything

(AMA) sessions with the software support team, the L&D team helped accelerate adoption and reduce clinician frustration.

Build a Framework for Collaboration

Stakeholder collaboration is essential to confirm that learning investments connect with real business needs, and for that purpose, you need a deep, well-structured approach—a framework—to guide collaboration. Begin by establishing the right mindset, and then embed collaboration into your operating model.

Establish the Right Mindset

Stakeholder collaboration isn't just about gathering input; it's about positioning L&D as a driver of business success. This requires shifting your mindset from reactively delivering training to actively shaping workforce strategy.

To approach stakeholder conversations with a business-first perspective, ask questions like:

- What business problems are keeping you up at night?
- Where do you see performance gaps in your team?
- What skills will be critical for success in the next 12 to 18 months?

These questions shift the conversation. Instead of discussing courses and content, L&D and business leaders should discuss outcomes, results, and growth.

Embed Collaboration in L&D Operations

By incorporating a few simple techniques for stakeholder collaboration into L&D operations, you can ensure that learning strategically supports business objectives. Those techniques include:

- **Regular strategy meetings.** Meet with business leaders to assess evolving priorities.
- **Learning advisory groups.** Have these groups provide ongoing input into training strategies.
- **Business performance reviews.** Use monthly business reviews (MBRs) and quarterly business reviews (QBRs) to track the effect of learning initiatives on key business outcomes.
- **Feedback loops.** These ensure training is solving real workforce challenges.

By embedding stakeholder collaboration into your fundamental L&D framework with the right mindset and through everyday operations, you can move beyond a support function and become a strategic enabler of business performance.

Pause to Reflect
How do you determine learning needs? Are you diagnosing business performance gaps or just responding to training requests?

A Business-Focused Learning Plan

A strong learning strategy is about building a sustainable, forward-thinking approach that ensures employees have the right skills at the right time to support business goals. If you try to proceed without a well-structured plan, you risk being reactive and responding to short-term demands without considering long-term workforce development. When L&D teams operate without a business-focused plan, the result is often a fragmented learning ecosystem in which training initiatives are disconnected from business priorities, resources are wasted, and learning has minimal effect.

On the other hand, a well-designed learning plan can provide clarity and direction, ensuring that learning investments are both strategic and scalable. A learning plan helps organizations balance short-term priorities (such as onboarding, compliance training, or immediate upskilling needs) with long-term workforce transformation (such as leadership development, digital skills growth, and succession planning). Most important, it aligns L&D initiatives with evolving business needs, ensuring that learning is a proactive driver of company success rather than an afterthought.

Build a Learning Road Map

Learning priorities must be structured carefully to ensure that L&D remains a strategic partner rather than a reactive function. The Learning Operations Blueprint introduced in chapter 1 provides the foundation. The timeline we'll discuss here ensures that L&D aligns with evolving business needs, balancing short-term needs with long-term workforce transformation.

Your learning road map should include three key phases—0 to 12 months, 12 to 18 months, and 18 to 36 months—with key activities linked to each:
- **At 0 to 12 months,** you should focus on immediate priorities:
  - Closing urgent skills gaps
  - Deploying business-critical training in areas such as compliance, regulatory, and systems training, as well as sales enablement
  - Addressing high-risk areas affecting productivity
- **At 12 to 18 months,** you should focus on midterm development:
  - Preparing employees for anticipated business shifts, such as adoption of new technology, expansion into new markets, or the evolution of key processes
- **At 18 to 36 months,** you should focus on future workforce readiness:
  - Building long-term capabilities such as leadership development and reskilling for automation
  - Engaging in succession planning

Each phase should have measurable outcomes tied to business results. For example, instead of measuring completion rates, L&D can track how targeted training efforts reduce operational errors, improve productivity, or increase customer retention. We'll dig into these details more in chapter 9.

A well-structured learning road map is your strategic vision for workforce development, but its effectiveness depends on establishing strong governance and accountability, ensuring agile and adaptable execution, and prioritizing what matters most. Without a structured approach to implementation, even the best-laid plans risk becoming disconnected from business realities.

Establish Governance and Accountability

To execute your learning plan, begin with a clear governance framework. You'll define ownership at multiple levels, including:
- **Strategic oversight.** Senior L&D leaders should work with business executives to review the road map's progress quarterly, ensuring learning investments continue to support evolving business goals.

- **Operational execution.** Functional L&D teams, HR partners, and business unit leaders should be responsible for implementing road map initiatives, tracking results, and ensuring learning content is delivered in ways that integrate seamlessly with daily work.
- **Managerial accountability.** People leaders play a crucial role in reinforcing learning. They should have access to coaching guides, learning reinforcement strategies, and data-informed insights to help their teams apply new skills effectively.

A governance framework should include checkpoints at a regular cadence, quarterly business reviews, performance data reviews, and stakeholder meetings to validate that learning initiatives remain relevant and effective. Without this structure, L&D risks falling back into a reactive mode, responding to ad hoc training requests rather than driving strategic business outcomes.

Ensure Agility and Adaptability

Your learning road map will never be static. It must be continuously reassessed and adapted to keep pace with business changes. This requires leveraging data insights from multiple sources, including:

- **Business performance metrics.** Track operational efficiency, revenue growth, customer satisfaction, and other business KPIs to assess whether learning initiatives contribute to measurable improvements.
- **Skills and workforce analytics.** Use skills gap assessments, talent mobility data, and succession planning insights to prioritize learning initiatives.
- **Employee and manager feedback.** Collect qualitative insights to ensure training addresses real workforce challenges and doesn't just deliver content.

By embedding real-time feedback loops into the execution of your plan, you can pivot more easily when priorities shift, whether that means accelerating digital skills development, adjusting leadership training for emerging challenges, or refining onboarding programs as the workforce evolves.

Prioritize What Matters Most

In chapter 1, we discussed viewing the business as the customer your L&D team serves and employees as the consumers of your products. Remembering this distinction will help you prioritize learning needs in your business-focused learning plan. Your L&D team can first assess whether closing a particular learning gap will have a measurable impact on key business metrics. Then, you can design learning experiences that are engaging and applicable to employees. This balance prevents L&D from becoming a compliance-driven cost center or an overly engagement-focused initiative with no clear business value. Here's a suggested progression of actions for customer-centric learning and consumer-driven priorities.

1. **To focus on customer-centric learning:**
   - Identify customer pain points and design learning initiatives that address them.
   - Develop training programs that enhance the customer experience, quality of service, and product knowledge.
   - Use customer feedback data to refine and iterate learning priorities.
2. **To focus on adapting to consumer-driven priorities:**
   - Adapt learning solutions to meet internal workforce needs.
   - Ensure that frontline employees and leaders have the skills needed to execute customer-centric strategies.
   - Develop targeted learning pathways that reinforce both employee performance and customer success.

A well-structured learning road map is the difference between a reactive training function and a proactive, strategic L&D organization. Without a road map, learning initiatives can become scattered, addressing short-term needs without building the long-term capabilities required for business success. A 12/18/36–month road map ensures that L&D efforts are responsive to immediate priorities and prepared for future workforce transformation. The key to success is balancing agility with discipline, ensuring that learning investments remain flexible enough to adapt to changing business needs while maintaining a clear trajectory for long-term influence.

For L&D leaders, the question is not "What training do we need next?" but rather "How do we ensure learning drives measurable business value over time?" Organizations can use a learning road map and the Learning Operations Blueprint to build a business-focused learning plan and maximize business value.

Pause to Reflect
Does your current learning strategy have a clear road map that balances short-term business needs with long-term workforce development?

The Power of Organizational Alignment

If you want to drive business value, you cannot design learning initiatives in a vacuum. Your work must be fully aligned with the organization's business strategy. True alignment requires weaving L&D into the fabric of corporate decision making and fundamentally shifting how L&D operates so it proactively shapes workforce capability in partnership with organizational leaders and contributes to long-term success, workforce agility, and sustained competitive advantage. The critical elements of organizational alignment include rooting L&D in business, talent, skills, and technology strategies.

Integrate L&D With Business Strategy

Many L&D teams talk about alignment with business strategy, but few truly integrate their work into the broader organizational ecosystem. Instead, they function as standalone entities, delivering training programs that may or may not support the company's goals. The problem with this approach is clear: If L&D is disconnected from the goals and purpose of the business, it will always struggle to prove its value.

Strategic integration with business strategy goes beyond aligning training topics with business goals; it requires L&D to proactively partner in workforce planning and organization development. This means understanding the company's objectives and identifying where workforce capabilities affect those goals. If the business is focused on scaling revenue, L&D should equip employees with the skills to improve sales performance and customer retention. If innovation is a priority, learning programs should focus on upskilling employees in emerging technologies and agile methodologies.

Measure Learning Outcomes Like Business Outcomes

Many organizations fall into the trap of assuming that as long as L&D aligns with general business objectives, it is doing its job. However, real integration means that learning outcomes are measured like business outcomes. For example, instead of tracking course completion rates, L&D should measure its influence on key business metrics like revenue growth, operational efficiency, or employee productivity.

The experience of one global retail company illustrates this well. Instead of launching generalized leadership training, the retail company's L&D team worked with senior executives to identify the biggest business challenges. Data showed that store managers who effectively coached their teams saw higher customer satisfaction scores and increased revenue per store. Based on this insight, L&D redesigned the leadership development programs to focus specifically on coaching behaviors that influenced business performance. Precision-driven integration like this ensures that learning isn't just a function within the company; it's a strategic lever for business success.

Embed L&D in Talent Strategy

Talent and L&D are often treated as separate functions, but in reality, they are deeply intertwined. A company's ability to attract, retain, and develop top talent depends on whether employees see a clear path for growth—and learning opportunities shape that path.

When L&D is embedded in the overall talent strategy, organizations can create structured learning pathways that support career mobility, employee retention, and leadership development. This integration ensures that learning isn't just about filling immediate skills gaps but also about preparing employees for future roles.

For example, companies that struggle with high turnover often overlook the role that L&D can play in retention. Employees who don't see growth opportunities are more likely to leave, yet many organizations fail to connect learning programs to career progression. Highly effective L&D teams work directly with HR and talent leaders to map out development frameworks that show employees exactly how training leads to new opportunities. By embedding learning into talent development, organizations ensure that employees don't just complete training; they see it as a key part of their long-term success within the company.

Align L&D With Skills Strategy

The rate of change in modern business is unprecedented, and it is *skills*, not job titles, that make up the foundation of workforce planning. As companies move toward becoming skills-based organizations, L&D plays a central role in ensuring that employees have the capabilities to meet evolving business demands.

A well-defined skills strategy allows L&D to target learning investments at the areas that have the biggest, most positive impact. Instead of focusing on creating broad training programs, organizations should use skills intelligence platforms and workforce analytics to identify which specific skills are most critical for business success. For example, an insurance provider might analyze claims processing times and customer feedback to reveal that underwriters need stronger skills in digital tools and risk communication. By targeting those gaps, L&D can help reduce processing delays and improve client retention.

A strong skills strategy also ensures that learning programs remain future-focused. Many organizations make the mistake of training employees only for today's needs rather than preparing them with the emerging skills that will drive future success. Forward-thinking L&D teams work closely with workforce planning leaders to anticipate skills gaps before they become problematic. By aligning L&D with skills intelligence, companies ensure that learning programs are future-proofing their workforce for long-term success.

Incorporate L&D in Technology Strategy

Technology is no longer only a delivery mechanism for learning content. It's now a strategic enabler that allows organizations to scale, personalize, and measure the effectiveness of L&D programs. Yet many companies fail to connect their learning technology strategy with the broader business technology strategy, which leads to inefficiencies, siloed systems, and missed opportunities. True integration means ensuring that learning technologies are:

- **Aligned with enterprise systems.** Learning platforms should seamlessly connect with HR systems, performance management tools, and workforce analytics to provide a holistic view of employee development.
- **Designed for scale and efficiency.** L&D should leverage automation, AI-enabled personalization, and adaptive learning technologies to reduce administrative burdens and improve learning effectiveness.

- **Data-informed.** Learning analytics should be tied to business intelligence platforms, allowing leaders to track how training affects key business outcomes in real time.

As organizations continue to invest in skills intelligence platforms, AI-enabled learning, and workforce analytics, the role of L&D will become even more intertwined with technology strategy. Companies that embrace this integration will improve learning efficiency and gain a competitive edge in workforce development. We'll explore this topic in greater depth in chapter 5.

Is Your L&D Function Disconnected?

Many organizations unintentionally treat L&D as a reactive service provider rather than a strategic partner. The symptoms of this disconnect are easy to spot if you look through the business lens we discussed at the beginning of this chapter. You will see:

- ▶ Training developed in response to ad-hoc requests rather than being guided by a proactive strategy
- ▶ Annual budgets fluctuating wildly, with L&D often being the first to face cuts when cost reductions are needed
- ▶ Measurement focused on activity metrics (like course completions and satisfaction scores) instead of business outcomes
- ▶ L&D leaders struggling to secure executive buy-in because learning initiatives are seen as nice to have rather than essential

This disconnect inevitably creates a vicious cycle. Because L&D is not fully integrated into the business's decision-making processes, its programs often fail to deliver measurable value. And because the impact isn't clear, executives are hesitant to invest, which then leads to reduced funding and influence.

Consider, for example, companies that roll out broad leadership development programs without tying them to specific business challenges. If your company struggles with low employee engagement and high turnover, a generic leadership course won't solve the problem. Instead, your L&D team needs to address the specific leadership behaviors that drive retention, such as coaching, feedback, and career development conversations.

Make L&D an Extension of Company Priorities— Not an Afterthought

Your L&D function probably struggles with the perception that it exists on the periphery of the business as a separate function responsible for training but not fully connected to core business functions. We've discussed many ways to address this misconception but haven't yet considered mindset as a barrier to L&D's ability to drive value. When leaders view L&D as an isolated function (an afterthought), it won't get the budget or attention it deserves.

Perhaps the most difficult hurdle to overcome is the pervasive notion that L&D strategy runs parallel to business strategy. In fact, L&D strategy should always be an extension of business strategy. Every investment in learning initiatives should directly support the company's strategic goals, ensuring that workforce development is fueling organizational success. When this mindset alignment happens—in addition to aligning with business, talent, skills, and technology strategies—your L&D team can transition from a transactional training provider to a critical enabler of business growth, innovation, and performance. You can link L&D with core company priorities by reframing learning as a driver of value, eliciting executive buy-in, fully integrating learning into business operations, and positioning L&D as a growth engine.

Reframe Learning as a Driver of Value

How can you, as an L&D leader, ensure that learning strategy is fully embedded in corporate priorities rather than operating in a silo? Reframe the L&D function's organizational role as a driver of value by:

- **Shifting from training-focused to performance-focused work.** L&D should not just deliver content—it should actively solve business problems.
- **Speaking the language of the business.** Executives don't care about learning hours; they care about revenue growth, customer satisfaction, and operational efficiency. L&D must frame its value in these terms.
- **Embedding learning into business processes.** Learning should be integrated into employees' daily workflows rather than being a separate activity.

Another step you can take to demonstrate how learning drives value is to support company priorities consciously and consistently. L&D leaders who can align learning initiatives with the company's most pressing priorities move their teams from isolation to integration within the company. While every organization has unique challenges, most corporate strategies focus on a few common themes you can look for and support, including:

- **Revenue growth and market expansion.** Focus on sales enablement, customer experience training, and upskilling employees in high-growth areas. For example, in a software company launching new products, you might ensure that all sales and customer support teams receive just-in-time product training, leading to faster adoption and higher customer satisfaction.
- **Operational efficiency and cost reduction.** Ensure that learning initiatives help employees work faster, smarter, and with fewer errors. For instance, if your manufacturing company is struggling with production delays, introduce microlearning or digital job aids for machine operators to reduce downtime.
- **Workforce agility and digital transformation.** Equip employees with missing and forward-looking industry or professional skills they need to keep pace. For instance, if you lead an L&D team at a healthcare company preparing for AI-enabled diagnostics, you could launch an upskilling program in data literacy and AI applications for clinicians, ensuring they can use new technology effectively.
- **Talent retention and leadership development.** Employees stay where they see career growth. L&D should strive to ensure that learning is clearly linked to internal mobility. For example, one large retail chain reduced store manager turnover by 30 percent by creating structured career development pathways, so employees could see exactly how progression worked in the organization.

By proactively addressing these four business priorities, L&D can move from delivering training programs to driving high-value business transformation.

Elicit Executive Buy-In

Even when L&D teams align their efforts with corporate strategy, they will never be fully integrated unless executive leaders champion learning as a business priority. Winning executive support requires the L&D team to shift from pumping out content on-demand to solving business problems. L&D leaders should approach conversations with the C-suite like they interact with any other business unit—by presenting a clear value proposition with measurable outcomes.

An effective way to elicit buy-in is through business case storytelling, or showing how learning initiatives have already driven measurable results. For example, instead of saying, "We trained 5,000 employees last year," a more compelling strategy would be to say, "By equipping our sales team with advanced negotiation skills, we increased the number of deals closed by 12 percent, leading to an additional $4.2 million in revenue."

When executives see L&D as a revenue driver, not a cost center, learning becomes a non-negotiable investment rather than a budget line item they can cut when times are tough.

Integrate Learning Into Business Operations

To be valued, learning must be embedded into how work gets done. To do so, you can:
- Design learning solutions that fit into employees' workflows rather than pulling them away from their jobs.
- Partner with business units to create just-in-time training content rather than relying only on scheduled courses.
- Leverage technology to personalize learning so employees get the right content at the right time.

What does this look like in the real world? A leading tech company successfully applied this approach when scaling its workforce during rapid global expansion. Instead of traditional onboarding, L&D embedded real-time learning content into each employee's first 90 days, using machine learning to push training content tailored to individual roles. As a result, new hire ramp-up time decreased by 22 percent, accelerating time-to-productivity.

Position L&D as a Strategic Growth Engine

By now, you can see that the ultimate goal for any L&D team should be seamless integration with corporate priorities to the point where learning isn't seen as a separate function but as a growth engine woven into the business itself. This shift requires L&D leaders to:

- Engage directly in business discussions to ensure learning supports key objectives.
- Move away from generic training programs and toward targeted initiatives that solve real workforce challenges.
- Adopt business metrics to prove value in ways executives care about.
- Align learning initiatives with business objectives to drive measurable results.
- Embed L&D into talent development to support employee growth and retention.
- Use skills intelligence to ensure learning programs address critical workforce capabilities.
- Leverage technology strategically to scale learning programs and enhance data-informed decision making.

Organizations that successfully integrate L&D into corporate strategy don't just build a learning culture. Instead, they build a high-performance culture in which every employee has the skills and knowledge to drive business success and L&D is able to shape the workforce strategy.

The first step for L&D teams looking to make this shift is to build deeper partnerships across the organization. Whether it's collaborating with business leaders, HR, workforce planning teams, or IT, L&D must become a strategic architect of workforce transformation. When L&D is fully integrated into business strategy, it stops being seen as an optional support function and becomes an indispensable driver of success.

 Pause to Reflect
How well is your L&D strategy integrated with business, talent, and technology priorities? Where are the biggest gaps?

The Bottom Line

Identifying and prioritizing business-critical learning needs isn't only about being strategic. It's about having a tangible influence on business performance. The most effective L&D teams don't just build training programs; they solve business problems. By linking learning initiatives with corporate objectives, using data to pinpoint true performance gaps, and collaborating with key stakeholders, L&D becomes a critical driver of organizational success.

The focus of this chapter has been the need to move from delivering standalone programs to aligning learning initiatives with business priorities, talent and skills strategies, and technology integration. This transformation positions L&D not just as a support function but as a valued growth engine within the organization. To effectively drive this transformation, L&D must be embedded in the business planning processes, ensuring that learning initiatives directly support organizational goals. Each learning needs analysis should begin by identifying business challenges, not just skills gaps, to ensure a learning solution produces tangible performance outcomes. Sustaining L&D's influence also requires ongoing partnerships with business leaders, HR, and IT, fostering collaboration that integrates learning with broader organizational strategies.

How to Take Action to Prioritize Business-Focused Learning Needs

The shift from reactive training delivery to a proactive business partnership requires the L&D function to adopt new habits and approaches. To put these ideas into practice, here are three actions you can take today:

- **The next time someone requests training, challenge yourself to go beyond the surface.** What performance issue is driving the request? Is training the right solution?
- **Pick a business KPI, such as sales performance, customer satisfaction, or error rates.** Explore whether a capability gap contributes to less-than-optimal results.
- **Instead of discussing training needs, start a conversation with a business stakeholder about their priorities.** What's keeping them up at night? Where are their employees struggling to deliver results?

By taking these steps, you'll move beyond traditional training models, positioning L&D as a proactive partner in driving business success. Remember, the goal isn't just to deliver learning content; it's to create measurable, strategic value. In part 2, we will explore how to standardize processes, manage learning portfolios, and leverage data and technology to increase efficiency without sacrificing effectiveness.

PART 2
Scaling Learning Operations

Chapter 3
Repeatable, Reliable, and Responsive Learning

When I joined the learning technology team at a multinational grocer, I inherited a challenge most L&D leaders will recognize: too many people doing the same work in different ways. We had more than 30 decentralized LMS administrators, each supporting their own region with their own processes. There were no intake standards, no shared expectations, and no consistent ways to track or resolve employee issues. If you were an employee trying to complete required training, your experience depended entirely on which part of the business you worked in.

Then came the mandate: Centralize it. All of it. Reduce 30 LMS admins to a single team of three learning technologists. Support more than 100,000 employees across more than 500 locations in three countries, and do it without creating a backlog of tickets or compromising the employee experience.

And we did it—through process improvement, governance, and automation.

We started by standardizing our core processes, defining how requests came in, how we triaged them, how work got done, and how long it should take. We simplified where we could, made self-service the default where it made sense, and automated everything else. We integrated with the company help desk, set service-level agreements, and built a Center of Excellence.

The result? Average support ticket time to resolution dropped by more than three days. Assignment errors decreased, and we saved $2.3 million in labor costs that first year without cutting corners.

The lesson my team took from that experience was that strategy means nothing without execution. You can have the most well-aligned learning road map in the world, but if your processes are inconsistent, your resourcing is unclear, or your intake is chaotic, you won't be able to deliver at scale, and you certainly won't be able to do it the same way twice.

After your L&D team has established a strategic, business-aligned learning road map (as discussed in chapter 2), your next challenge is executing at scale. This chapter explores how L&D can build a structured, scalable function that delivers value consistently while remaining agile enough to respond to evolving business needs.

Many L&D teams struggle with inefficiencies, inconsistent processes, and misalignment with organizational goals. Without a strong operational foundation, L&D teams risk becoming reactive, filling training requests without a clear strategy when they should be acting as business partners driving measurable results. To avoid these common problems, your organization must establish repeatable, scalable processes that align with business priorities, optimize resources, and enhance speed to market. Therefore, this chapter will also explore how standardized governance, prioritization frameworks, and customer-centric methodologies enable L&D to function with the same level of rigor as other business units. This includes how to create service-level agreements (SLAs).

By structuring your L&D operations around efficiency, consistency, and business alignment, you can ensure that learning initiatives deliver measurable results, strengthen workforce capabilities, and maximize the return on learning investments. Remember: Efficiency isn't just about cost savings; it's about giving L&D the bandwidth to focus on high-value, business-critical initiatives rather than leaving it trapped in reactive execution.

Building Your Learning Operations

A well-run L&D function operates as an internal service provider and a strategic partner to the business. By embedding a customer-centric approach, you can ensure processes align with business expectations and drive measurable value. By establishing business-first learning priorities, including implementing standard operating procedures, structured intake processes, and prioritization frameworks, your team will enhance consistency and reliability. By using technology strategically as part of overall resource management, you can ensure that your team will maximize their effectiveness. And by focusing on customer-centric processes, you will help connect learning initiatives with business goals. By embracing all these principles, you can move beyond being a reactive training provider to becoming a strategic enabler of business performance.

Aligning L&D Processes With Business Expectations

For L&D to be truly effective, it must operate with the same level of rigor as other business units. Establishing SLAs with stakeholders sets clear expectations on deliverables and timelines. Regular stakeholder check-ins help maintain alignment with business priorities, while tracking and reporting on KPIs demonstrates L&D's influence on business performance. Embedding these practices ensures that L&D is viewed as an essential driver of organizational success rather than a reactive support function.

Establishing Business-First Learning Priorities

L&D functions often face the challenge of balancing training needs with business goals. Training initiatives can become disconnected from the organization's strategic direction without a structured approach. You must engage stakeholders early to define learning priorities, conduct regular strategy meetings with department heads, and integrate training objectives with business outcomes.

Your success metrics for all L&D efforts should extend beyond completion rates to include indicators such as productivity improvements, employee retention, and customer satisfaction. Embedding learning into business workflows through just-in-time tools and on-the-job training is especially helpful for increasing relevance.

Using Technology Strategically

Learning technology and data analytics have made it easier for L&D teams to manage and prioritize training requests. For example, integrated learning platforms and workforce analytics tools provide real-time insights into:
- Employee skills gaps based on performance data and assessments
- Training completion rates and effectiveness metrics
- Business impact measures, such as improved productivity and reductions in errors

By leveraging technology, your L&D team can move beyond making intuition-based decisions and instead use empirical data to prioritize learning initiatives more effectively.

Focusing on Customer-Centric Processes

Prioritizing customer value requires your L&D team to operate as a strategic partner. The organization can enhance customer focus by engaging stakeholders in co-designing learning solutions; establishing SLAs to define response times, deliverables, and quality expectations; and leveraging data to anticipate learning needs rather than waiting for requests.

SLAs help your L&D team operate with the same discipline as other business units. By setting clear expectations with business leaders and your primary customers, you reinforce your role as a value-generating function rather than an administrative cost center. SLAs also play a crucial part in setting clear expectations for training development timelines, service delivery standards, and measurable impact metrics.

For example, an SLA might specify that:

- New training requests receive an initial response within 48 hours.
- Program design will be completed within 30 days.
- Employee satisfaction will be tracked to support L&D's goal of a minimum 90 percent engagement score.

An SLA for escalation procedures would ensure that urgent business needs—such as addressing a sudden spike in customer complaints—receive prioritized support. With an SLA in place, business leaders can see the L&D team's commitment to responsiveness, quality, and continuous improvement, reinforcing your role as a strategic enabler of customer success. (You can find a sample SLA template in Tool 3-1 at the end of this chapter.)

Using Structured Governance Models for Your L&D Initiatives

A structured governance model helps keep L&D initiatives focused, accountable, and connected with business priorities. Along with that model, decision-making committees consisting of L&D leaders, HR professionals, and business executives can provide oversight for training initiatives. In addition, a clear intake and approval process will direct resources to highly effective programs rather than ad hoc requests. Regular strategy reviews conducted quarterly or biannually will help you assess training effectiveness and refine priorities as business needs evolve.

Governance frameworks also prioritize customer value. Without clear governance, organizations risk misallocating resources, responding reactively to training requests, and failing to achieve meaningful business outcomes. Your L&D function can enhance efficiency, effectiveness, and alignment with organizational goals by establishing a governance structure that prioritizes customer value.

Additionally, governance frameworks drive L&D accountability. An effective structure includes leadership committees that provide strategic direction, as well as defined roles and responsibilities for decision making and execution. Performance monitoring mechanisms also help track the effectiveness of training programs against business objectives. Finally, defined roles and responsibilities should clarify accountability for budgeting, implementation, and quality assurance, while careful performance monitoring and reporting ensure that training effectiveness is assessed through KPIs rather than just completion rates.

Your organization should schedule periodic reviews of governance structures and training programs to maintain their effectiveness. These audits help identify areas for improvement so you can adjust policies to reflect changing business needs. A proactive governance approach keeps learning initiatives relevant so they drive measurable business value.

Creating Governance Committees to Support L&D's Investments

Without governance, your L&D team risks being pulled in multiple directions, diluting its influence. By implementing structured decision-making processes, you can ensure that learning investments continue to support evolving business priorities, increasing your ability to scale value.

Start by clearly defining your purpose and structure to establish and operationalize an effective governance committee. A governance committee should typically include representatives from key stakeholder groups, including L&D leaders, HR leaders, senior business leaders, and SMEs from various departments.

Diverse representation ensures a comprehensive understanding of business priorities and workforce needs and informs decisions.

The committee's primary functions include prioritizing training initiatives, approving budgets and resources, and monitoring the alignment of learning strategies with organizational objectives. To help clarify accountability and promote effective collaboration, assign specific roles within the committee, such as:

- A chair to lead discussions
- A record keeper to document decisions
- Members who are responsible for representing their functional areas

Your governance committee should meet regularly, with the frequency determined by the pace of organizational change and the number of L&D initiatives. For example, quarterly meetings may be effective for strategic oversight, while monthly subcommittee meetings might be needed to address tactical issues. All meetings should follow a structured agenda, including:

- Updates on current initiatives
- New training request reviews
- Key performance metrics discussions

The committee can also implement a standardized scoring framework that evaluates requests based on strategic alignment, potential ROI, and urgency.

By adhering to these practices, your governance committee can be a vital mechanism for ensuring your L&D efforts consistently deliver value and adapt to evolving business needs. We'll dive deeper into this topic later in the chapter.

Governance for Organizational Growth

As organizations expand, governance structures need to evolve to accommodate the increase in complexity. Scaling governance structures requires a balance of centralized oversight and decentralized decision-making processes. By empowering divisional or departmental learning leaders within a corporate governance framework, businesses can speed up decision making while maintaining alignment with the overall strategy.

Technology plays a crucial role in scaling governance. LMSs and project management tools can help you track training approvals and outcomes, ensuring efficiency. Standardized best practices across business units also provide consistency while allowing flexibility for localized training needs.

If you are part of a growing organization, try to implement governance models that support adaptability while reinforcing corporate learning strategies.

Avoiding 5 Governance and SLA Pitfalls

Governance models and SLAs are essential for standardized and effective L&D operations, but poor implementation can lead to inefficiencies and unmet expectations. Let's try to understand (and avoid) these five most common pitfalls:

- **Lack of clear definitions and scope.** Vague SLAs and unclear governance structures are easily misinterpreted. Ambiguous expectations, such as undefined response times, frustrate stakeholders. Focus on establishing precise agreements and specifying timelines, responsibilities, and escalation paths to promote efficiency and collaboration.
- **Failure to align with business needs.** Rigid governance frameworks detached from business objectives slow down decision making and hinder responsiveness. Focus instead on engaging stakeholders early to ensure alignment with operational realities. Then, conduct regular reviews to keep SLAs and governance relevant.
- **Overly bureaucratic structures.** Excessive layers of approval can delay critical training initiatives. Focus on a balanced approach that categorizes initiatives by complexity and risk, applying streamlined oversight where necessary. Tiered approvals will allow you to remain both accountable and agile.
- **Inconsistent enforcement and accountability.** Governance structures lose credibility without proper monitoring. Many organizations fail to track SLA adherence or address deviations. Focus on regular audits, dashboards, and feedback loops to ensure compliance. Identifying the root causes of SLA breaches and implementing corrective actions strengthens trust and performance.
- **Poor communication and change management.** Governance structures and SLAs require stakeholder buy-in. Without clear communication, employees may ignore new processes. Focus on proactive engagement through training, townhalls, and feedback sessions to foster understanding and continuous improvement.

Building a customer-centric learning operation requires more than just delivering training; it demands a strategic approach that links L&D with business priorities, governance structures, and measurable results. By embedding learning within business workflows, establishing clear governance, and leveraging technology, you can transform your L&D function into a proactive business partner. Keep in mind that your goal is to ensure learning initiatives drive performance improvements, enhance workforce capabilities, and contribute directly to organizational success.

Pause to Reflect

How do your current L&D processes ensure alignment with business priorities? Where can you strengthen governance to enhance your effectiveness?

Developing Scalable L&D Processes

As organizations grow and evolve, the need for scalable, efficient L&D processes is increasingly critical, and that requires standardization. Standard operating procedures, intake forms, and prioritization frameworks will form the foundation of your structured, repeatable, and adaptable L&D processes and allow you to respond with agility to emerging business needs and pivot as priorities shift. Review the simple phased approach and scorecard in Tool 3-2 at the end of the chapter and consider how you could adapt it to your own organization.

The Value of Standard Operating Procedures

Standard operating procedures (SOPs) are essential for creating a well-structured and efficient L&D function. They provide consistency, clarity, and a shared understanding of how tasks should be performed. By documenting and standardizing workflows, organizations can eliminate ambiguity, reduce redundancies, and improve overall operational effectiveness.

A well-developed SOP ensures that every phase of the learning life cycle—including needs assessment, design, development, delivery, and evaluation—is standardized and repeatable. This consistency enhances learning quality and ensures training initiatives support broader business goals. SOPs will also help you mitigate risks by establishing compliance guidelines so training content meets industry standards and regulatory requirements.

The Role of SOPs in L&D Efficiency

L&D teams operate in fast-paced environments, managing multiple training programs simultaneously. Without documented procedures, teams may struggle with inefficiencies, miscommunication, and errors. SOPs can serve as a blueprint, outlining step-by-step instructions that standardize how your tasks should be completed, and this uniformity reduces variability and enables your team to deliver training initiatives at scale while maintaining high quality.

A key advantage of SOPs is their ability to streamline decision making. When employees have a clear reference guide for handling specific tasks, they spend less time waiting for approvals or resolving misunderstandings. This improved efficiency translates to faster course development cycles, quicker responses to business needs, and a more agile L&D function overall.

Onboarding and Training New L&D Team Members

As organizations grow, new L&D professionals must be onboarded quickly and efficiently. SOPs can facilitate this process by providing a clear map for managing training initiatives. Instead of relying on word-of-mouth knowledge transfer, your new team members can refer to SOP documentation to understand workflows, expectations, and best practices.

For example, if your team develops e-learning modules, an SOP can outline the instructional design framework, authoring tools, and quality assurance processes to follow. This level of detail helps new hires get up to speed faster, reducing onboarding time and ensuring a seamless transition into the team's existing processes.

A Mechanism for Continuous Improvement

SOPs are not static documents; they must evolve as business needs change. Your organization should establish regular review cycles to ensure procedures remain relevant and effective. By incorporating feedback from L&D, its stakeholders, employees, and industry trends, your team can refine its processes and integrate new industry best practices.

One way to facilitate continuous improvement is through *process audits*, which involve conducting periodic reviews of SOPs to identify inefficiencies, redundancies, or outdated practices. L&D leaders should encourage teams to document lessons learned and update procedures to reflect new insights. This iterative approach ensures that your SOPs are dynamic tools that drive operational excellence.

Technology's Role in Standardizing Procedures

Technology plays a critical role in the development, storage, and execution of SOPs. Many organizations use tools like Microsoft SharePoint or Confluence to manage their SOPs. In addition, they may hold function-specific SOPs in specialized software, such as sales enablement training SOPs in the customer relationship management (CRM) software. These platforms give you a centralized location where employees can easily access documentation, ensuring processes remain transparent and readily available.

For example, a company implementing a blended learning strategy might use a project management tool to track the various stages of training development. The SOPs within the system could outline roles, timelines, and approval workflows, helping the team stay on schedule and ensuring that training programs are executed efficiently.

Ensuring Organizational Buy-In for SOPs

The success of SOP implementation relies on organizational buy-in. Leaders and stakeholders must recognize the value of standardized processes and support their adoption across the organization. One way to gain buy-in is by demonstrating how SOPs contribute to business outcomes, such as improved training effectiveness, controlled labor budgets, and enhanced employee performance.

Your L&D team should collaborate with department heads and SMEs to tailor learning program SOPs to your specific needs. Engaging stakeholders in the development process fosters a sense of ownership and makes it more likely they will adhere to standardized practices. Providing training on effectively using SOPs ensures that employees understand their purpose and application.

Capture the Right Information From the Start

Intake forms play a crucial role in the efficiency and effectiveness of your L&D function. A well-designed intake form acts as a filter, capturing essential details about training requests, preventing misaligned efforts, and enabling L&D teams to focus on highly effective projects. Just as product teams use customer feedback to prioritize feature development, your team can apply a structured intake process to ensure training investments align with the needs of your business customers.

The Purpose and Benefits of Intake Forms

The primary function of an intake form is to collect the necessary information to evaluate, prioritize, and design training initiatives. These forms standardize the request process so all stakeholders provide consistent and relevant data. Streamlining this process allows L&D teams to make informed decisions based on business needs, employee profiles, and expected outcomes. The key benefits of a structured intake process include:

- **Alignment with business goals** ensures that requested training initiatives contribute to overarching business objectives, preventing you from developing training programs that lack strategic relevance.
- **Resource optimization** enables your team to allocate resources efficiently by assessing each request's urgency, scope, and potential effects.
- **Clearer expectations** help stakeholders define their training needs more precisely, reducing ambiguity and preventing miscommunication.
- **Prioritization of learning requests** allows your organization to filter and rank training requests based on urgency, alignment with strategic priorities, and projected ROI.

Key Components of an Effective Intake Form

An intake form should gather comprehensive information, but be as simple and intuitive as possible. Overly complex forms can deter stakeholders from submitting requests, but insufficient detail can lead to vague or misaligned training initiatives. Use these components to make sure your intake forms serve their intended purpose:

- **Requester information:**
  - Name, department, and contact details
  - Role in the organization and relationship to the training request

- **Business objective and justification:**
  - Clear articulation of the business problem or opportunity that the training request aims to address
  - Expected influence on productivity, efficiency, compliance, or other KPIs
- **Target audience:**
  - Roles, departments, and locations of the intended employees
  - Experience levels and any prior knowledge or training that's relevant to the request
- **Training scope and requirements:**
  - Preferred modality (such as instructor-led, e-learning, or blended learning)
  - Estimated number of participants and frequency of training sessions
  - Any specific tools, technologies, or content areas that need to be covered
- **Urgency and timeline:**
  - Expected delivery date and any hard deadlines
  - Level of priority and flexibility in scheduling
- **Measurement and success criteria:**
  - KPIs for evaluating training effectiveness
  - How success will be measured (such as knowledge assessments, behavioral changes, or business impact)
- **Approval and budget considerations:**
  - Confirmation of funding sources and budget approval
  - Manager or department head sign-off to validate business necessity

Best Practices for Implementing Intake Forms

To maximize the effectiveness of intake forms, they should be well-integrated into your existing workflows and easy for stakeholders to complete. Try these best practices:

▶ **Automate the intake process.** Use digital tools whenever possible—Smartsheets, workflow automation software like Power Automate, or Microsoft Forms, for example—to streamline submission and tracking.

- ▶ **Educate stakeholders on proper use.** Guide effective completion of the form and make sure managers understand their roles in linking training requests with business needs.
- ▶ **Regularly review and update the forms.** Ensure that forms evolve alongside business priorities and remain relevant as organizational needs change.
- ▶ **Leverage data analytics.** Use insights from completed intake forms to identify trends in training requests, optimize learning strategies, and forecast future training needs.

Enhancing Training Alignment Through Structured Intake Forms

Let's consider the case of a midsize financial services company that faced challenges managing a high volume of training requests from various departments. The L&D team frequently received informal requests via email and verbal communications, which led to inefficiencies and misalignment with business objectives. To address these challenges, they implemented a standardized training intake process using a structured intake form.

The form required stakeholders to provide essential details, such as business objectives, target audience, urgency, and expected outcomes. The L&D team used this information to prioritize requests based on strategic alignment and resource availability. Within six months, the company observed a significant reduction in ad hoc requests, improved alignment of training programs with business goals, and more effective resource allocation.

By establishing a formal intake process, the team was able to transform its L&D function into a reliable business partner that could ensure learning initiatives directly contributed to business success. This structured approach allowed the L&D team to focus on highly effective learning initiatives while minimizing unnecessary training expenditures.

The Future of Intake Forms in L&D

As organizations continue to embrace digital transformation, the role of intake forms will expand beyond simple data collection. AI-powered analytics, chatbots, and predictive modeling can further enhance the effectiveness of training requests by providing real-time recommendations and aligning learning initiatives with workforce development trends. Integrating these technologies will allow L&D teams to make even more data-informed decisions, ultimately improving the effectiveness of corporate learning strategies.

Prioritization: Aligning L&D With Business Strategy

Prioritization frameworks are essential for L&D teams to maximize their influence by allocating resources to initiatives that deliver the highest value. Without a structured approach, training requests can become scattered and reactive. A well-designed prioritization framework allows organizations to make data-informed decisions, optimize resource use, and create training programs that contribute meaningfully to business success.

In chapter 2, we established that you should prioritize your learning investments based on their measurable impact on business objectives. Here, we take the next step by building your prioritization framework, which is now possible because you have established a foundation of standardized governance.

Establishing Criteria for Prioritization

L&D teams should establish clear, objective criteria to effectively assess and rank training requests. Factors you will often find in prioritization frameworks and questions you can ask yourself when considering those factors include:

- **Strategic alignment.** Does the training initiative directly support the company's key business objectives, such as revenue growth, product line, customer satisfaction, or operational efficiency?
- **Regulatory or compliance requirements.** Is training legally mandated or necessary to mitigate risk?
- **Potential ROI.** Will training result in measurable improvements in productivity, quality, or cost savings?
- **Scalability and sustainability.** Can you easily adapt or reuse the program across multiple departments or locations?
- **Urgency and business impact.** Does training address an immediate need or critical skills gap that could affect performance?

Use these criteria to prioritize highly effective training requests while minimizing ad hoc, low-value initiatives.

Implementing a Scoring System

Assigning numerical scores to each criterion is an effective way to apply a prioritization framework. For example, you can create a weighted scoring model in which each factor is assigned a specific value based on its importance to the business. Requests with the highest cumulative score get priority, ensuring that learning investments are focused on the areas of highest value. Consider the example in Table 3-1.

Table 3-1. A Weighted Scoring System for Prioritizing Learning Investments

Criteria	Weight	Score (1–5)	Weighted Score
Strategic alignment	30%	4	1.2
Compliance requirement	20%	5	1.0
Potential ROI	20%	3	0.6
Scalability	15%	4	0.6
Urgency	15%	2	0.3
Total	100%		3.7

A structured scoring approach ensures that decisions are objective, transparent, and defensible, which reduces the risk of subjective prioritization.

Leveraging Stakeholder Input

Your L&D team should always collaborate closely with key stakeholders to ensure you're addressing business needs. Your stakeholders include HR leaders, department heads, and executives who can provide insights into business priorities and workforce challenges. Regular prioritization meetings with these stakeholders can help validate rankings, adjust for changing business conditions, and encourage buy-in for L&D initiatives.

You may want to create a cross-functional steering committee to further enhance the effectiveness of your efforts with ongoing guidance and oversight. This committee can review and approve high-priority training initiatives that support broader corporate strategies and workforce development goals.

Navigating Conflicting Priorities

You will need to do more than just assign scores to ensure prioritization is effective; you also need a structured approach to keep up with evolving business needs. Your L&D team should revisit prioritization scores quarterly, assessing whether shifts in strategic goals, market conditions, or workforce demands require adjustments. Regular review cycles prevent outdated priorities from dictating resource allocation and allow your team to proactively support emerging business challenges. Engaging key stakeholders during these reviews also ensures transparency and reinforces your department's role as a strategic partner.

When conflicts arise between business units, such as competing requests for high-priority training, you can leverage your governance framework to achieve a resolution to those conflicts. A cross-functional learning council or steering committee can evaluate competing requests against company-wide objectives, ensuring alignment with the overarching business strategy rather than individual departmental interests.

By establishing clear escalation pathways, you also allow senior leadership to weigh in on high-stakes decisions, and by embedding these mechanisms into the prioritization process, your team can consistently ensure that learning investments drive the greatest value across the organization.

Balancing Short-Term Needs With Long-Term Planning

Reflecting back on creating your learning road map, remember that prioritization frameworks can help address immediate training demands, but they should also support long-term workforce development. Often, organizations focus too heavily on resolving current urgent skills gaps but fail to invest in future capabilities. Your L&D team should maintain a balanced portfolio of training initiatives across its road map, including:

- **Training programs for immediate needs,** which address pressing skills gaps, compliance requirements, and urgent business initiatives.
- **Initiatives in midterm development,** which prepare employees for anticipated business shifts, such as adopting technology or process improvements.
- **Programs focused on future workplace readiness,** which develop leadership skills, digital literacy, and other capabilities that are essential for long-term organizational success.

By integrating immediate and strategic needs into your prioritization framework, you can create a sustainable learning ecosystem that drives continuous business growth.

Summing up, we know that scalable L&D processes ensure consistency, efficiency, and alignment with organizational goals, and SOPs streamline workflows and reduce reliance on institutional knowledge while maintaining quality. Intake forms capture key details to connect training initiatives with business priorities so you don't waste resources. And prioritization frameworks enable your team to allocate resources effectively, focusing on highly effective initiatives that support strategic objectives.

 Pause to Reflect
How well do your current L&D processes balance efficiency, consistency, and business alignment? Where can you make improvements to enhance scalability?

Managing and Allocating Resources

Effective resource management and allocation ensures that the right resources are allocated to the right priorities, amplifying your L&D function's ability to drive business results rather than just delivering training. Whether you're managing a small team with limited resources or a global department with multiple initiatives, optimizing how you allocate resources ensures learning programs support priorities, remain cost-effective, and meet organizational goals.

Resource Constraints

Challenges in resource management—including limited budgets, competing priorities, and fluctuating demand for training—will arise in most organizations. Without a structured approach to allocation, all teams risk over-committing resources to ineffective initiatives while neglecting strategically important programs. Some key resource constraints include:

- **Budget limitations.** These usually top the list of constraints that dictate the scope of training programs, making it essential to connect investments with business priorities.
- **Team capacity.** Your team's workload plays a crucial role in execution, requiring careful distribution across its members.
- **Technology and tools.** LMSs, digital platforms, and other tools can streamline content delivery and tracking, ensuring that training initiatives are scalable and effective.
- **Time constraints.** These further complicate resource allocation and require a prioritization model that focuses on initiatives with the highest ROI.

Strategic Planning to Allocate Resources

Strategic resource planning involves assessing your organization's training needs and distributing resources accordingly. You must use a data-informed approach that leverages business goals, workforce analytics, and learning effectiveness metrics to inform decision making.

However, resource allocation is not just about optimizing individual learning programs; resources must also be evaluated across the entire learning portfolio. In chapter 4, we'll explore the critical role resource allocation plays in strategically managing L&D investments. For now, know that programs that consume too many resources without delivering measurable business results must be reevaluated, optimized, or retired.

Just as prioritization frameworks help determine where your resources should be allocated within a single training initiative, portfolio management scales these principles so L&D's resources are distributed effectively across multiple programs and initiatives. Without this broader portfolio perspective, your team risks spreading resources too thin, supporting redundant programs, or underinvesting in critical business priorities.

Needs Assessment

Conducting a training needs assessment is an important step in ensuring that your learning initiatives target critical business objectives. Mapping resources to priorities involves assigning instructional designers, trainers, and platforms based on the urgency and complexity of projects. A resource allocation matrix can provide a structured framework for ranking your initiatives based on strategic importance, available resources, and expected outcomes. Flexible resource pools—such as groups of internal SMEs, contract trainers, and digital content providers—can expand your training capacity when needed, preventing bottlenecks in program execution.

Effective Tools and Strategies

Optimizing L&D resource management requires a combination of strategic planning, technological tools, and adaptable processes. A well-defined approach allows your organization to meet its learning objectives while maximizing efficiency and minimizing waste. You can solve one-off needs with separate systems to bring your Learning Operations Blueprint to life. If those systems already exist in your organization, this might be a great way to maximize your budget and build a strong business case for learning operations. However, there are also digital platforms that combine all the learning operations' principles into a singular tool, which gives you greater integration, efficiency, and analytics capabilities as your learning operations function matures.

You can also implement several strategies with existing in-house resources, including:

- **Capacity planning model.** This is one of the most effective strategies because it helps you evaluate current and future resource needs by assessing workload distribution, identifying gaps, and reallocating personnel to vital areas. Workforce analytics play a crucial role in this process, offering insights into how your resources are used and where you need to make adjustments.
- **Centralized resource management system.** Another key strategy involves using a cloud-based project management tool (like Asana, Monday.com, ClickUp, or Jira) to track real-time assignments, deadlines, and resource use. These tools enable better coordination and can reduce bottlenecks by providing visibility across multiple training initiatives.
- **Content repurposing.** Your organization also can enhance efficiency with content repurposing. Rather than developing new training programs from scratch, your team can leverage existing materials, modifying them to meet new learning objectives. Curation and reuse save time and effort and ensure consistency in messaging and instructional quality.

- **Flexible staffing models.** Many organizations leverage gig economy trends by employing contract trainers and external consultants to handle fluctuating training demands. This approach prevents your core L&D staff from being overburdened while providing access to specialized expertise as needed.
- **Scenario planning.** By modeling different business scenarios—such as workforce expansion, budget reductions, or shifts in strategic priorities—you can proactively adjust resource plans for your L&D department to accommodate changing conditions.
- **Embed L&D resources within other business units.** Rather than maintaining a centralized training function, a decentralized or federated/hybrid approach can allow for closer collaboration between L&D teams and functional departments, ensuring that training initiatives align more closely with business needs.

Leverage Technology for Efficiency

We've established that technology plays a crucial role in optimizing L&D resource allocation. For example:

- Learning platforms, content authoring tools, and AI-enabled analytics can enhance training development and delivery.
- Automated administrative tasks for enrollment, tracking, and reporting (through learning platform automation) reduce manual workload, allowing L&D teams to focus on high-value activities.
- Data-informed decision making uses workforce analytics to provide insights into employee performance, ensuring that resources are allocated where they are needed most.
- Blended learning approaches—incorporating e-learning, virtual instructor-led training, and self-paced courses—optimize facilitator time while maintaining employee engagement.
- Cloud-based collaboration tools—such as Microsoft Teams, Slack, or Trello—enhance coordination among L&D teams and stakeholders, ensuring seamless execution of training initiatives.

You and your team may also be experimenting with and integrating AI and machine learning to help kickstart new efficiency models. AI-enabled analytics can predict training needs, recommend optimal learning pathways, and automate administrative tasks such as scheduling and reporting.

These capabilities free up the L&D professionals on your team to focus on more strategic initiatives rather than manual, time-consuming tasks. We will discuss this topic in more detail in later chapters.

Measure and Optimize Resource Use

Resource allocation should be an ongoing process that evolves based on your organization's needs. Establishing KPIs helps confirm you're using resources effectively. Knowing the training cost per employee lets you evaluate the financial efficiency of training initiatives, while time-to-competency measures how quickly employees gain proficiency from training.

The utilization rate of L&D personnel points to how effectively you're assigning trainers and designers to projects, ensuring a balanced workload distribution. And, of course, employee engagement and completion rates provide insights into the effectiveness of training programs, guiding adjustments to enhance their value.

Regularly reviewing these metrics allows you to make informed adjustments, reallocate resources to highly effective initiatives, and phase out low-value training efforts. Portfolio performance reviews should be conducted quarterly to identify trends and inefficiencies so your learning initiatives remain aligned with business goals.

Effective resource management and allocation are invaluable in running an efficient L&D function that delivers measurable business value. By assessing training needs, leveraging technology, and using data-informed planning, you can optimize resources to support business goals. A structured approach strengthens your learning initiatives so they remain highly effective, scalable, and connected to organizational priorities. Continuous evaluation of resource utilization allows you and your team to make strategic adjustments, ensuring that resources are directed toward the initiatives with the greatest potential value.

 Pause to Reflect

How effectively does your L&D team allocate resources? Where could technology or strategic planning improve efficiency?

The Bottom Line

Standardizing core processes within L&D is not just about efficiency; it is about creating a function that delivers consistent, strategic value to the organization. A well-defined governance model, clear SLAs, and data-informed prioritization ensure that learning initiatives align with business objectives and drive measurable results.

By embedding learning into everyday workflows and leveraging technology to streamline operations, you can enhance your team's responsiveness and effectiveness. Moving beyond a reactive approach allows you to proactively partner in business success. Organizations that commit to these principles will see improvements in workforce readiness, operational efficiency, and overall business performance. A structured, scalable L&D function is not just a support mechanism, but a critical enabler of sustainable growth and competitive advantage.

Your next step is to ensure that learning investments are actively managed like a portfolio, linked to business strategy, optimized for effectiveness, and continuously refined to meet evolving needs.

How to Take Action When Designing Your Learning Operations

To put the ideas of this chapter into practice, here are three actions you can take now:

- Schedule a 30-minute meeting with a key business partner to discuss their top training needs and define mutual expectations for L&D support.
- Create and share a simple, one-page training request form to ensure all incoming requests include necessary details for evaluation.
- Identify one repetitive L&D task, such as sending training reminders, and automate it using an existing tool like an LMS or email scheduler.

Tool 3-1.
Sample Service Level Agreement for L&D Teams

Use this sample SLA to help your team set clear expectations with business leaders and your primary customers.

Effective date:
Review date:
Version:

Purpose
This service level agreement (SLA) establishes expectations between the L&D team and its business partners. It defines the scope, response times, deliverables, and performance metrics for training requests, ensuring alignment with business priorities and operational efficiency.

Stakeholders
The parties involved include:
- L&D team: [*Team or department responsible for training delivery*]
- Business unit: [*Requesting department or function*]
- Approving authority: [*HR, business leaders, or L&D governance committee*]

Scope of Services
The L&D team provides the following services:
- Training needs assessment
- Learning program design and development
- Instructor-led training (ILT), virtual instructor-led training (vILT), e-learning, or blended learning
- Content curation and management
- Learning technology support
- Performance support and just-in-time learning
- Evaluation and metrics reporting

Service Request Process
Request submissions must be submitted:
- Using the L&D intake form
- At least [*number of weeks*] in advance for new content and [*number of weeks*] in advance for modifications to existing content

This information is required in each request:
- Business need and expected outcome
- Target audience (including job roles, locations, and number of employees)
- Preferred learning modality
- Requested completion date and urgency
- Approval from department leader

Service Response and Resolution Times

Service Type	Initial Response Time	Estimated Completion Time
Simple training request (off-the-shelf)	3 business days	2 weeks
Custom e-learning development	5 business days	6–12 weeks
ILT scheduling	2 business days	4 weeks
Learning technology support	1 business day	3–5 business days
Training data and reporting	3 business days	1 week

Note: Completion times may vary depending on complexity, business priority, and resource availability.

Roles and Responsibilities

Stakeholder	Responsibilities
L&D team	• Assess, design, and deliver learning solutions. • Maintain training quality standards. • Ensure alignment with business needs. • Report on training effectiveness.
Business partners	• Provide clear learning objectives and expected business outcomes. • Ensure employee participation in training. • Collaborate to evaluate training results.
Approving authority	• Prioritize and approve training initiatives. • Ensure training aligns with business goals.

Performance Metrics and Reporting

The effectiveness of L&D services will be measured using the KPIs listed here.

Metric	Target Benchmark
Training request response time	___% within the SLA timeframe
Training completion rate	___% of employees who complete required training
Stakeholder satisfaction score	___% satisfaction (post-training survey)
Business impact measurement	___% improvement in the targeted performance metric

Escalation Process

If the SLA's expectations are not met, the escalation steps are:
- Level 1: Contact the L&D coordinator at [email and phone number].
- Level 2: Escalate to the L&D manager at [email and phone number].
- Level 3: Involve the L&D governance committee or HR business partner.

Review and Continuous Improvement

This SLA will be reviewed [quarterly or annually] to ensure continued alignment with business needs. All parties will discuss and agree upon any necessary updates.

Tool 3-2.
A Phased Approach to Scaling Your L&D Processes

Use this simple phased approach and scorecard to begin developing scalable L&D processes at your organization.

Phase 1. Assess the current state:
- Conduct stakeholder alignment meetings to identify business-critical learning needs.
- Audit existing L&D processes, technology, and governance frameworks.
- Identify inefficiencies in intake, prioritization, and resource allocation.

Phase 2. Define the Learning Operations Blueprint:
- Establish governance models for learning initiatives.
- Develop SOPs for intake, project prioritization, and execution.
- Align L&D investments with business unit OKRs and KPIs.

Phase 3. Implement, measure, and scale:
- Pilot test standardized learning workflows and refine them based on feedback.
- Introduce data dashboards for real-time tracking of a learning initiative's effectiveness.
- Scale best practices across business units.

Your Learning Operations Self-Assessment Scorecard

A structured scorecard will help L&D leaders assess the maturity of their learning operations across six dimensions: strategy alignment, governance, process efficiency, technology integration, impact measurement, and agility.

How to use the scorecard:
- **Assess your current state.** Score each dimension on a scale from Level 1 to Level 4.
- **Identify gaps.** Focus on areas in which your organization is at Level 1 or 2.
- **Set goals.** Create an action plan to move toward Level 4 across all dimensions.

Dimension	Level 1 (Basic)	Level 2 (Emerging)	Level 3 (Mature)	Level 4 (Optimized)
Strategy alignment	No clear alignment with business goals	Some alignment, but learning initiatives are reactive	Learning strategy is developed in partnership with business leaders	Fully integrated into business planning and decision making
Governance	No defined governance model	Informal governance that lacks consistency	Defined governance with clear decision-making processes	Governance fully embedded in corporate strategy
Process efficiency	Ad hoc, inconsistent processes	Some standardization, but gaps remain	Well-documented, scalable processes	Fully optimized and automated where possible
Technology integration	Basic LMS is in place but not widely used	Some integration with business systems	Integrated learning technology ecosystem	AI-enabled learning and skills intelligence platforms in use
Impact measurement	Focus on completion rates and satisfaction surveys	Some linkage to business metrics	Clear KPIs tied to business outcomes	Predictive analytics used to forecast results
Agility	Slow response to business changes	Some ability to pivot learning initiatives	Regular updates based on evolving needs	Fully agile, continuous learning integrated into daily workflows

Chapter 4
Your Learning Portfolio

The majority of learning leaders are flying blind, unsure of where their efforts are creating value and where they're quietly draining resources. According to research by BCG, nearly 70 percent of L&D teams cannot identify which of their current learning programs are underperforming or redundant (BCG Henderson Institute 2020). What if your CFO said they didn't know which product lines were profitable? Or what if your operations leader admitted they had no idea which facilities were performing below expectations? That seems unthinkable, doesn't it? Yet this is often the reality for L&D. Programs are launched with good intentions, but few are revisited, evaluated, or sunsetted. Over time, the whole group of programs, which I refer to as a *learning portfolio*, becomes bloated, misaligned, and impossible to defend. Lack of visibility is not just a measurement problem; it's a management problem.

Most L&D teams juggle multiple programs, initiatives, and learning solutions, but few manage them like a financial planner would manage a portfolio of strategic investments. Instead, learning programs exist in silos, competing for resources without a clear connection to business priorities. This fragmented approach leads to inefficiencies, redundant content, and training that fails to move the needle on organizational goals.

Managing your learning portfolio means treating L&D initiatives as investments that you actively manage, optimize, and align with the business strategy. A well-run portfolio ensures that learning programs deliver measurable business value, remain relevant, and balance short-term needs and long-term workforce development. This chapter explores the principles of learning portfolio management and how to leverage data to measure success. It also offers tips to help you scale and adapt a learning portfolio to your needs. By taking a disciplined, portfolio-based approach,

L&D leaders can make informed decisions that maximize their positive influence and eliminate waste.

Principles of Managing a Learning Portfolio

A learning portfolio comprises all the programs, initiatives, and platforms an organization uses to develop its workforce. Like a financial portfolio, it should be actively managed to ensure the right mix of investments, avoid duplication, and maximize returns. An effective learning portfolio must support strategic business goals, maintain a balance of learning initiatives, undergo regular optimization, and be scalable to accommodate business growth. Building on the prioritization frameworks introduced in chapter 3, portfolio management applies these principles at scale, ensuring that resources are allocated to the most effective programs while eliminating redundancy and waste.

Managing a learning portfolio as a strategic investment requires taking an intentional approach to evaluating, prioritizing, and optimizing training initiatives. You will need to identify and manage risks, regularly audit your portfolio, and make sure you maximize the return on your learning investment.

Who Owns Your Organization's Learning Portfolio?

Effective portfolio management is not the sole responsibility of L&D. While L&D plays a central role in strategy, execution, and measurement, multiple stakeholders share ownership of the portfolio to help drive influence and accountability, including:

- ▶ **Your L&D team.** You should be responsible for designing and delivering high-quality learning experiences, ensuring they support business goals, and tracking program effectiveness based on data.
- ▶ **Other business unit leaders.** On the other hand, these leaders define learning priorities and fund development initiatives that support strategic objectives. Their engagement is critical to ensure that learning solutions address genuine business needs and drive measurable outcomes.
- ▶ **HR.** These folks will connect learning initiatives to workforce planning so training supports talent development, succession planning, and skills forecasting. Your organization can proactively address skills

gaps and enhance employee career growth by integrating learning with broader operations and HR strategies.

▶ **Employees.** As active participants in the learning portfolio, employees provide feedback, engage in upskilling, and apply newly acquired skills in the workplace. Their involvement ensures that learning programs remain relevant, engaging, and effective in driving individual and organizational growth.

By fostering strong collaboration among L&D, business unit leaders, HR, and employees, organizations can create a dynamic learning portfolio that continuously evolves to meet business demands and workforce expectations.

Let's delve into how your structured learning portfolio can follow a disciplined investment model by focusing on risk assessment and performance tracking. You can maintain a balance between immediate operational needs and long-term workforce development if you first categorize your learning programs based on their contributions to the business. Options include:

- **Foundational programs.** These might include compliance training or onboarding, which are essential for keeping the business running smoothly.
- **Operational programs.** These support current performance needs, such as upskilling customer service teams to meet new quality standards.
- **Strategic programs.** These focus on future growth, like leadership pipeline development or reskilling efforts that support digital transformation initiatives.

Identify and Manage Risks

Managing risks in your learning portfolio requires a proactive approach to identifying, assessing, and mitigating potential threats that could undermine the effectiveness of your learning initiatives. A structured framework, such as the risk rubric in Table 4-1, allows you to categorize risks based on their likelihood and impact to help guide your mitigation strategies. This approach also helps you prioritize your responses and implement targeted mitigation actions. There are six types of risks you need to consider:

- **Adoption risks**—such as low employee engagement or resistance to change—can be mitigated through stakeholder alignment, clear communication, and behavioral nudges like gamification and recognition programs.
- **Content relevance risks** require governance mechanisms that ensure regular updates and the use of modular learning design to facilitate quick revisions.
- **Business alignment risks** require ongoing collaboration with leadership and the integration of learning metrics into broader organizational performance tracking.
- **Cost and resource risks** can be addressed through budget forecasting, vendor audits, and leveraging technology to optimize efficiency.
- **Learning fatigue risks** can be addressed by balancing the employee learning workload, coordinating across business units to prevent too many learning programs from launching simultaneously, and regularly reviewing feedback to detect early signs of disengagement.
- **Scalability risks** require learning program design that can expand usage without major revisions by using modular content, automation, and infrastructure that supports consistent delivery across roles and divisions.

To effectively manage all these risks, you will need a structured approach to resource allocation, as discussed in chapter 3.

Once you've completed Table 4-1, use this scoring guide to assess your risks:

- **Low risk.** If a program's total score is 6–9 points, it is stable and well-managed. Monitor performance, ensure continuous improvement, and maintain alignment with business goals.
- **Medium risk.** If the total score is 10–15 points, you should make minor adjustments to the program to improve effectiveness. Identify areas for adjustment, implement corrective measures, and track progress over time.
- **High risk.** If the total score is 16–21 points, the program will require some major interventions to address risk areas. Conduct an in-depth review, escalate concerns to stakeholders, and implement major improvements.

- **Critical risk.** The program may need to be overhauled or discontinued if its total score is 22–24 points. Consider redesigning the program, reallocating resources, or phasing out initiatives that no longer provide value.

By systematically assessing and addressing risks using a structured framework and updating materials to engage employees, you can safeguard your learning investments and ensure programs remain meaningful, scalable, and strategically aligned with business priorities.

Table 4-1. A Learning Portfolio Risk Rubric

Type of Risk	Low Risk (1 Point)	Medium Risk (2 Points)	High Risk (3 Points)	Critical Risk (4 Points)	Score
Adoption	High employee engagement and adoption	Some resistance to adoption and moderate engagement	Low engagement and widespread resistance	Adoption failure and program abandonment	
Content relevance	Content is up-to-date and highly relevant	Some content updates needed with minor gaps present	Outdated content and significant gaps present	Irrelevant or obsolete content	
Business alignment	Fully aligned with business priorities	Moderate misalignment with business priorities	Major misalignment with business needs	No alignment with business strategy	
Cost and resource	Budget well-managed with no resource constraints	Some budget overruns or inefficiencies	Severe budget issues and resource shortages	Severe financial mismanagement that's unsustainable	
Learning fatigue	Balanced learning workload and no signs of fatigue	Minor employee fatigue reported	Significant employee fatigue and disengagement	Widespread burnout and disengagement	
Scalability	Learning programs scale seamlessly	Scalability requires moderate adjustments	Programs struggle to scale and major barriers exist	Scalability impossible and major redesign needed	
				Total	

Your Learning Portfolio

Audit Your Learning Portfolio

Portfolio audits help you evaluate whether current resource allocation strengthens strategic business priorities, identify gaps and redundancies, and make informed decisions about when to scale, update, or retire programs. This will keep your learning investments financially sustainable and positioned to deliver measurable value.

Portfolio audits should always incorporate resource use data, examining whether learning programs consume too many resources relative to their business value. Programs that consistently exceed their budgets, have low adoption numbers, or require disproportionate maintenance may need to be redesigned, consolidated, or phased out.

Let's walk through the audit process, which includes creating an inventory of existing programs. Start by cataloging all active learning programs and classifying them based on their purpose and audience. Common categories include:

- **Compliance and regulatory training**—legally required or policy-driven programs
- **Foundational and onboarding programs**—essential training for new hires or role transitions
- **Technical and functional skills training**—job-specific capability-building initiatives
- **Leadership and professional development**—programs that support career growth and succession planning
- **Strategic and innovative learning**—future-oriented initiatives tied to business transformation

A complete inventory provides visibility into the full scope of L&D initiatives and helps assess whether the current mix supports organizational needs.

Evaluate Your Programs

As part of your audit, you should ask questions to evaluate each learning program in your portfolio. Use these prompts to assess whether programs are aligned, effective, and meeting expectations.

- **To evaluate business alignment, ask:**
  - Is this program directly tied to a current business goal, KPI, or workforce capability priority?

- Can you clearly articulate how this program contributes to workforce performance or risk reduction?
- Has a business leader validated the program's relevance?
- **To evaluate effectiveness and engagement, ask:**
  - Are employees completing the program and applying what they have learned on the job?
  - What do performance metrics show before and after training?
  - Are you collecting and acting on employee and manager feedback?
- **To evaluate SLA performance, ask:**
  - Are you meeting agreed-upon timelines and deliverables with your business stakeholders?
  - Is satisfaction with the learning experience high across all user groups, including employees, managers, and sponsors?
  - Have any programs consistently missed deadlines or failed to deliver expected value?

Use quantitative data (such as participation rates, assessments, and business KPIs) and qualitative feedback (such as surveys, interviews, and focus groups) to answer these questions. The goal is to identify which programs deliver measurable value and which need to be optimized or sunsetted.

Identify Redundancies and Gaps

An effective portfolio has good coverage of topics without unnecessary duplication. As part of the audit, analyze whether:

- **Multiple programs address the same skills or topics,** which may reveal opportunities to consolidate or streamline content.
- **Some skills are overemphasized while others are underrepresented,** which could indicate that some business capabilities are missing from your current learning strategy.
- **Certain programs are underused**—in which case, the low engagement may indicate irrelevant programs, poor promotion, or a mismatch between content and employee needs.

Your portfolio audit can help you allocate resources strategically, ensuring that learning investments drive meaningful business results and your L&D team maintains a dynamic, high-performing learning ecosystem that continuously evolves to meet business needs while maximizing the return on learning investments.

Maximize ROI

ROI in L&D goes beyond efforts to reduce costs. ROI means maximizing the value generated from your learning investments. To achieve a high return:

- **Align learning content to business KPIs.** Training programs should contribute to business metrics, such as productivity, customer satisfaction, revenue growth, and employee retention.
- **Measure learning impact effectively.** Move beyond traditional completion rates and satisfaction surveys. Instead, track:
    - *Productivity improvements post-training.* For example, a sales team increased deal velocity by 18 percent within 90 days of being trained in a new sales enablement process.
    - *Employment retention rates for training participants.* For example, a call center determined that customer support representatives who completed the new career pathway initiative had a 32 percent higher retention rate over 12 months.
    - *Performance improvements in key job roles.* For example, new managers at a supply chain management company who attended a leadership boot camp scored 20 percent higher on quarterly performance evaluations than their peers who did not attend.
- **Optimize learning modalities.** Use cost-effective and scalable methods, such as digital learning, microlearning, and AI-enabled adaptive learning.
- **Leverage new learning technologies.** AI, automation, and data analytics can drive efficiency, personalize learning, and provide real-time insights into program effectiveness.

Use Portfolio Management to Address High Employee Turnover

Imagine an organization struggling with high turnover among frontline employees. A traditional approach might involve rolling out generic training modules without assessing their effectiveness. A better option would be to apply a portfolio-based approach:

- ▶ Conduct a portfolio audit to identify redundant or outdated onboarding programs.
- ▶ Use data analytics to determine key skills gaps and knowledge retention challenges that slow down speed to proficiency for new hires.

- ▶ Launch a pilot microlearning series focused on core job functions with embedded assessments.
- ▶ Measure retention and speed to proficiency improvements to determine ROI.

By treating learning as a portfolio investment, you will direct resources toward vital areas, ensuring learning initiatives actively contribute to business goals.

Align Learning Objectives With Strategic Business Goals

If you want a learning portfolio that drives tangible business outcomes, it must be tightly integrated with strategic business objectives. This requires ongoing collaboration between L&D and business stakeholders to ensure learning investments support broader organizational goals.

Start with a comprehensive assessment of business priorities, identifying critical skills gaps, and determining which learning programs directly contribute to achieving corporate goals. As an L&D leader, you will need to engage other business leaders, HR teams, and department managers to map learning initiatives to business performance indicators, such as revenue growth, operational efficiency, and workforce agility.

Assess Strategic Learning Priorities

Your strategic learning portfolio should be built around three categories of initiatives:

- **Business-critical training** includes programs that address immediate compliance, regulatory, and operational needs.
- **Capability development** includes learning initiatives focused on upskilling and reskilling to meet evolving business demands.
- **Strategic workforce enablement** includes leadership development, innovation training, and programs designed to future-proof the organization.

By categorizing training programs in this way, your L&D team can prioritize investments and ensure that resources are allocated effectively to support short- and long-term business objectives.

Create a Performance-Based Learning Framework

To measure the effectiveness of learning programs, you will need to move beyond traditional L&D vanity metrics such as completion rates and satisfaction scores. Instead, focus on performance-based indicators that demonstrate tangible business results. Key metrics include:

- **Workforce productivity,** which measures improvements in job performance and efficiency post-training.
- **Operational KPIs,** which track reductions in errors, downtime, and inefficiencies as a result of training programs.
- **Revenue impact,** which assesses whether sales training, customer service enhancements, or innovation programs contribute to business growth.
- **Talent retention and engagement**, which allows you to evaluate whether professional development opportunities increase employee retention and job satisfaction.

A structured measurement approach ensures that learning initiatives contribute to the organization's overall success.

In short, effective portfolio management treats learning programs as business investments, ensuring that resources are allocated where they have the greatest influence. By evaluating programs based on strategic alignment, cost, and measurable outcomes, you can optimize your portfolio to maximize ROI, allowing you to move beyond reactive program development and drive sustained business value.

 Pause to Reflect

How well does your current learning portfolio align with your company's strategic priorities? What adjustments could improve its overall effectiveness?

Leverage Data to Measure Success

Data-informed decision making is a core component of effective learning portfolio management. Organizations that fail to connect learning programs to business outcomes often struggle to justify L&D investments. By leveraging company-wide analytics, you can move beyond traditional training metrics and demonstrate clear value on the profit and loss (P&L) statement.

Establish a data framework that tracks learning outcomes at multiple levels, including:
- **Learning engagement metrics** (completion rates, assessment scores, and participation levels)
- **Behavioral change indicators** (manager feedback, workplace observation, and self-reports)
- **Business impact measures** (productivity efficiency, customer satisfaction, and cost reduction)
- **Financial outcomes** (revenue growth, risk mitigation, retention, and cost savings)

To operationalize this approach, your L&D team should follow four key practices:
- **Align learning metrics with business objectives.** This ensures that data reflects progress toward KPIs and strategic priorities.
- **Use dashboards to deliver real-time insights to both L&D and business stakeholders.** This enables faster, more informed decisions.
- **Automate data collection.** Integrate your learning platforms with your organization's data warehouse and business intelligence tools.
- **Apply predictive analytics.** Forecast training effectiveness, identify highly effective programs, and optimize resource allocation.

When learning data is integrated with company-wide performance metrics, L&D can demonstrate not only activity but results. This will build and support the case for continued investment and value.

Measure the Financial Value of Learning

A healthy approach to financial measurement extends beyond traditional calculations and incorporates a more comprehensive view of L&D's contribution to business outcomes. Here are some ways to get a clearer picture of L&D's financial value:
- **Cost-benefit analysis evaluates the financial return on learning investments by assessing cost per employee against revenue.** It includes direct costs (such as content development, platform expenses, instructor fees) and indirect costs (like employee time

spent in training). Comparing these costs to business outcomes (such as increased sales, improved customer satisfaction, or reduced compliance risks) helps demonstrate the value of learning programs.

- **Workforce productivity metrics measure improvements in efficiency and operational effectiveness.** Key indicators include reductions in rework, faster time-to-proficiency for new hires, and increases in employee output post-training. Analyzing these metrics helps you quantify the tangible effects of learning on workforce performance.
- **Strategic value metrics assess the long-term benefits of learning initiatives, including their effect on innovation, leadership pipeline development, and organizational agility.** Programs that contribute to talent retention, succession planning, and the ability to adapt to market changes provide critical business advantages that extend beyond immediate financial returns.

Using these financial measurement approaches will help you articulate the value of learning investments, ensuring continued support and alignment with broader business objectives.

Balance Business Needs With Employee Engagement

As we've discussed, L&D operates at the intersection of business needs and employee engagement. Striking the right balance between these two priorities is critical to ensure that training delivers organizational value and a positive employee experience.

Organizations often face a tough dilemma because business stakeholders prioritize measurable outcomes—such as productivity, compliance, and operational efficiency—while employees seek engaging, relevant, and accessible learning experiences. To reconcile these perspectives, your L&D team must design programs that are aligned to the business and employee centric. Table 4-2 shows a few data-informed practices that can help you accomplish this.

Achieve Sustainable Learning Results

Balancing business objectives with employee engagement requires continuous collaboration with stakeholders and an intentional, data-informed approach. Here's how to make it actionable:

- **Engage leadership and managers.** Ensure that executives and managers actively champion learning by linking training to measurable business outcomes. For example, if a sales team leader sees a 12 percent increase in closed deals after employees complete targeted objection handling training, this should prompt a broader rollout.
- **Make learning a performance enabler.** Shift from compliance-first thinking to designing programs that directly support job performance. For example, instead of a generic soft skills course, an L&D team could launch a customer escalation training program for the customer support team, which would lead to a drop in support tickets escalated to management.
- **Build a learning culture.** Encourage everyday development through embedded practices, not standalone events. For example, a company might embed micro-coaching prompts into weekly team check-ins and track manager usage and effectiveness via pulse survey data.

Table 4-2. Business and Employee Benefits of Data-Informed Practices

Data-Informed Practice	Business Benefit	Employee Benefit
Dual-value approach	Develops critical skills aligned to KPIs	Supports career development and engagement
Personalization and adaptive learning	Ensures training supports business goals based on role and function	Delivers relevant, individualized learning experiences
Multimodal learning	Improves scalability and access	Creates accessibility for all and supports diverse learning preferences
Moment of need learning	Increases productivity and performance at the point of need	Delivers help when employees need it most
Feedback loops	Enable program agility and alignment	Create responsive learning programs

By combining companywide analytics with learning programs designed to meet and achieve business needs and employee expectations, L&D can improve adoption and drive tangible outcomes.

Pause to Reflect
What key data points are you tracking? How effectively do they inform strategic learning decisions?

Scale and Adapt Your Learning Portfolio

An effective learning portfolio is not static; it must evolve with your business. As market conditions, organizational priorities, and workforce dynamics shift, learning initiatives must be agile enough to keep pace. Scaling and adapting your learning portfolio requires a proactive approach in which you are continuously assessing its value, integrating emerging learning technologies, and aligning with evolving business strategies.

Build an Agile Portfolio

By now, you know that effective learning requires more than just increasing the number of training sessions. It involves developing an agile framework that enables rapid adjustments to program offerings, resource allocation, and delivery methods. The most important elements of an agile learning portfolio include:

- **Modular learning design.** Breaking down learning content into smaller, reusable modules allows organizations to update or reconfigure training programs without overhauling entire courses. This ensures content remains relevant and linked to shifting business needs. For instance, a financial services company created an agile portfolio by modularizing its regulatory compliance training. Instead of redeveloping full courses when regulations changed, the company's L&D team broke the content into bite-sized components tied to specific rules. When updates were needed, the team revised only the affected modules, cutting update time from three months to two weeks.
- **Scalable infrastructure.** Cloud-based learning platforms and online content providers allow organizations to scale learning initiatives efficiently, enabling just-in-time learning and real-time content updates.
- **Continuous needs assessment.** Regularly engaging with stakeholders and leveraging workforce analytics ensures that

learning programs align well with skills gaps and forecasting, as well as emerging business priorities.
- **Iterative program development.** Agile methodologies, such as rapid prototyping and feedback loops, allow organizations to continuously test and refine learning initiatives.

Integrate Emerging Learning Technologies

As technology continues to reshape how we do business, leveraging new learning technologies becomes even more critical for scalability and adaptability. Organizations must be strategic in their adoption of new tools to enhance learning effectiveness while ensuring cost-efficiency. Technologies that support scalable learning include:

- **AI-enabled personalization.** Adaptive learning platforms use AI to tailor training content based on individual employee progress, performance, and preferences, ensuring more relevance and engagement. One global logistics organization, for instance, used this approach in its frontline onboarding program. By integrating an AI-enabled learning platform, new hires received personalized content based on role, geography, and tested prior knowledge. Ramp-up time dropped by 30 percent and completion rates rose by 22 percent, which freed field trainers to focus on high-value coaching.
- **Learning platforms.** The market keeps evolving from LMSs and learning content management systems (LCMSs) to LXPs and headless platforms. No matter which you choose, these platforms are designed to help curate learning content and deliver it in more accessible and relevant ways.
- **Virtual and augmented reality.** Immersive learning environments enhance experiential training, particularly for complex skills, technical training, and high-risk environments.
- **Automation and chatbots.** AI-enabled chatbots provide on-demand learning support, answer employee questions, and guide them through training modules.

By monitoring, experimenting, and integrating these technologies, L&D leaders can create scalable, engaging, and responsive learning experiences that support diverse learning needs quickly and effectively.

Ensure Alignment With Business Strategy—Again

A scalable learning portfolio must align tightly with your organization's strategic goals. To achieve this, you can take these three steps:

1. **Establish a governance framework.** As discussed in chapter 3, a structured governance model ensures that learning initiatives will support your business objectives, maintain stakeholder involvement, and facilitate ongoing prioritization of learning investments.
2. **Create learning dashboards.** Using real-time analytics, organizations can track learning effectiveness, measure workforce readiness, and adjust programs based on performance data. To illustrate this, a healthcare system piloted a dashboard that combined learning platform data with performance metrics from its EHR system. It tracked training completions, time-to-proficiency for new nurses, and clinical error rates at a handful of locations. By monitoring this data, the L&D team was able to identify specific learning modules that correlated with faster ramp-up and reduced errors and scale them across the organization.
3. **Embed learning in workforce planning.** Partnering with HR and business leaders ensures that learning programs anticipate workforce shifts, helping organizations stay ahead of industry disruptions and emerging talent needs. For example, at an insurance company I worked with, workforce planning uncovered an upcoming shortage of midcareer underwriters due to planned retirements. The L&D team was able to proactively design a career acceleration program for internal candidates, compressing a typical five-year development path into two years. This ensured operational continuity and reduced the number of external hires needed to fill vacancies.

Mentioning governance in the same breath as agility may seem counterintuitive. However, governance is not just about structure; it is also about enabling agility. As discussed in chapter 3, standardized processes, intake frameworks, and SLAs create operational efficiency, empower L&D teams to make informed decisions, and shift resources and priorities quickly when business needs change. Without governance guardrails in place, your portfolio decisions can become fragmented, leading to reactive boondoggles rather than strategic learning investments.

A well-defined governance structure ensures that learning portfolio decisions are proactive, data-informed, and responsive to emerging business priorities. For example, when a new strategic initiative is proposed, governance committees can evaluate whether existing programs could be adjusted or expanded instead of defaulting to creating new training initiatives from scratch. By balancing structured decision making with flexibility, L&D teams can scale learning initiatives efficiently while maintaining strategic focus.

Overcome Barriers to Scaling Learning

Scaling learning isn't just a matter of adding more content or increasing headcount. It means building an infrastructure that can support consistent, high-value learning at speed, even as business needs shift. To do that, you need to anticipate and address common roadblocks.

Start by securing leadership support. Demonstrate how scalable learning solutions like those we have discussed reduce time-to-productivity, improve workforce readiness, and contribute to business KPIs. When executives and managers see the connection between learning and business outcomes—like faster time-to-productivity or increased customer satisfaction—they are more likely to invest.

At the employee level, resistance often stems from information overload and competing priorities. A content curation strategy helps cut through the noise. Focus on relevance: What do employees need to know to do their job better right now? Use data to identify high-value content and remove content that fails to drive performance. Reinforce engagement through small but powerful levers like recognition programs, peer learning groups, and real-time nudges delivered through organizational tools that are already in place, like email or Microsoft Teams.

Future-Proof Your Portfolio

The ability to scale and adapt learning programs is essential for long-term organizational resilience. To future-proof your learning portfolio, consider these strategies:

- **Build a skills taxonomy.** Mapping organizational competencies ensures that learning initiatives remain targeted and address evolving skills demands. For example, the commercial fleet division at an insurance company created a skills taxonomy to map critical claims processing and data analytics skills across roles. This enabled them to align development programs with future automation plans and guide reskilling efforts during a claims processing system overhaul.
- **Emphasize lifelong learning.** Encourage employees to take ownership of their development and foster a self-directed learning culture.
- **Stay ahead of industry trends.** Engaging in continuous benchmarking and external learning partnerships will help you anticipate future skills needs and adjust learning investments accordingly.

By developing an adaptive, technology-enabled, and business-aligned learning portfolio, organizations can make sure their workforce remains competitive and equipped to meet the demands of a rapidly changing business environment.

As business needs evolve, so must your learning portfolio. A scalable yet adaptable approach ensures L&D can respond to organizational shifts while maintaining efficiency. Standardized processes, governance frameworks, and automation play a critical role in sustaining a learning portfolio that is agile and aligned with business objectives.

 Pause to Reflect

What barriers prevent your L&D team from scaling learning initiatives efficiently? How could better portfolio management help overcome them?

The Bottom Line

Managing your learning portfolio as a strategic investment ensures that learning initiatives are aligned with business priorities, resources are used efficiently, and programs drive measurable results. By taking a disciplined, data-informed approach, you should be able to eliminate redundancies, optimize learning solutions, and make smarter decisions about where to invest.

Small but intentional actions can set the stage for a more strategic and well-managed learning portfolio. Instead of overhauling everything at once, start with the simple steps discussed in this chapter, and you'll make immediate progress.

How to Take Action to Manage Your Learning Portfolio

Now that we have discussed the need for managing your learning portfolio, here are a few actions you can take today to put these insights into motion:

- **Look at engagement, completion rates, or feedback from a program you suspect isn't delivering results.** Does the data confirm your concerns? If so, flag it for further review or start a conversation about whether it should be optimized or retired.
- **Send a quick email or Slack message to a key stakeholder.** Try something like: "What's the most pressing workforce challenge on your plate right now? I want to make sure our learning efforts are aligned with your business needs." The answer may help you refocus your portfolio on what matters most.
- **Pick a learning program designed a year or more ago and evaluate its effectiveness.** Are the business needs, skills, or performance challenges that it addresses still current? If not, note it for an update or refresh.

PART 3
Driving L&D Innovation

Chapter 5
Emerging Technologies

The pitch was slick. The demo was flawless. And the promise? Transform frontline safety training with cutting-edge virtual reality (VR) simulations. The L&D leader at a global manufacturing firm was sold and so was the executive team. Half a million dollars and six months later, the pilot launched.

But usage lagged. Plant managers didn't push it. Frontline teams didn't have time to use it. And when the CFO asked, "Did this reduce incidents? Did it save us money?" no one had a clear answer. What went wrong?

It wasn't the technology. The VR content was well-designed, the user feedback was positive, and the potential was real. The problem was upstream: No business problem had been clearly defined, no metrics agreed upon, and no operational integration planned. The result? A missed opportunity to prove value and a hesitancy to invest again.

Now, contrast that with a three-person L&D team at a regional healthcare network. Instead of starting with tools, they started with a problem: Patient documentation errors were increasing, leading to billing delays and compliance risks. After reviewing workflows and shadowing staff, they pinpointed a learning gap tied to a new system. Rather than overhauling their LMS or investing in new software, the team pilot tested a microlearning solution embedded in the platform itself—short, task-based prompts triggered by system actions.

Within 60 days, documentation accuracy improved, billing cycles shortened, and compliance issues declined. The solution wasn't flashy, but it worked because it was built around a real business problem, tested quickly, and tied directly to measurable outcomes.

The difference between these two teams wasn't budget or headcount; it was mindset. Emerging technology can accelerate learning, reduce friction, and introduce entirely new ways of solving problems, but only if it's applied with intent. When tech is chosen to support a business outcome, rather than to chase innovation for its own sake, it becomes a strategic asset.

Let's start by looking at how some high-performing teams are experimenting with new tools in ways that add value, not noise.

Innovating With Learning Technologies

The real challenge in learning technology adoption isn't access to new tools; it's knowing how to implement them strategically to improve workforce performance and business outcomes. While emerging technologies like AI, automation, and immersive learning offer exciting possibilities, they can also become expensive distractions if they're not effectively integrated into a structured L&D strategy.

Organizations that view technology adoption as a business decision grounded in operational efficiency, governance, and measurable value can drive sustainable learning transformation. However, investing in technology without a clear plan for implementation, adoption, and scalability leads to wasted resources, disengaged employees, and fragmented learning ecosystems.

Integrate Tools and Learning Strategies

Adopting new learning technologies is about transforming how organizations approach skills development and knowledge transfer. Companies that fail to modernize their L&D strategies risk inefficiencies, disengagement, and an inability to adapt to industry disruptions. When applied strategically, emerging technologies can improve accessibility, boost engagement, and enhance learning retention by catering to different learning styles and needs.

Moreover, organizations that embrace innovation in learning technology foster a culture of continuous improvement and agility. By investing in emerging solutions, companies can create dynamic learning tech ecosystems in which employees are encouraged to take ownership of their development. Learning becomes an ongoing, embedded process rather than a one-time event, ensuring that employees remain adaptable and equipped to handle evolving challenges in their respective industries.

No More Wasted Resources

Simply acquiring new tools without a strategic need can lead to wasted resources and disengaged employees. The key to success lies in integrating these technologies into a broader learning strategy aligned with business goals, employee needs, and measurable outcomes.

To avoid acquiring technology for technology's sake, start with a clear understanding of the skills your organization needs to develop, the challenges it is addressing, and the business outcomes it aims to achieve. Only then should you evaluate if technology can support those goals.

The Role of Leaders in Driving Innovation Through Technology

Executive leaders need to do more than just sign-off on budget requests for L&D teams to effectively leverage emerging technologies, whether that means AI, immersive learning, automation, or next-generation learning platforms. Executives need to set the vision, secure investment, model digital fluency, and ensure accountability. Without strong executive engagement, even the most promising learning technologies can become underfunded, deprioritized, and disconnected from business strategy.

Use a Business-First Lens

Leaders should evaluate potential investments through a business-first lens to ensure emerging technologies support long-term business success. Before committing to any learning technology, executives need to ask:

- **Does it address a business-critical skills gap or performance challenge?** For example, will AI-enabled analytics help you quickly identify and close workforce capability gaps?
- **How will you measure its impact on workforce capability?** For example, will VR-based training lead to measurable improvements in safety, compliance, or leadership skills?
- **Can you integrate it into existing systems without creating redundancies?** For example, does this new tool complement your current LMS or LXP ecosystem, or does it duplicate existing functionality?

Leaders who apply these criteria can ensure their technology investments serve a strategic purpose rather than becoming expensive, underused tools.

The first step in successful adoption is articulating a clear vision for how emerging technologies will enhance learning and workforce capability.

If you are an executive, position innovation as a driver of business agility, workforce readiness, and competitive advantage rather than a tool for delivering training. Instead of focusing on how technology can improve training efficiency, shift your conversations to discussing how immersive simulations accelerate leadership development, how automation frees instructional designers for high-value projects, or how next-generation platforms enable continuous upskilling. When you frame learning technology as a tool for business transformation, you'll help elevate L&D from a cost center to a strategic enabler of growth.

Invest in Innovation

Beyond setting a vision, executives play a pivotal role in securing investment for innovation. Many L&D teams struggle with adoption because emerging technologies often fall outside traditional L&D budgets. As a forward-thinking leader, build in dedicated funding for experimentation and pilot programs, whether that's VR-based training, intelligent content curation, or AI-powered workforce analytics.

A budgeting practice you can try is *iterative funding*, which involves releasing investment in phases based on pilot group outcomes rather than requiring full commitment upfront. This method enables L&D teams to test new solutions, measure effectiveness, and scale based on data-informed success. Ensure cross-functional collaboration in funding decisions by working with IT, HR, and business units to co-fund learning technologies that benefit the broader organization.

Be a Tech Role Model

Equally critical for executives is modeling digital fluency and championing adoption. Employees and managers are far more likely to embrace new technologies when they see senior leaders actively engaging with them.

As a tech role model, you might participate in VR-based leadership simulations, leverage adaptive learning pathways, or experiment with skills-mapping tools to inform workforce planning. As a leader, you should also encourage senior managers to embed emerging technologies into team development strategies, reinforcing their importance beyond the L&D function. Moreover, try to foster a culture of experimentation in which trying, testing, and refining new learning technologies is encouraged rather than seen as risky or disruptive.

Recognizing and rewarding teams that successfully integrate technology into learning programs sends a strong signal that innovation is not only supported but expected.

Measure Technology's Effectiveness

Finally, as a leader you must ensure that your team is measuring technology adoption for real results. Too often, emerging learning technologies are evaluated on engagement metrics rather than their influence on workforce capability and business performance.

Hold L&D accountable for tracking clear success metrics, such as reduced time-to-proficiency, increased skills retention, performance improvements, and alignment with business objectives. Regular reporting, through quarterly business reviews or live dashboards, helps sustain momentum and ongoing refinement. As a leader, you should safeguard against unintended risks so learning technologies support equity, accessibility, and ethical standards in workforce development.

When you actively support L&D experimentation, secure flexible funding, engage with new technologies firsthand, and measure business results, you will ensure that your organization maximizes the benefits of learning innovation. You will also position your organization for continuous learning, workforce adaptability, and sustained competitive advantage. In doing so, you can help create an organization in which learning is not just a function but a strategic capability that drives business success.

Without strong leadership, L&D technology adoption risks remaining underfunded, siloed, and disconnected from enterprise strategy. Your commitment as a leader will lay the foundation for successful technology adoption, but execution depends on the L&D team's skills and capabilities. Investing in AI, immersive learning, or automation is pointless if L&D professionals can't leverage these tools effectively. The next step is to build internal expertise by fostering a culture of experimentation, structured upskilling programs, and data-informed learning design.

Learning Technologies for Scalability

Even with executive sponsorship and a clear vision, integrating new learning technologies effectively requires structured implementation, governance, and ongoing optimization. Many organizations struggle because they focus too much on launching new tools rather than embedding them into existing learning workflows and business processes. The real challenge is ensuring that a new technology will deliver sustained value by becoming a seamless part of the organization's learning ecosystem.

Prioritize Governance, Scalability, and Measurement

To successfully operationalize emerging technologies, L&D teams must approach implementation with a disciplined strategy that prioritizes governance, scalability, and performance measurement to ensure long-term success. Your organization risks creating redundancy, disjointed user experiences, and disengaged employees without a clear governance framework. Misaligned or fragmented adoption can overwhelm employees rather than enabling them, turning what should be a strategic asset into a frustrating inefficiency. And without continuous performance tracking, even the most well-intended innovations can fade into irrelevance.

A strong governance model ensures that new learning technologies can integrate seamlessly into the existing infrastructure rather than creating silos or redundant systems. To achieve that kind of seamless integration, the L&D leaders must work closely with IT, HR, and business stakeholders to align new tools with enterprise-wide learning platforms, such as LMSs, LXPs, HR information systems (HRISs), and knowledge management systems. Governance helps prevent disjointed and disconnected systems while creating a cohesive employee experience. At the same time, by defining clear ownership and decision-making responsibilities, you will create accountability and prevent ad-hoc tech investments that fail to scale.

However, governance alone is not enough. Your adoption strategies must be equally intentional. Technology-driven learning initiatives often fail, not because the tools themselves are ineffective, but because they are not introduced in a way that encourages sustained engagement.

Simply rolling out an AI-enabled analytics platform or a VR-based leadership training program does not guarantee success. Employees need structured support to integrate these tools into their daily work. A phased rollout strategy, starting with small pilot programs before expanding company-wide, will allow your organization to refine its approach, address potential barriers, and generate early success stories that can drive broader adoption. Companies that integrate technology into existing learning support structures—such as internal learning communities, peer mentoring, and real-time performance feedback loops—see stronger engagement and long-term technology adoption.

But without measuring results, even well-adopted tools can fail to drive meaningful change. Many organizations assess learning technology success based on usage rates or employee satisfaction surveys. These surface-level metrics do not capture real business value. Instead, you'll need to track whether specific tools reduce time-to-proficiency, enhance productivity, or contribute to business-critical KPIs like customer satisfaction, workforce agility, and employee retention. Analytics dashboards that track engagement, skills application, and performance shifts tied to technology implementation will allow your organization to refine content delivery, optimize learning pathways, and demonstrate tangible ROI to business leaders.

If your organization takes a structured approach to operationalizing learning technologies through strong governance, intentional adoption strategies, and continuous measurement, you will move beyond short-lived implementations to create a foundation for sustainable learning innovation. However, technology alone does not transform learning. Your organization must also invest in the right skills, experimentation frameworks, and an adaptive learning culture to realize its full potential. The next section explores how organizations can develop the capabilities needed to ensure that emerging technologies enable workforce development.

 Pause to Reflect
If you paused all learning technology purchases today, would your current ecosystem still be capable of scaling learning programs and developing your workforce over the next three years?

Upskilling and Experimenting With Future-Forward Tools

AI, extended reality (XR), and adaptive learning platforms are at the forefront of learning technology transformation. AI-powered tools enable personalized learning by analyzing employee data and tailoring content to individual needs. Chatbots, AI tutors, and intelligent coaching systems enhance employee engagement and retention. Meanwhile, VR and AR create immersive, hands-on experiences that accelerate skills acquisition in high-risk and complex environments, such as healthcare, manufacturing, and customer service.

To successfully integrate these technologies, you'll need to foster a culture of experimentation. Encourage L&D teams to pilot test AI and XR initiatives and assess their effectiveness before full-scale implementation. You must also upskill the L&D professionals on your team because equipping them with the knowledge to leverage AI-enabled analytics, data visualization, and immersive learning design allows them to create more effective learning solutions. AI-powered analytics can help assess skills gaps, recommend learning pathways, and measure results in real-time. By embracing a test-and-learn mindset, you'll stay ahead of technological shifts, ensuring that your learning strategies remain relevant and effective.

How to Upskill Effectively

A successful L&D upskilling strategy requires the same methods and tools we use for employees as a whole, including structured learning, hands-on experimentation, and real-time feedback. As L&D professionals, we need to create space to build those capabilities inside our teams. AI-enabled tools like recommendation engines and content generators are not just things we implement—they are tools we need to learn to use effectively. That means running internal cohorts, experimenting in controlled environments, and building fluency before we scale. If we expect to lead transformation, we have to invest in transforming ourselves.

Another critical component of successful upskilling is fostering a culture of digital curiosity and resilience across the L&D function. Encourage your team to experiment, learn from failure, and iterate new approaches. Try implementing sandbox environments, internal hackathons, and low risk pilot tests that give them hands-on exposure to emerging technologies in low-risk settings. By creating an environment within L&D that supports innovation, it becomes easier to lead transformation with credibility and confidence.

Collaboration across functions is also essential for the seamless adoption of emerging technologies. Cross-functional teams that include IT, business operations, HR, and other business units should work together to identify relevant use cases, design small-scale pilot programs, and assess what works. Upskilling doesn't happen in a vacuum. Building fluency with emerging tools requires the same cross-functional coordination we expect in broader enterprise initiatives.

What Leaders Do

The role of leadership in transforming organizations through technology cannot be understated. As a leader, you must model a forward-thinking approach by promoting technology adoption, using emerging tools to support organizational goals, and actively engaging in AI, VR, and AR learning initiatives. When you prioritize your own upskilling, your employees are more likely to follow suit, creating a top-down culture of continuous learning.

Partnerships with external experts and technology vendors can also accelerate the learning curve. You can stay informed about the latest advancements and best practices in AI and XR learning applications by collaborating with industry leaders, educational institutions, and technology providers. Collaboration will allow you to leverage external expertise while continuously refining your internal learning strategies.

Ethical Questions

Your organization should be aware of the ethical implications that come with emerging technologies like AI. As AI-enabled tools become more sophisticated, you'll need to make sure they are used responsibly. For example, address bias in AI algorithms, data privacy concerns, and equitable access to technology to build trust and maximize the benefits of these innovations. Any L&D team that uses AI recommendation engines in learning platforms to create personalized learning paths for employees should periodically audit the system recommendations to detect and correct any potential bias that could disadvantage certain employee groups or worker class. Likewise, it is necessary to establish clear data governance policies to protect personal employee data, comply with privacy laws where you do business, and give employees equitable access to the necessary tools.

Measure the Impact

Finally, your organization should establish robust metrics to measure the effectiveness of learning initiatives driven by emerging technology. To refine your approaches and make sure that tech investment delivers solid, measurable returns, track engagement levels, skills acquisition rates, and business impact.

Continuous assessment and iterative improvements will help your company maximize the benefits of emerging technologies and drive long-term workforce transformation. However, while emerging technologies present exciting possibilities, their success hinges on your thoughtful implementation. To avoid inefficiencies, ethical and security risks, and wasted resources, resist rushing into adopting emerging technology before first assessing your organization's readiness.

Pilot Programs for Learning Tech Adoption

Integrating new learning technologies without disrupting business operations requires careful planning. Pilot programs provide a structured approach to help you test feasibility, usability, and ROI before committing to full-scale implementation. A well-designed pilot program validates real-world results by assessing how effectively a specific tool integrates with your learning workflows, enhances engagement, and supports business goals. Your successful pilot test will begin with:

- Identifying business-critical challenges
- Defining clear objectives that are aligned with workforce skills gaps or performance goals
- Selecting a small, diverse user group

A diverse pilot group will ensure representation from different roles and functions so you can capture varied insights into user experience and effectiveness. During your pilot phase:

- Simulate real-world application scenarios to determine whether the technology improves productivity, enhances knowledge retention, or reduces training time.

- Use structured feedback mechanisms, including surveys, interviews, and real-time performance tracking. An open feedback loop between users, developers, and the L&D team allows you to make iterative refinements before widely deploying your program.
- Elicit buy-in and visible support from organizational leaders to drive adoption. That way, information you gain from the pilot program will translate into actionable strategies when you're ready for broader implementation.

When You're Ready to Scale

Scaling your pilot program will require a phased approach. Begin with controlled expansion, gradually increasing the number of users while continuously monitoring performance metrics. Put robust training and support structures in place to address potential adoption barriers so your program can realize the full effect of the technology.

By treating technology adoption as a continuous, data-informed process, you'll minimize risks while maximizing the benefits of innovation. Pilot programs help you bridge experimentation and operationalize the tool, transforming innovative ideas into scalable, sustainable learning solutions. Tool 5-1 outlines a structured approach to testing learning technologies. (You'll find it at the end of this chapter.) This framework can help your organization move forward confidently because it's backed by real-world data on effectiveness, adoption, and integration challenges.

This approach to pilot testing your project should ensure that your L&D team minimizes risk, maximizes value, and makes data-informed decisions before committing to a full-scale rollout.

Strong Leadership Is a Must

Investing in learning technology is never enough on its own. Without executive leadership driving your strategy, new tools can become distractions rather than solutions. The real differentiator isn't the technology itself; it's how well it solves business problems, supports workforce capabilities, and integrates with existing systems. Leaders in the C-suite can make sure that technology adoption aligns with business needs. They should ask the right questions before approving investments, including:

- What problem are you solving?

- How will you measure success?
- Does this tool enhance, not duplicate, your current learning ecosystem?

By maintaining a business-first mindset, your organization's executives can prevent technology from becoming a costly experiment with no clear return.

Experiment!

Fostering a culture of experimentation is as important as good leadership. Test your emerging solutions in targeted pilot groups, evaluate results against measurable outcomes, and refine before scaling. If you support an iterative approach to adoption, rather than rushing to deploy the latest trends, you will help your organization maximize results while minimizing risk.

Pause to Reflect

How can your organization create an environment in which employees are empowered to experiment with and adopt new learning technologies?

Prioritizing Business Problems

While emerging technologies present exciting possibilities, many organizations fall into the trap of "shiny object syndrome," or investing in new tools without a clear business case. Without a structured approach, learning technology adoption becomes reactionary rather than strategic, leading to fragmented systems, low adoption rates, and minimal business value.

Technology Is a Tool, Not a Strategy

Running L&D like a business means treating technology as a tool, not a strategy. Organizations that successfully integrate new learning technologies recognize that it must serve the business, not the other way around. This means that before selecting any solution, you must ensure that it supports workforce development priorities, business needs, and operational capabilities.

L&D teams that operate within a learning operations model embed technology adoption into repeatable, scalable processes that maximize efficiency and minimize risk. This disciplined approach prevents ad-hoc purchasing decisions and ensures that every investment supports long-term workforce capability goals. Your organization can reduce waste, improve adoption, and align innovation with measurable outcomes by treating learning technology as a strategic business investment rather than a standalone initiative.

The Learning Operations Decision-Making Model

A learning operations approach to technology adoption helps you focus on business results rather than novelty. Begin with these steps:

1. **Identify specific workforce challenges**—such as reducing time-to-proficiency for new hires or improving sales performance—before selecting a technology solution.
2. **Evaluate whether the technology in question integrates seamlessly into your existing systems to support long-term growth.** A poorly integrated tool can create operational bottlenecks and increase administrative overhead, making it a burden rather than a solution.
3. **Get employees involved.** Seek a user-centric design approach in which employees are engaged in the selection process. This promotes adoption and improves usability by ensuring that the technology meets real learning needs. When you prioritize strategic alignment over trend adoption, you will see greater returns on your learning technology investments.

New tech tools emerge constantly, but not every innovation strengthens business priorities or integrates smoothly into existing systems. Without a structured evaluation process, organizations risk adopting technology that adds cost and complexity without delivering meaningful value. The Learning Operations Decision-Making Model™ shown in Table 5-1 clarifies this process by guiding you through a structured assessment of technology investments. Instead of making decisions based on trends or vendor promises, the model helps your team evaluate solutions based on strategic fit, feasibility, and measurable results. The goal is to adopt technology that serves a business purpose, scales effectively, and delivers tangible results.

Table 5-1. The Learning Operations Decision-Making Model at a Glance

Step	Key Questions	Application to Technology Adoption
1. Define the business need.	What business challenge or performance gap does this technology address?	Is this technology solving a business-critical issue or is it just a "shiny object"?
2. Assess alignment with strategy.	Does this technology align with enterprise learning and business priorities?	Will this technology integrate with existing systems and address business needs?
3. Evaluate feasibility and fit.	Can this technology be effectively implemented within the organization?	Does the organization have the technical infrastructure, governance, and resources for adoption?
4. Measure impact and ROI potential.	How will success be measured? What is the expected ROI?	What are the expected productivity, efficiency, or cost savings from this technology?
5. Governance and approval.	Does this technology pass compliance, budget, legal, and executive review?	Are budget, legal, and IT governance approvals in place? Are ongoing maintenance costs sustainable?

Of course, a structured decision-making model is only as effective as its execution. A framework can help you evaluate technology with clarity, but the real test comes when you apply it to actual business challenges. Many organizations struggle to balance innovation with practicality and as a result adopt tools that seem promising but fail to deliver results at scale. This is why I came up with this decision-making model. Let's consider an example of how a data-informed approach works.

Case Study: A Data-Informed Approach to Learning Tech Investment

A global IT services company known for its strategic approach to workforce development allocated 2 percent of its annual revenue to training, ensuring that every investment in learning aligned with business objectives. Rather than adopting new learning technologies based on trends, the leadership team took a structured, data-informed approach to evaluating and scaling learning initiatives.

Instead of chasing every new platform on the market, the company treated learning technology decisions like any other core business investment. Each initiative had to prove its value through measurements like accelerate workforce readiness, ability to scale efficiently, and deliver measurable results. Here are some other key elements of the company's approach to structured learning technology adoption:

- **Pilot programs preceded full-scale deployment.** New learning technologies were tested within targeted training programs, ensuring they met business objectives before a broader rollout. This prevented unnecessary investment in tools that didn't address workforce needs.
- **Success metrics were well-defined.** Each initiative measured the influence on the business (such as improved workforce readiness and reduced time-to-proficiency) and culture (such as employee engagement and career mobility).
- **The learning technology strategy was well-integrated.** The company leveraged blended learning—by combining classroom, online, and self-directed learning methods—which ensured scalability and accessibility across the organization.

Lessons for Structured Learning Tech Adoption

The approach used by this organization aligned closely with the Learning Operations Decision-Making Model because it covered:

- **Business impact.** The company addressed specific performance gaps and alignment with business objectives before investing in new learning tools.
- **Scalability.** Its new learning initiatives had to integrate with existing technology ecosystems to ensure long-term sustainability.

By following a structured, data-informed framework, the organization ensured that its learning technology investments drove measurable results, reinforced workforce capability, and integrated seamlessly into its learning operations strategy. This case study underscores why organizations should avoid shiny object syndrome by taking a methodical approach to technology adoption and validating business results before making large-scale investments.

Too often, organizations get caught up in the excitement of new learning technologies without first defining the problems they need to solve. That approach, however, leads to wasted budgets, fragmented learning ecosystems, and underused tools that fail to drive real results. Shifting to a business-first mindset ensures that technology has a strategic purpose rather than becoming another disconnected expense.

Prioritizing business problems *before* tech adoption requires discipline. It starts with understanding the organization's biggest workforce capability gaps and performance challenges. For example, you need to get answers to these questions:

- Are employees struggling with compliance?
- Is leadership development failing to produce measurable results?
- Are customer-facing teams missing critical skills that affect revenue?

Identifying these core issues means that any technology investment is rooted in business value.

Leaders must also resist the pressure to move fast without clear alignment. The most effective L&D strategies involve structured needs assessments, cross-functional collaboration, and a phased approach to implementation. Testing solutions in real-world scenarios before scaling prevents costly missteps and ensures that chosen technologies integrate seamlessly into existing systems.

Organizations can maximize the return on their learning investments by leading with business needs. Instead of chasing trends, they should deploy technology purposefully, driving measurable improvements in workforce capability and organizational performance. The next step is ensuring that these investments are operationalized effectively, creating a learning ecosystem that is scalable, sustainable, and aligned with long-term goals.

 Pause to Reflect
How does your organization currently evaluate new learning technologies? What changes could you make to ensure a more structured, business-aligned decision-making process?

The Bottom Line

Successfully integrating emerging technologies into L&D is not about chasing trends; it's about running L&D like a business. This means confirming that every investment in learning technology aligns with your business goals, scales efficiently, and delivers measurable value. Organizations that take a structured approach to operationalizing learning technologies through strong governance, intentional adoption strategies, and continuous measurement can move beyond short-lived implementations to build a sustainable, business-driven learning ecosystem.

However, adopting new technology is only part of running L&D as an effective business function. Real value comes when the technology, process, and methodology are incorporated into a cohesive learning operations strategy. Without the right methodologies in place, even the most sophisticated technologies will fail to improve your workforce capability and business performance.

In short, technology enables efficiency, but methodologies ensure effectiveness.

This is why learning methodologies should evolve alongside technology adoption. If you want to scale learning programs, you will need to go beyond traditional content delivery models and leverage modern, research-backed methodologies that prioritize the employee experience, personalization, and business performance. Emerging technologies such as AI, immersive simulations, and adaptive learning platforms are only as powerful as the instructional strategies that support them.

Organizations that align technology, methodologies, and operational strategies under a well-structured learning operations model will scale their L&D efforts and create a learning function that drives real business results. This is the future of L&D, not just as a support function but as an integrated, strategic business driver.

With emerging technologies embedded in your L&D strategies, the next step is ensuring that you select the right learning methodologies to drive measurable results. While AI, automation, and immersive learning tools transform how organizations deliver training, their success depends on how effectively they use learning methodologies like adaptive, social, and experiential learning. In the next chapter, we'll explore how to integrate these methodologies with business strategy and examine real-world examples.

How to Take Action to Embrace Emerging Technologies

Take these three actions to put the ideas of this chapter into practice:

- **Look at the learning tech ecosystem your organization is using.** Do all the elements support business goals, or were they adopted because they seemed innovative at the time?
- **Before committing to a new learning technology, run a small pilot test to see if it actually solves a business problem.** Choose a single use case, define success metrics, and gather feedback from a small, diverse group before expanding. The pilot program framework for learning technology adoption in Tool 5-1 can guide you.
- **Start a conversation about strategy with L&D, IT, HR, and business leaders to align on how learning technology supports business goals.** Position technology adoption as an operational decision, not just an innovative effort, by focusing on governance, scalability, and ROI.

Tool 5-1.
A Pilot Program Framework for Learning Technology Adoption

This structured approach to pilot testing learning technologies can help your organization move forward confidently because it's backed by real-world data on effectiveness, adoption, and integration challenges. Answer each question in detail for the best results.

Step 1. Define the Business Problem and Objectives
Ask a few essential questions:
- What is the core business challenge this technology is solving?
- What specific outcomes should this pilot achieve?
- What business priorities and L&D strategy are these objectives supporting?
- What are your success metrics (e.g., engagement, efficiency, knowledge retention, or business impact)?

Key deliverable: Pilot objectives and a success criteria document

Step 2. Identify Stakeholders and Champions
Who needs to be involved? If specific people are key to your success, identify them:
- L&D team
- IT and security
- Business unit leaders
- Pilot participants (target employees)

Who owns the pilot?
- Assign a project lead.
- Identify internal champions who will advocate adoption.

Key deliverable: A stakeholder engagement plan

Step 3. Select a Pilot Group and Define Its Scope
First, choose a small but representative group of employees (10–20 percent of the target audience). Ensure diversity in roles, locations, and learning needs, and limit the scope to a specific learning use case (such as onboarding, compliance training, or leadership development). Finally, define the timeframe; for example, six to 12 weeks.

Key deliverable: A defined pilot scope and participant selection

Step 4. Develop an Implementation Plan

The technology setup period will include:
- Integrating with your organization's LMS or LXP (if needed)
- Addressing security and compliance concerns
- Ensuring content readiness by customizing learning modules for pilot users
- Providing orientations to show participants how to use the tool

Key deliverable: A pilot execution plan and timeline

Step 5. Run the Pilot Test and Monitor Results in Real-Time

Conduct a kickoff meeting with participants and then provide ongoing technical and instructional support. Gather real-time feedback via:
- Usage analytics
- Participant surveys
- Focus groups or interviews

Key deliverable: Weekly pilot performance reports

Step 6. Collect and Analyze Data

Compare your collected data against the success criteria defined in step 1 using a pilot evaluation scorecard (qualitative and quantitative metrics) that includes:
- Adoption rate and engagement
- Learning retention and behavior change
- Productivity impact
- Cost-effectiveness

Key deliverable: Pilot evaluation report

Step 7. Scale, Iterate, or Sunset?

Based on the data you've collected and analyzed, decide whether you need to:
- Scale up by expanding adoption across teams or business units.
- Iterate by making adjustments and retesting.
- Sunset the project if it is ineffective, and document lessons learned before discontinuing it.

Use this final decision framework to help determine your next step.

Pilot Outcome	Next Step
≥ 80% success	Scale to full rollout
50–79% success	Revise and extend pilot
< 50% success	Discontinue and reassess

At the end, present your findings to executive sponsors with a clear recommendation.

Key deliverable: Pilot findings and adoption decision report

Chapter 6
Modern Learning Methodologies

A few years ago, I walked into a project that was already on fire. The company had rolled out a multimillion-dollar leadership development program. It had the right branding, a sleek digital experience, and a vendor that promised "transformational outcomes." The learning experience was well-designed, cohort-based, and complied with what the executives said they wanted. But no one had validated whether those methods were the right tools for the job. Frontline managers weren't having better performance conversations. Turnover hadn't improved. And within six months, the program was shelved. It wasn't because the content was bad. *It was because the instructional methods didn't fit the business problem.*

This happens more often than we would probably like to admit. L&D teams feel pressure to modernize and innovate, so they chase what's new, what's trending, and what's easy to deploy without stepping back to ask two essential questions:

- What kind of change does the business actually need to see?
- Which learning methods are best suited to drive that change, given the working environment?

Choosing the right method starts with understanding the job to be done. Does the business need people to think differently? Behave differently? Move faster? Slow down and make better decisions? The right method isn't the one with the most features; it's the one that delivers the outcome with the fewest barriers between learning and application.

With carefully chosen technology embedded in your L&D strategies, as discussed in chapter 5, the next step is to ensure that you choose the right learning methodologies to drive business results. We know that traditional learning approaches often fall short in work environments, and this is why many organizations are turning to the following three learning strategies:

- **Adaptive learning** leverages AI, system logic, and workforce data to personalize learning paths, ensuring employees develop the right skills at the right time.
- **Social learning** fosters a culture of continuous development through collaboration, mentorship, and peer-driven knowledge sharing.
- **Experiential learning** focuses on real-world application, helping employees build confidence and competence in critical skills through hands-on practice.

These methodologies are not standalone solutions but complementary approaches that, when integrated effectively, form a holistic learning ecosystem that aligns with employee and business needs.

In this chapter, we'll explore what these learning methodologies are and how each addresses workforce needs and business priorities. We'll also consider how to standardize your process for selecting a methodology. Not every methodology is right for every challenge, but if you select yours with purpose, it can accelerate results, reduce friction, and make learning a more natural part of how work gets done. Finally, we'll consider how to create a multimodal approach to learning modeled on portfolio management principles. This approach can enhance engagement while supporting business objectives such as upskilling, innovation, and performance improvement. The portfolio approach also ensures that your employees receive the right type of learning at the right time, leading to higher retention, improved performance, and a stronger connection between learning and business outcomes.

Learning Approaches and Business Priorities

Different business challenges call for different approaches to learning. Let's dissect three of the most prominent strategies that organizations are adopting today to determine how each aligns with common business priorities and discuss how to enhance each methodology for maximum effectiveness.

What Is Adaptive Learning?

Adaptive learning is a data-informed, highly personalized approach that tailors learning experiences to the individual needs of employees. It leverages AI, machine learning, system logic, and real-time analytics to dynamically adjust content, ensuring employees receive material suited to their competency levels and knowledge gaps. Unlike a traditional learning approach, which applies a one-size-fits-all model, adaptive learning enables organizations to provide a scalable, flexible, and meaningful learning environment that meets individual and business objectives.

Advantages of Adaptive Learning

You can use adaptive learning as a strategic tool to bridge skills gaps, improve workforce agility, and drive performance outcomes. By integrating adaptive learning with business priorities and workforce planning, you can align training initiatives with KPIs, such as operational efficiency, talent retention, compliance, and productivity enhancement. Through AI-enabled analytics and machine learning models, you will be able to adjust learning content dynamically to fit the specific needs of each employee, ensuring engagement and maximizing retention.

Successful implementation of adaptive learning requires your organization to embed solutions within its LMS, LXP, or broader talent development frameworks. AI-enabled personalization will help you assess individual skills gaps, track progress, and adjust learning content in real time. By using competency-based learning paths, you can make sure that employees acquire the relevant skills that support business goals; by deploying microlearning and just-in-time training strategies, you will allow employees to access tailored learning initiatives precisely when needed, reinforcing knowledge application.

Challenges of Adaptive Learning

Despite its advantages, adaptive learning presents several challenges for L&D teams. Data privacy and ethics are significant concerns because your organization must demonstrate transparency in how it's collecting, storing, and analyzing employee data. Technology integration can also present hurdles. You'll need seamless connectivity between adaptive learning systems and your enterprise platform to prevent inefficiencies.

In addition, the role of instructors is evolving, and many L&D professionals may need to transition into coaching and the facilitation of adaptive learning to fully support employees. A final significant challenge for implementing adaptive learning is demonstrating ROI. You will need to establish clear metrics to measure business results.

Implement Adaptive Learning

Because adaptive learning personalizes content to meet each employee's unique needs, content must be updated in real-time so employees receive the right information at the right time, based on their current skill level. Put simply, adaptive learning is best for:

- Technical skills development requiring mastery of foundational knowledge
- Compliance training in which comprehension must be verified
- Scaling training solutions consistently across distributed workforces
- Situations with significant knowledge gaps between employees

As you implement adaptive learning in your organization, you should adopt best practices that align learning objectives with business KPIs to maximize its effectiveness, including:

- Leverage advanced analytics dashboards to provide valuable insights into employee progress and identify skills gaps.
- Promote accessibility and inclusivity by creating content for diverse learning needs that complies with the Web Content Accessibility Guidelines (WCAG).
- Encourage a culture of employee autonomy to foster self-directed development and empower employees to take control of their learning journeys.
- Implement effective communication strategies.
- Secure leadership buy-in to drive greater adoption and sustained engagement.

How to Enhance Adaptive Learning

Adaptive learning can be even more effective when combined with rapid, scenario-based decision-making exercises that simulate real-world challenges. For example, an employee might encounter real business scenarios within their learning path, prompting them to make quick decisions before receiving technology-driven feedback. Such scenario-based decision making helps employees practice applying knowledge in real-world situations, reinforcing learning through practical application. Your learning tools should adjust content dynamically, based on employee performance using machine learning or AI, to offer personalized feedback that improves knowledge retention.

Let's consider a more specific example: A compliance training program uses adaptive learning to assess an employee's baseline understanding of regulatory guidelines. After the learning system's assessment identifies knowledge gaps, it presents a *compliance incident scenario* requiring the employee to choose the correct response to a compliance issue. Based on their answers, the employee will get feedback that reinforces the learned content and adjusts future lessons accordingly.

By integrating scenario-based decision making and adaptive learning, your organization can maximize knowledge retention and ensure employees develop the skills they need to apply their knowledge effectively in real-world scenarios.

What Is Social Learning?

Social learning is a powerful method that leverages peer-to-peer knowledge exchange, collaborative problem solving, and mentorship to enhance learning experiences. Unlike traditional learning methods that rely on instructor-led sessions or static content, social learning integrates real-world interactions, discussion forums, and on-the-job collaboration to create an engaging and sustainable learning environment.

Advantages of Social Learning

Aligning social learning with business strategy helps employees absorb the knowledge and develop the critical thinking, communication, and teamwork skills that are essential for business success. When supported by corporate objectives, social learning enhances workforce adaptability, strengthens internal networks, and accelerates knowledge retention across teams.

Challenges of Social Learning

Your organization may face challenges in adopting social learning, including a lack of engagement, difficulty measuring effectiveness, and resistance to nontraditional learning models. To overcome these barriers, it's important to integrate social learning into existing workflows, recognize and reward knowledge contributors, and establish clear objectives that tie learning outcomes to performance improvements. For example, discussion boards may go quiet without active moderation or visible incentives, leading to low participation. Similarly, without clear success metrics, it's difficult to demonstrate how peer collaboration contributes to business outcomes, making it harder to secure executive buy-in.

Implement Social Learning

Your organization can implement social learning by embedding collaborative tools within its learning ecosystem, creating mentorship programs, and fostering communities of practice that encourage continuous knowledge sharing. Social learning is best for:
- Culture change initiatives
- Innovation and problem-solving challenges
- Knowledge retention and transfer (particularly with a retiring workforce)
- Leadership development and team collaboration

To address some of the challenges we've discussed as you implement social learning in your organization, adopt these best practices:
- Leverage enterprise collaboration platforms.
- Structure peer-led coaching programs.
- Embed social learning into leadership development initiatives.
- Encourage employees to learn in the flow of work by integrating learning discussions into team meetings, project debriefs, and peer-review sessions.

These practices foster a culture of continuous learning and organizational agility. Companies that embrace social learning create an environment in which knowledge transfer becomes organic, self-sustaining, and strategically linked with business priorities.

How to Enhance Social Learning

Social learning is most effective when knowledge sharing is structured rather than left to chance. While informal peer learning happens naturally, organizations can amplify its effectiveness by embedding structured peer coaching, mentoring programs, and collaborative decision-making exercises into the learning strategy. For example, employees could engage in real-world scenarios through structured peer coaching and team discussions. Your company might also use mentorship programs to create long-term knowledge transfer, particularly for leadership development. Live case-study exercises and decision-making scenarios could encourage cross-functional learning and innovation.

Imagine a global technology firm rolling out a new leadership development program and implementing a peer coaching model in which managers meet biweekly to discuss real challenges they face. Each session includes a case incident exercise in which managers analyze a workplace scenario, propose solutions, and receive feedback from peers, reinforcing leadership skills through real-world application.

By integrating structured collaboration into social learning, organizations enhance knowledge retention, problem solving, and leadership development, ensuring that employees retain what they've learned and apply it in a peer-driven, real-world context.

What Is Experiential Learning?

Experiential learning immerses employees in real-world scenarios, promoting deeper understanding and practical skill application. This methodology bridges the gap between theory and practice through immersive, hands-on experiences that solidify learning outcomes. Unlike traditional passive learning methods, experiential learning requires active participation, which increases retention and the ability to apply skills in professional environments.

Advantages of Experiential Learning

Organizations implementing experiential learning report higher engagement, improved problem-solving capabilities, and stronger job performance among employees (Merriam and Baumgartner 2020). People who learn through hands-on experience tend to retain knowledge more effectively and apply it confidently.

Experiential methods also accelerate the speed to competence by allowing employees to practice in realistic but risk-free settings. Whether through XR simulations or on-the-job immersion, employees can make mistakes, receive feedback, and refine their skills without jeopardizing real outcomes. Experiential learning builds confidence and reduces the learning curve for critical roles and scenarios.

Challenges of Experiential Learning

While experiential learning offers clear benefits, it can also be resource intensive to design and scale. Simulations, role plays, and hands-on projects often require significant coordination, facilitation, and time away from daily work. Additionally, without structured reflection or clear performance ties, the learning experience may not translate into lasting behavior change. To overcome these challenges, organizations should embed experiential learning into real workflows, set clear objectives, and pair experiences with coaching or debriefs that connect lessons to job performance.

Case Study: VR Training for Experiential Learning

A multinational retailer's large-scale adoption of VR demonstrates how experiential learning can enhance skills development and workforce readiness when supported by emerging technologies. Faced with the challenge of preparing employees for high-pressure retail scenarios, the L&D team integrated VR simulations across tens of thousands of stores to create risk-free, immersive learning experiences.

By leveraging Oculus Go headsets, the organization provided employees with real-world simulations, such as handling customer interactions, navigating high-traffic retail situations (like Black Friday), and responding to store emergencies. The interactive nature of these VR modules meant that employees were making real-time decisions, receiving instant feedback, and practicing their responses in a controlled environment.

This initiative's results were significant:

- ▶ Knowledge retention increased by double percentage points compared with traditional training methods.
- ▶ Training time was reduced, enabling employees to become productive faster.
- ▶ Employee engagement improved as employees actively participated in scenario-based learning.
- ▶ Workforce readiness was enhanced, ensuring the staff was prepared for critical retail events and customer interactions.

This case exemplifies how experiential learning, powered by technology, drives employee engagement and business performance. By embedding decision-making exercises within VR modules, the company ensured that employees learned policies and procedures and then applied them in a simulated real-world context.

Implement Experiential Learning

Experiential learning is most powerful when employees actively engage with real-world scenarios rather than passively absorbing information. This type of learning is best suited for:

- High-stakes roles in which mistakes have serious consequences
- Complex decision-making scenarios requiring judgment
- Customer-facing skills development
- Process improvements that require practice to master

Common experiential learning approaches include:

- **Simulations and role-playing.** Employees can practice decision making in risk-free environments, building confidence and competence in critical job functions
- **On-the-job learning.** Structured learning can be integrated directly into daily responsibilities, ensuring practical and immediate application.
- **Project-based learning.** Employees can solve real business challenges, fostering innovation, creativity, and problem-solving skills.
- **Immersive technologies.** VR and AR can create realistic training experiences, particularly in industries requiring hands-on skills development.

How to Deepen Experiential Learning

While it is commonly used for hands-on training, you can maximize an experiential learning solution's effectiveness by embedding simulations, on-the-job learning, and project-based problem-solving into a variety of structured learning programs. For example, employees could practice real-world tasks in a controlled environment before applying them on the job, and you could use simulations, role playing, and VR to create risk-free spaces for developing complex skills. You might also try using project-based learning to encourage employees to solve real business challenges, reinforcing problem-solving and critical thinking skills.

Imagine a healthcare provider implementing experiential learning for new nurses by introducing a VR simulation in which the nurses practice high-risk medical procedures in a virtual setting. The VR environment would allow them to make mistakes and refine their skills before performing real-life patient care.

By using structured experiential learning opportunities, your organization can help employees develop confidence and proficiency in high-risk roles, ensuring that theoretical knowledge translates into real-world expertise.

Pause to Reflect

How can you incorporate adaptive, social, or experiential learning into your L&D strategy?

Choose a Learning Methodology

When it's time to choose a methodology, your decision isn't just about weighing innovation and engagement. The selection requires the same kind of disciplined governance as the technology adoption process. Just as you would evaluate technologies based on business needs and feasibility, you should assess learning methodologies carefully through structured intake, prioritization, and governance frameworks.

Applying a standardized decision-making process helps you connect your methodologies with your business objectives, confirm they're scalable, and integrate them seamlessly into the broader learning ecosystem. Governance mechanisms—such as stakeholder committees, approval gates, and data-informed reviews—help prevent ad-hoc decisions and ensure that investments in learning approaches yield measurable results.

Attend to the Needs of the Business and Employees

Finding the right balance between business objectives and employee needs is critical when choosing the right learning methodologies and designing effective and sustainable learning programs. As we've discussed, you must recognize that while the business is the *customer* (funding learning initiatives, driving the learning agenda, and expecting ROI), employees are the *consumers* who engage with and apply the learning content. To achieve a good balance:

- **Align learning content with business KPIs.** Learning initiatives should directly contribute to strategic goals, such as revenue growth, customer satisfaction, and operational efficiency.
    Defining success in business terms promotes executive buy-in and continued investment in L&D.

- **Personalize learning pathways.** Employees engage more with learning content when it's relevant to their roles and career growth. Adaptive learning, in particular, tailors content dynamically so each employee receives instruction suited to their skill level and business function.
- **Establish real-world applications of learning.** Learning solutions must bridge theory and practice. Social learning, for example, provides opportunities for peer engagement and knowledge sharing. In contrast, experiential learning immerses employees in work-based scenarios that enhance problem-solving skills.
- **Monitor feedback and opportunities for iteration.** Establish continuous feedback loops to assess the effectiveness of learning initiatives. Measuring employee engagement, business results, and skills application allows your L&D team to refine strategies and maintain long-term relevance.
- **Balance efficiency and engagement.** While cost-effective and scalable solutions appeal to business leaders, engagement and knowledge retention matter to employees. Immersive learning and peer coaching can provide highly effective experiences without sacrificing efficiency.

Ultimately, organizations that integrate customer business priorities and consumer employee needs can create sustainable learning ecosystems in which employees feel supported in their growth while driving measurable business outcomes.

Try a Multimodal Learning Strategy

Successful organizations integrate adaptive, social, and experiential learning into a multimodal learning strategy like this:

- **Employ adaptive learning for foundational knowledge.** Employees will be able to efficiently build baseline competencies.
- **Use social learning for deeper understanding.** Reinforce learning through peer discussions, mentorship, and shared experiences.
- **Adopt experiential learning for application.** Provide real-world scenarios in which employees can apply learned skills and develop proficiency.

Tie Engagement to Business Strategy

As we've learned, engagement isn't just about participation; it's about ensuring employees gain the right skills at the right time to contribute to business success. No matter what learning modality you choose, think beyond engagement as an employee experience metric and treat it as a business driver. Running L&D like a business means:

- **Defining engagement in business terms.** Rather than focusing on completion rates or employee satisfaction, link engagement with business-critical KPIs, such as productivity, retention, and operational efficiency.
- **Ensuring engagement translates into measurable outcomes.** High employee engagement with the content is not enough; they need to apply the information in ways that improve business performance.
- **Prioritizing scalable and repeatable engagement strategies.** As your organization scales operations, you'll need to scale learning methodologies that sustain engagement without increasing complexity or cost.
- **Aligning engagement strategies with business priorities.** Engagement shouldn't be about what's hot or new in learning but what drives business growth, innovation, and workforce capability.

Engagement is about ensuring that learning drives real behavior change and measurable business results. By leveraging adaptive, social, and experiential learning strategies, you can create a learning ecosystem in which employees remain actively involved in their development while gaining the skills they need to succeed. For instance:

- **Adaptive learning keeps engagement high** by delivering personalized learning paths so employees receive content that is relevant, timely, and appropriate to their knowledge level. Rather than forcing employees through material they already know, adaptive learning keeps them challenged without overwhelming them, increasing motivation and retention.
- **Social learning enhances engagement** by making learning collaborative, which allows employees to learn from one another through structured mentorship, peer coaching, and group problem

solving. When learning is embedded in real-world conversations and shared experiences, it becomes more meaningful and immediately applicable.
- **Experiential learning helps translate engagement into action** by immersing employees in real-world challenges that allow them to practice making decisions and developing problem-solving skills in safe, controlled environments. Hands-on learning boosts confidence, accelerates competency, and drives long-term retention.

Business-First Decision Making

Organizations too often select learning methodologies based on what has always been done, industry trends, or popular formats, rather than focusing on measurable business results. While employee engagement is important, the primary criterion for choosing a learning method should be its ability to drive results that matter to the organization. When learning methodologies support business needs, engagement follows naturally because employees see direct value in applying their new skills.

A Structured Process

A business-first approach to choosing a learning methodology goes beyond selecting the right format; it requires embedding methodology selection into L&D's standardized processes to promote scalability, consistency, and value. Don't decide on a learning methodology in isolation or based on individual requests. Instead, follow a structured process that is integrated within a broader learning operations framework and supported by intake, governance, portfolio management, and technology strategy. You can maximize business value in the selection process by using a decision matrix.

A Learning Methodology Decision Matrix

While it's tempting to get caught up in what's new and trendy or to rely on personal favorites rather than consistently applying a standardized process to determine what will drive results, if you're running L&D like a business, every methodology decision should start with the business problem you need to solve and proceed through evaluation and assessment of risks to the final decision. This approach prevents ad-hoc decision making and reinforces L&D's role as a strategic business partner.

Let's examine how you can use the Learning Operations Decision-Making Model to evaluate which learning approach to implement. Table 6-1 shows how you can adapt the questions in the model to focus on learning methodologies. Use this matrix as a practical guide to evaluate each learning methodology against your business and operational needs.

Table 6-1. The Learning Methodology Decision-Making Matrix

Step	Key Questions	Application to Learning Methodologies
1. Define the business need	What business challenge or performance gap does this methodology address?	Is this methodology addressing a performance gap or improving a business process?
2. Assess alignment with strategy	Does this methodology align with enterprise learning and business priorities?	Is this methodology aligned with business goals and existing learning strategies?
3. Evaluate feasibility and fit	Can this methodology be effectively implemented within the organization?	Does the methodology fit the employee audience, existing content, and L&D capabilities?
4. Measure impact and ROI potential	How will success be measured? What is the expected ROI?	How will this methodology improve employee performance and contribute to business success?
5. Governance and approval	Does this methodology pass compliance, budget, and executive review?	Does this methodology have leadership buy-in, instructional feasibility, and scalability?

A Risk Assessment Matrix

Selecting a learning methodology always involves trade-offs. After defining the business problem, you want to address, you'll need to weigh four key factors:
- Investment risk
- Implementation complexity
- Expected business impact
- Adoption likelihood

After using the decision-making matrix in Table 6-1 to determine whether an adaptive, social, or experiential methodology is the best fit for your business problem, move to the risk assessment matrix in Table 6-2.

This matrix can help you assess the four critical factors for each learning methodology you are considering and ensure it aligns with your business constraints and opportunities. Score each methodology across all four factors using a 5-point scale (low = 1 point, medium = 3 points, and high = 5 points). Then, prioritize the methodologies with a strong balance of business impact and feasibility.

Table 6-2. A Learning Methodology Risk Assessment Matrix

Learning Methodology	Investment Risk (Cost and Time)	Implementation Complexity	Business Impact (ROI)	Adoption Likelihood
Adaptive learning				
Social learning				
Experiential learning				

You can mitigate risks by always addressing technology gaps, cost constraints, and adoption challenges. For example, as an L&D leader you might present a risk assessment matrix to a group of stakeholders to help justify an investment in adaptive learning rather than VR simulations. The assessment would showv that while VR offers a high business impact, the complexity of technology integration and investment risks outweigh its feasibility at your particular stage of business development.

Technology Alignment

Another critical consideration in choosing your methodology is technology alignment. Always select a learning methodology that considers your organization's learning technology ecosystem. Before committing to a specific approach, your L&D team must ask some basic questions to assess whether your existing LMS, LXP, collaboration platforms, or immersive tools support the methodology. For example:

- **Adaptive learning depends on logic statements, machine learning, and AI-enabled personalization.** Does the company's learning platform offer enhanced employee data feeds, real-time analytics, and intelligent recommendations?
- **Social learning depends on knowledge-sharing infrastructure.** Does the organization have an internal community platform or digital collaboration tool?
- **Experiential learning tools such as AR and VR require simulation capabilities.** Does the business case justify investing in these tools if they are not already available?

If you see a technology gap, review your methodology selection within your organization's broader L&D technology landscape to ensure alignment with existing capabilities and planned investments. For instance, if your organization lacks an AI-enabled platform, implementing adaptive learning may require significant additional investments. In contrast, using existing video conferencing tools for peer coaching may provide a low-cost, immediate alternative for social learning.

Learning Impact Measurement

Measurability is another essential consideration in methodology selection and must be integrated into your operational decision-making and risk-assessment processes. Business leaders expect you to tie learning impact to performance metrics that align with measurable business results rather than relying solely on participation rates or course completions.

To ensure that your methodologies are business-driven, your L&D team must link learning outcomes directly to KPIs such as efficiency gains, revenue growth, compliance adherence, and quality improvements. Choose methodologies with on-the-job application in mind so employees can practice and refine their skills in real-world contexts.

Without structured reinforcement and measurement of KPIs, learning remains purely theoretical and results in poor retention and limited impact. This is another reason that methodology selection can't be a one-time decision for your department and should be integral to L&D's standardized intake, governance, and performance-tracking processes.

Beware of Siloed Decision-Making Processes

In an approach driven by learning operations, your decisions about methodology should never be made in a silo or based solely on immediate stakeholder requests. Always integrate your decisions into intake, governance, portfolio management, and technology planning, ensuring that every decision contributes to scalable, measurable business outcomes.

First, embed the selection of learning methodology within your company's intake and governance processes. Rather than allowing training requests to dictate a learning format, your L&D team should require stakeholders to articulate the:

- Business challenge
- Performance gap
- Expected impact

This will help you choose methodologies based on strategic alignment, speed, resource efficiency, scalability, and measurability rather than personal preference.

Then, apply the learning methodology decision matrix consistently in intake reviews. The governance structure should vet major methodology choices to ensure alignment across the organization. For example, instead of defaulting to e-learning for compliance training, a governance review may determine that an adaptive learning model with AI-enabled assessments is better at ensuring comprehension and retention.

Build Your Business Case for Stakeholders

Once you've used the decision-making matrix and identified the most appropriate learning methodology in a process informed by learning operations, you need to build a compelling case that speaks to business stakeholders by addressing:

- **Problem-solution alignment.** Show how the methodology addresses the specific business challenge.
- **Resource requirements.** Detail the technology, people, and time you'll need.
- **Expected timeline.** When will the business see initial and then full ROI?

- **Success metrics.** How will success be measured in business terms?
- **Risk mitigation.** What challenges might arise, and how you will address them?

Considering and addressing all these issues clearly demonstrates that you have selected learning methodologies based on business results rather than learning trends. It gives you a defensible rationale for your choices and aligns your decision-making process with the way other business functions approach investments.

Once you've selected the learning methodologies, it's time to manage them. In the next section, we'll explore how to do this as part of an L&D portfolio, much like managing business investments.

Pause to Reflect

If asked, could you confidently explain how your chosen learning methodologies support your company's goals?

A Portfolio-Based Learning Strategy

Now that you have a better understanding of three key learning methodologies and have some tools to evaluate and choose the best methodology for your business needs, it's time to consider how to manage a variety of learning methodologies at once. In a business-aligned L&D model, learning initiatives should be treated like an investment portfolio. Just as a company balances financial investments across different risk categories, your L&D team must balance learning methodologies based on business needs, risk appetite, and strategic priorities.

First, you will need to categorize each methodology based on its role in driving business results. For example:

- **Adaptive learning**—which is a stable investment—ensures consistency and efficiency in technical training. This makes it ideal for large-scale, high-compliance environments.

- **Experiential learning**—such as simulations or hands-on practice—has varied risk but is essential for high-stakes decision-making roles in which theoretical knowledge alone isn't enough.
- **Social learning**—which leverages peer coaching and collaboration—is often a low-cost, highly effective strategy for leadership development, culture transformation, and knowledge transfer.

A company scaling operations globally, for example, could prioritize adaptive learning for consistent technical training across regions while using social learning to build knowledge-sharing networks among global teams. By mapping the methodologies to business priorities, you can create a balanced portfolio that maximizes ROI.

Divide Learning Methodologies Into Three Portfolio Categories

In developing a learning portfolio, you'll need to assess all methodologies under consideration. The first step is to categorize each one into an investment category based on risk versus effectiveness:

- **Stable investments are low-risk and offer high predictability.** They are considered consistent and scalable, with a proven ROI. The learning methodologies that fit this category include adaptive learning for technical and other hard skills.
- **Growth investments are moderate risk and offer scalable, broad results.** Learning methodologies that fit this category include social learning for leadership development and cohort-based training.
- **High-return investments are also high risk.** They often include unproven innovative or experimental methodologies with strong potential. Learning methodologies in this category include experiential AR and VR simulations as well as AI-enabled learning.

Balance stable, growth, and high-return investments to support your business priorities, and then track their effectiveness over time to determine whether each methodology should be scaled, refined, or retired. For example, a global manufacturing firm adopted a portfolio-based learning strategy using adaptive learning (stable investment) for technical training, social learning (growth investment) for leadership development, and VR simulations (high-return investment) for safety training in high-risk environments. Integrating adaptive, social, and experiential learning shifts L&D offerings from traditional, one-size-fits-all training content to a dynamic, business-aligned learning ecosystem. Each methodology serves a distinct purpose but they work best when strategically combined to enhance engagement, retention, and real-world application:

- **Adaptive learning** personalizes training by identifying knowledge gaps and tailoring content to individual needs to ensure employees build competencies efficiently.
- **Social learning** reinforces knowledge through peer collaboration, mentoring, and team-based problem solving to drive engagement and knowledge transfer.
- **Experiential learning** provides hands-on practice, which allows employees to develop confidence and competence through real-world application.

Selecting the right approach requires a structured decision-making process that aligns learning initiatives with business goals. Your organization needs to move beyond seeing learning methodologies as standalone tactics to maximize effectiveness and instead integrate them into a cohesive learning strategy that directly supports business priorities.

Pause to Reflect

What criteria does your organization currently use to select learning methodologies? How could they be improved?

The Bottom Line

By embedding methodology selection into intake, governance, portfolio management, and technology strategies, your L&D team can move further away from reactive, trend-driven decision making and toward choosing methodologies based on business priorities, scalability, and measurable results. A business-first selection process ensures that learning investments drive tangible results while efficiently leveraging existing infrastructure.

Instead of choosing methodologies based on engagement alone, follow a learning operations approach so learning methodologies are:

- Aligned with business priorities
- Scalable and resource-efficient
- Measurable for business impact

- Integrated with existing technology

By treating methodology selection as a structured, operationalized process, your team will also scale its influence while maintaining agility, which is a crucial capability for responding to business pivots (a topic we'll explore in the next chapter).

Embedding methodology selection into learning operations mirrors L&D's broader portfolio management strategy, balancing investments in different methodologies based on their expected results. When you follow a structured decision-making approach to choose a learning methodology, you will enhance efficiency and strengthen L&D's role as a business enabler rather than a reactive service provider.

With this foundation in place, we now turn to the next challenge: How can your L&D team pivot quickly when business needs shift? Selecting the right learning approach is just a starting point. Even the most well-planned learning strategies must flex with shifting market conditions, executive priorities, and emerging needs. That's where agility comes in.

How to Take Action With Modern Learning Methodologies

You can start putting the ideas in this chapter into action today by taking three simple steps:

- **Look closely at your existing learning programs.** Are they designed solely for engagement, or do they also directly support critical business outcomes? Use the learning methodology decision-making matrix to evaluate whether your current mix of adaptive, social, and experiential learning supports your business needs.
- **Identify a pressing business challenge.** Whether you need to onboard new employees faster, improve compliance adherence, or support a major transformation, select a learning methodology that could show an immediate result and sketch out a small-scale pilot program to test its effectiveness.
- **Schedule a conversation with a business leader to discuss their biggest workforce challenges.** Instead of leading with learning trends or training requests, ask about their top priorities and where skills gaps may limit results. Use these insights to rethink how your learning strategies can be positioned as a business accelerator.

PART 4
Navigating Agility and Change

Chapter 7
Strategic Agility

In 2024, 60 percent of learning leaders reported significant shifts in business priorities, and nearly half admitted their teams struggled to respond quickly or effectively (RedThread Research 2024). What's more, only one in five said they had a structured process in place to reprioritize learning initiatives in real time.

That's not a gap. It's a risk.

When business strategies change and learning doesn't keep up, your credibility can erode quickly. L&D teams keep building programs that no one needs anymore, and stakeholders go silent. Budgets disappear.

Business pivots are inevitable. Market conditions shift, leadership changes, and product road maps get rewritten. Organizations must continuously adapt to market shifts, regulatory updates, and evolving customer expectations, and learning strategies need to move just as quickly. L&D can no longer afford to rely on rigid, long-term plans. The question isn't whether your learning priorities will need to change; it's how fast your team can shift when change happens.

Being agile means your L&D team is ready to pivot and deploy solutions at the speed of change rather than reacting too late. However, agility doesn't mean abandoning structure. You need to embed flexibility into how you operate so training initiatives continue to support business needs while maintaining quality and effectiveness. This requires responding to shifts in the business environment and developing mechanisms for rapid deployment of training to meet changing business needs.

Responding to Shifts in the Business Environment

Business priorities evolve rapidly because they're often driven by market fluctuations, regulatory changes, competitive pressures, and emerging technologies. In response, your L&D function must move beyond static learning road maps and cultivate an adaptable strategy so employees are always equipped with the skills they need. Without this responsiveness, organizations risk delivering outdated or misaligned learning solutions, which diminishes your credibility as a business enabler.

Many traditional L&D functions struggle to keep pace with business changes because they operate under rigid training cycles that fail to account for midyear pivots. Some overengineer structured learning road maps that take months to develop only to become irrelevant by the time they launch. Others rely on historical training priorities rather than real-time data, making it difficult to proactively address emerging skills gaps.

When L&D Fails to Adapt

Organizations that treat L&D as a fixed function that's locked into rigid annual training plans often fall behind. Many traditional L&D functions overemphasize structured, long-term skills-building without embedding mechanisms for real-time shifts. These models typically suffer from:

- Fixed learning road maps that don't adapt to market needs
- Slow response times to emerging business challenges, which leads to lagging workforce readiness
- Lack of real-time data, which prevents proactive identification of skills gaps before they become business risks

In all these cases, L&D becomes a bottleneck. Employees are left without the knowledge and skills they need to perform at the pace of change. This leads to missed opportunities, inefficient operations, and a loss of competitive advantage.

A Model of Learning Agility

Some organizations do successfully embed learning agility into their workforce strategy. One multinational IT services giant exemplifies this approach. In an industry with constantly shifting technology, client, and workforce demands, this organization has built a highly adaptable L&D framework that ensures its employees always stay ahead of change. Here are the steps it took:

- **Establish business-aligned learning functions.** Each business unit has a dedicated L&D function so training priorities are directly linked to evolving business needs.
- **Use real-time skills intelligence.** The organization uses workforce analytics to identify capability gaps before they become a problem, ensuring L&D initiatives are always timely.
- **Create a balanced learning strategy.** Rather than relying solely on structured programs, the company combines formal certification programs with continuous, informal learning, empowering employees to upskill to meet changing business demands.
- **Support "learnability" as a core value.** Employees are held accountable for continuous learning, and L&D is positioned as a proactive business enabler, not a reactive training provider.

As a result of this approach, this multinational IT services company maintains a highly agile workforce that can pivot quickly to new client demands, adopt new technologies faster than its competitors, and sustain long-term growth.

Proactive Agility

L&D teams should be deeply integrated into business strategy discussions to stay ahead and capture early signals of change. One way to do this is by engaging in continuous business reviews with leaders across functions to track evolving priorities and workforce capability needs. These conversations should go beyond tactical training requests and focus on forecasting skills gaps, emerging performance challenges, and shifts in business strategy. By treating learning priorities like a product road map, L&D can refine training offerings continuously rather than adhering to a rigid annual plan.

Another key tactic is implementing a *rolling learning backlog*, which is a prioritized queue of learning initiatives that L&D can adjust in real time as business needs change. Instead of relying on set content cycles, learning teams can adopt rolling content refreshes to ensure training remains relevant and effective. For example, suppose a company pivots its go-to-market strategy midyear. In that case, L&D should be able to reprioritize sales enablement training within weeks, not months. This approach prevents lagging initiatives and equips employees with the skills they need precisely when they need them.

Real-Time Data Informs Decision Making

Data plays a critical role in enabling L&D responsiveness to business needs. Many organizations track employee completion rates and satisfaction scores, but these metrics offer little insight into whether training solves real business problems. Instead, L&D teams should monitor KPIs such as sales growth, customer retention, workforce productivity, and compliance adherence to align learning efforts with measurable business outcomes.

Leveraging skills intelligence platforms and workforce analytics allows L&D teams to identify emerging capability gaps before they become urgent business risks. By analyzing trends in business performance, employee engagement, and operational inefficiencies, L&D can ensure that training priorities remain proactive rather than reactive.

For example, an organization may notice an increase in customer complaints related to a subpar understanding of its product line. In that case, L&D could quickly deploy a targeted microlearning solution rather than wait for the next quarterly training cycle. Likewise, if sales data reveals performance gaps in a new market segment, L&D can use AI-enabled insights to customize coaching for underperforming sales teams.

To illustrate how data-informed learning initiatives drive measurable results, let's look at two organizations that successfully used real-time performance data to refine their L&D strategies.

A Construction Firm Boosts Knowledge Retention With Bite-Sized Learning

A global construction firm discovered that traditional training methods were not effectively engaging its workforce, leading to low retention and poor application of skills on the job. Rather than continuing with long-format training sessions, the company analyzed workforce engagement data and found that employees learned best when training was delivered in short, digestible pieces.

The L&D team transformed its training approach by implementing bite-sized, mobile-friendly learning modules inspired by TikTok and Instagram. Employees could take training courses in short bursts during their workday, improving retention without disrupting productivity.

This data-informed pivot dramatically expanded each training program's reach. Afterward, 10 percent of the company's learning budget benefited 700 employees per month, which was significant when compared with previous investments that served far fewer staff members. The shift also improved engagement and knowledge application, leading to higher productivity in the field.

Key takeaway: By tracking learning engagement data, the company was able to identify an ineffective training method, adjust its approach, and increase L&D's influence without additional investment.

A Pharmaceuticals Manufacturer Addresses Workforce Skills Gaps With AI

Like many global enterprises, a large pharmaceutical company needed a scalable approach to upskilling employees so training could continue supporting evolving business demands. Instead of relying on a one-size-fits-all training model, it used AI-enabled workforce analytics to detect skills gaps before they became critical.

The company implemented AI-enabled talent analytics to automatically match employees with relevant upskilling opportunities based on job roles and skill proficiency. It deployed targeted training materials and immersive simulations, allowing employees to practice new skills in a low-risk environment before applying them on the job. This real-time skills intelligence enabled the company to deliver highly personalized training content, ensuring employees developed the right skills at the right time. Early feedback showed that these AI-enabled initiatives significantly improved workforce readiness and internal talent mobility, reducing reliance on external hiring.

Key takeaway: Instead of relying on periodic skills audits, the company used real-time AI analytics to drive training decisions so its workforce remained agile and prepared for future business needs.

A KPI-Driven Approach for Your L&D Team

The organizations we've discussed highlight the power of using real-time data to shape effective learning strategies. When you proactively monitor business KPIs and adjust training efforts accordingly, you can:

- Ensure learning solutions address real business challenges, not just compliance requirements.
- Use data-backed insights to determine when to invest in new training versus refreshing existing programs.

- Demonstrate the ROI of your L&D initiatives in measurable business terms, strengthening your team's credibility as a strategic function.

By integrating AI-enabled workforce analytics, real-time skills assessments, and performance-driven learning strategies, you can transform your L&D function from a static, content-delivery function into a dynamic enabler of business capability. In other words, you'll shift from being a training provider to a strategic performance driver so your learning initiatives are always relevant, timely, and effective.

L&D and Cross-Functional Teams

In addition to incorporating real-time data, L&D must also shift from operating as an isolated department to becoming an integrated business partner. Many organizations still treat training as an afterthought, only consulting L&D teams after a significant change has already occurred. To be more responsive, L&D professionals should be embedded within cross-functional teams, such as business transformation initiatives, product development teams, and operations task forces.

By participating in senior leadership and cross-functional business meetings, your L&D team gains a window into shifting priorities and skill requirements. This proactive approach ensures learning initiatives align with business needs before performance gaps occur. Some organizations take this a step further by appointing L&D business partners for each division, mirroring HR business partner models. These dedicated L&D professionals work directly with key business units as learning consultants who help shape real-time workforce capability strategies.

Another effective approach is leveraging internal networks of SMEs who can provide rapid insights into emerging knowledge gaps. SMEs can be engaged to co-develop training content or lead microlearning sessions, allowing L&D to move faster without waiting for full course development.

Business priorities are constantly evolving, and L&D must be able to evolve at the same time. The key to your success will be employing a responsive learning strategy that continuously reassesses priorities and an effective communication plan that drives employee adoption. By embedding structured adaptability into L&D operations, organizations can prioritize keeping their learning programs relevant, effective, and aligned with business needs. The ability to pivot while maintaining quality and engagement is what differentiates high-performing L&D teams from those struggling to keep up. Organizations that master flexible learning design, business driven prioritization, and proactive workforce development will be able to successfully support business pivots.

Pause to Reflect

How well does your L&D function anticipate and respond to shifting business priorities? What changes could you make to enhance its ability to pivot effectively?

Developing Mechanisms for Rapid Deployment of Training

When a business makes a critical pivot—whether it's responding to a new compliance requirement, a leadership transition, a product launch, or a shift in customer engagement strategies—your L&D team must be able to deploy learning solutions quickly without sacrificing quality. Traditional instructional design cycles are often too slow, which leads to training delays that can affect performance and business outcomes. To facilitate rapid training deployment, you must integrate a tiered learning response, streamlined content development, just-in-time learning, and adaptive delivery models.

A Tiered Learning Response Model

Not every business shift requires a full-scale learning program. L&D must differentiate between urgent training needs and those that can be addressed through faster solutions. A tiered learning response model allows organizations to deploy training at the right level of complexity and speed. This model could include:

- **Quick job aids and performance support.** When minor process updates or knowledge gaps arise, you can use templates to develop

job aids, FAQs, quick-reference guides, or short videos instead of full training courses.
- **SME-led discussions or knowledge-sharing sessions.** If employees need context but not structured learning, SMEs can lead short virtual discussions or Q&A sessions to transfer knowledge quickly.
- **Targeted microlearning modules.** When employees need structured training quickly, you can use microlearning to ensure immediate application without long courses.
- **Fully developed training programs.** If a business shift fundamentally changes workflows, regulations, or job responsibilities, a more comprehensive, structured learning program may be necessary. However, even in these cases, you should use an iterative development approach rather than waiting to launch a complete program at once.

By implementing this tiered approach, L&D can avoid overengineering learning solutions and ensure that employees receive only what they need when they need it.

As you start implementing a tiered learning response model, use this structured framework to determine the fastest, most effective learning solution based on business urgency and complexity:

- **Tier 1: Instant solutions (self-service knowledge access).** Use these solutions when employees need quick answers for routine, repetitive challenges. Leverage AI-enabled knowledge hubs, chatbots, FAQs, and job aids. For example, if a customer support rep forgets how to process a return, they can find the answer using Microsoft Copilot.
- **Tier 2: SME-led discussions and quick coaching.** Use these solutions when knowledge exists internally but needs context. Conduct peer learning, SME Q&A sessions, and leadership coaching. For example, if sales managers notice reps are struggling with a new product pitch, L&D can facilitate a 30-minute expert Q&A session on Slack.
- **Tier 3: Microlearning and scenario-based training.** Use these solutions when employees need structured learning but the organization cannot afford downtime. Deploy interactive

microlearning modules, scenario-based videos, or VR simulations. For example, if a retail chain sees a 20 percent spike in customer complaints about a new product, L&D can push a five-minute microlearning refresher.

- **Tier 4: Formal training and certification programs.** Use these solutions when employees require in-depth skill building for long-term capability shifts. Conduct structured workshops, simulations, certifications, or blended learning. For example, if a cybersecurity breach exposes a compliance gap, L&D can launch a mandatory certification program for all IT staff.

The Tiered Learning Response Model in Action

Imagine a large global clothing store facing a surge in customer complaints about a newly launched product. Here's an example of how an L&D team could respond using the tiered learning response model:

- ▶ **Tier 1 (instant solution).** Store associates could first search the AI-enabled knowledge hub for answers. If information exists, they could resolve the issue themselves without further support.
- ▶ **Tier 2 (SME-led coaching).** A regional sales leader could host a 20-minute coaching session on Teams, allowing store associates to ask real-time questions.
- ▶ **Tier 3 (microlearning initiative).** After noticing persistent knowledge gaps, L&D could deploy a five-minute mobile microlearning module that reinforces key product details.
- ▶ **Tier 4 (formal training).** If complaints continue over time, L&D could launch a structured blended learning course for all customer-facing employees, ensuring long-term retention.

The advantage of this model is that instead of defaulting to expensive, time-consuming formal training, L&D can quickly escalate solutions based on complexity, which then allows them to resolve challenges faster without disrupting operations.

Solutions for Content Development Bottlenecks

A significant barrier to rapid training deployment is the time it takes to create and approve learning content. L&D teams often get caught in bureaucratic approval cycles, lengthy SME reviews, and rigid instructional design processes. To move faster, you can try one of these effective solutions:

- **Use prebuilt modular content.** Instead of creating training from scratch, maintain a library of modular, reusable learning assets that you can quickly adapt for new business needs.
- **Streamline approval processes.** Establishing clear governance on who approves training content and how long it takes can significantly reduce delays. Fast-moving organizations often preapprove content templates and set time limits for SME reviews to prevent bottlenecks.
- **Have SMEs generate content.** SMEs can provide frontline knowledge more quickly than traditional instructional design teams. You can train SMEs to create basic learning materials—like short video walkthroughs or annotated slide decks—which your L&D team can refine before deployment.
- **Adopt AI-assisted content development.** AI-powered tools can accelerate training creation by generating first drafts of job aids, quizzes, and interactive scenarios, reducing manual effort for L&D teams.

Technology-Enabled Just-in-Time Learning

Instead of pulling employees into formal training courses, try embedding learning into their daily workflow so they have access to knowledge precisely when needed. Just-in-time learning is a game-changer for agility. When business priorities shift suddenly due to compliance updates, new product launches, or changes in customer engagement strategies, you'll be able to deploy solutions in real time.

For example, when a global retail chain launched a new product feature, in-store employees needed immediate guidance. Instead of scheduling workshops, L&D leveraged its performance support platform and pushed searchable job aids to the employee's handheld devices. Customer complaints were reduced by 18 percent in just two weeks. To enable just-in-time agility, you should:

- **Embed learning into digital workplace tools.** Deploy microlearning content through Slack, Teams, and CRM platforms so employees can learn without leaving their workflow.

- **Leverage knowledge hubs.** Allow employees to access instant, role-based answers to work-related questions. Many platforms incorporate search based on natural language processing (NLP), and more are adding AI agents.
- **Automate adaptive learning paths.** Push the right training to the right employees based on real-time data signals.

By integrating learning into daily workflows, L&D ensures that employees receive training at the point of need rather than being pulled into unnecessary classroom sessions. (For a deeper look at how learning methodologies can drive value, see chapter 6.)

We know that speed alone is not a helpful goal, but by implementing a tiered learning response model, reducing content development bottlenecks, and embedding just-in-time learning into the flow of work, you will help employees get the right information at the right time and in the right way. Organizations that shift to a structured, rapid-response approach—leveraging SMEs, microlearning, AI-enabled content recommendations, and embedded workflow training—can deliver learning at the speed of change and drive real, measurable results and value.

 Pause to Reflect
When urgent business needs arise, how quickly can your L&D team deliver effective training solutions? What barriers might be slowing you down?

Responding to Shifting Customer Priorities

Successfully making the kind of learning pivots we've discussed in this chapter requires more than just creating new content; it demands a strategic, proactive approach to reprioritizing learning efforts and encouraging employee adoption. This involves adjusting learning strategies to match business priorities and effectively communicating about the business pivots to drive engagement and adoption.

How L&D Should Adjust

To keep up with shifting business dynamics, you'll need to develop business-integrated flexibility that allows your team to pivot alongside the business while maintaining efficiency and alignment. As we've discussed, you must move beyond static learning road maps and adopt a rolling prioritization model. Unlike traditional training calendars that lock learning initiatives into preplanned cycles, a rolling learning backlog allows L&D to dynamically reprioritize training efforts based on evolving business needs. This means regularly assessing learning programs to determine which ones should be accelerated, paused, or redesigned to match organizational priorities.

Business Alignment Embedded in Learning Strategy

One of the most effective ways to ensure L&D stays in sync with shifting business goals is to treat training initiatives like a *product road map*, which is a document that outlines the objectives and key results (OKRs), features, initiatives, and timelines of a product. High-performing L&D teams maintain a continuous feedback loop with business stakeholders so learning priorities can evolve quickly. Instead of waiting for an annual needs assessment, L&D should conduct quarterly or even monthly reviews of training results. Start by asking these questions:

- Are current learning programs driving measurable business results?
- Have new strategic initiatives emerged that require rapid upskilling?
- Which existing programs need to be adapted, expanded, or deprioritized?

By integrating business-aligned OKRs into training design, you can tie learning efforts directly to performance outcomes rather than operating in isolation.

You will also need to shift from long-cycle development to *iterative learning sprints*, which means working on smaller, agile learning deployments that respond rapidly to new business needs, rather than spending months developing extensive learning programs that may become outdated quickly. By working in two- to four-week content development cycles, your L&D team can continuously test, refine, and iterate learning solutions while keeping pace with business shifts.

A structured governance model also plays a role in your ability to adapt quickly. Organizations should establish a prioritization committee or advisory board that includes L&D leaders, HR, and key business stakeholders to review and approve training priorities on a rolling basis. This can prevent resource misallocation and confirm whether training efforts directly support pressing business needs.

Data to Inform Learning Adjustments

Business conversations are crucial, but data-informed decision-making processes separate reactive L&D teams from strategic enablers of business success. You must continuously monitor both learning effectiveness metrics and business KPIs to identify where shifts and revisions to your plans are needed. Some valuable data sources include:

- **Business KPIs.** If your organization sees declining customer satisfaction or increased employee turnover, L&D must determine if training gaps are contributing to the issue.
- **Skills analytics platforms.** AI-enabled tools can track emerging skills gaps across the workforce, enabling you to pivot proactively before those gaps affect business performance.
- **Employee learning engagement and performance data.** If completion rates are high but on-the-job application remains low, you may need to adjust your training methods.
- **Feedback loops.** Collecting real-time employee and stakeholder feedback helps training content remain relevant. You can do this through pulse surveys, manager debriefs, and peer learning sessions.

By combining business intelligence with workforce learning analytics, you can continuously refine training priorities, ensuring they align with business needs and deliver measurable results.

Adjusting to shifting business priorities is no longer optional for L&D; it's necessary to maintain relevance and effectiveness. Rather than relying on static learning road maps, your team can integrate continuous business alignment into your strategy, moving beyond annual training plans and adopting a rolling prioritization model to dynamically reassess which learning programs you should accelerate, adapt, or retire. By embedding real-time data insights, fostering strong cross-functional partnerships, and ensuring clear communication about learning pivots, you can avoid being seen as a reactive function and become a strategic driver of workforce agility.

Pause to Reflect
When business priorities shift, how does your L&D team reassess and adjust its learning initiatives to stay aligned? What processes could improve your responsiveness?

Communicating Effectively to Ensure Consumer Adoption

Even the most well-designed learning programs can struggle if they're not positioned well or don't communicate effectively. L&D teams often invest significant effort in building courses but assume that simply making them available is enough.

It's not.

Without a well-structured communication and engagement strategy, your learning initiatives may suffer from several challenges, including:

- **Low awareness.** Employees aren't aware of the program or don't understand its relevance.
- **Minimal participation.** Employees don't prioritize it because they don't see an immediate benefit.
- **Lack of reinforcement.** Managers aren't engaged, so training is seen as optional rather than essential.
- **Missed business impact.** Learning doesn't translate into performance improvement without proper adoption.

So, how can you ensure that your learning initiatives aren't just seen as static content in the LMS and are actually embraced and applied? Let's discuss a few strategies.

A Go-to-Market Strategy for L&D

In product marketing, a *go-to-market* (*GTM*) *strategy* ensures that a company builds and successfully launches new products that reach the right audience, drive engagement, and ultimately generate revenue. L&D needs the same approach. Without a structured rollout plan, even the most well-designed learning programs risk being overlooked, underused, or forgotten.

A GTM strategy for learning programs ensures that training initiatives are created, deployed, actively promoted, adopted, and reinforced across the organization.

By implementing a repeatable, structured process, you can drive awareness so employees and managers understand the value of a training initiative before it even launches. A well-executed GTM plan also fosters strong adoption, positioning learning as relevant, timely, and essential to employees' roles rather than just another training requirement.

Executive and manager support is critical because leadership endorsement significantly increases the likelihood of successful implementation. When leaders actively promote and reinforce learning within their teams, the perception of training shifts from an optional resource to an organizational priority. Most important, an L&D GTM strategy facilitates measurable results by linking participation to real business outcomes such as improved performance, behavior change, and organizational growth.

L&D cannot afford to take a passive approach to communication. Simply making training available is not enough; employees and managers must see the value, relevance, and urgency of engaging with it. To achieve this, L&D teams should operate like marketing and product teams, leveraging strategic messaging, multichannel promotion, and leadership advocacy to build excitement, reinforce relevance, and drive adoption. By integrating a GTM approach into learning initiatives, L&D shifts from being a content provider to a strategic enabler of business success.

A successful L&D GTM strategy consists of five key elements:
- Framing the learning initiative as a business priority
- Building a repeatable GTM playbook for learning adoption
- Structuring the right communication plan
- Tiering GTM efforts based on program size
- Activating managers and internal champions

Let's discuss each component in more detail.

Framing the Learning Initiative as a Business Priority

Before launching any learning program, you must position it as essential to both the business (your customer) and the employee (your consumer). Consider questions such as:
- Why does this learning initiative matter?

- What business problem does it solve?
- What's the risk if employees don't participate?
- Will it affect revenue, efficiency, or compliance?
- How does it benefit the business and the employees?
- Does it improve job performance, career growth, or skill development?

If employees don't see the relevance, they won't engage with the learning content. If managers don't see the urgency, they won't reinforce it.

Building a Repeatable GTM Playbook for Learning Adoption

A successful GTM strategy ensures that learning initiatives don't just exist in the LMS but are actively adopted, reinforced, and applied. However, creating a GTM plan from scratch for every new learning program can become time consuming and inconsistent. To streamline this process and improve efficiency, your team should develop a set of GTM templates that you can quickly customize for each launch. These templates should include:

- **Messaging frameworks**—prebuilt narratives that can be adapted to position training as a business priority
- **Communication plans**—ready-to-use email sequences, internal social media posts, and leadership talking points
- **Stakeholder engagement playbooks**—guidance for activating managers and leaders to reinforce learning
- **Promotion and awareness materials**—standardized launch kits, including quick-reference guides, intranet banners, and microvideos
- **Reinforcement strategies**—post-training follow-ups, pulse surveys, and coaching recommendations to sustain results

By leveraging these GTM templates, you can accelerate the rollout of new learning programs while maintaining consistency and engagement across initiatives. Instead of reinventing the wheel, your team can focus on refining and adapting proven approaches, leading to faster adoption, better alignment, and greater business value.

Structuring the Right Communication Plan

Different stakeholders require different messaging and channels to drive adoption. A one-size-fits-all email isn't enough. Depending on your audience and the focus of your message, you'll have different options for the best communication tools.

- **If your audience is executives and business leaders:**
    - Your message should be about business results and ROI.
    - Your best communication tools are leadership briefings, KPI and OKR dashboards, and strategy meetings.
- **If your audience is managers:**
    - Your message should be about how to reinforce learning.
    - Your best communication tools are manager toolkits, talking points, and coaching guides.
- **If your audience is employees:**
    - Your message should be about the relevance and application of learning.
    - Your best communication tools are email campaigns, internal social media, and direct nudges from managers.

A multichannel approach helps your learning initiatives gain visibility and engagement across the organization. Teasers—such as internal communications, short videos, and leadership endorsements—help generate early interest and set the stage for adoption. Emails tailored to specific employee roles provide targeted messaging to help people understand the relevance of the training program.

In addition to direct communication, internal social and collaboration tools like Teams or Slack provide dynamic platforms for promoting discussions, sharing success stories, and reinforcing key messages. Live kickoff sessions, including webinars and manager briefings, allow leaders to introduce the training program, highlight its business value, and encourage participation. Finally, embedded nudges within existing workflow tools—like learning reminders in CRM systems, intranet banners, or automated follow-ups—help reinforce training content as part of daily work rather than a separate, isolated task. By leveraging multiple communication channels, you can make learning initiatives visible, relevant, and accessible, driving higher adoption.

Tiering GTM Efforts Based on Program Size

Not every learning initiative requires the same level of promotion. By categorizing GTM efforts, you can allocate resources efficiently while maximizing their value. Different stakeholders require different messaging and channels to drive adoption. So, depending on your audience and the focus of your message, you have different options for the best communication channels:

- **Use a small GTM communication strategy**—with targeted emails, job aids, and LMS notifications—for compliance updates and microlearning.
- **Use a medium-sized GTM communication strategy**—with email series, manager endorsements, and quick-start guides—for new tools training and manager enablement.
- **Use a large GTM communication strategy**—with executive sponsorships, internal campaigns, and multichannel rollouts—for leadership programs and company-wide initiatives.

By segmenting your efforts, you can ensure high-priority learning programs get visibility while optimizing efforts on lower-impact initiatives.

Activating Managers and Internal Champions

Managers play a critical role in driving adoption. Employees are far more likely to engage when their manager:

- Discusses the training in one-on-one meetings
- Integrates learning into team goals and OKRs
- Reinforces key concepts in real work scenarios

This means that you should equip managers with:

- Talking points and FAQs to explain the program's value
- Coaching guides to connect learning to job performance
- Recognition tools to encourage participation (such as leaderboards and spot bonuses)

In addition, identifying *learning champions*—employees who advocate for training programs within their teams—can increase peer-driven engagement.

From Awareness to Adoption

An L&D GTM strategy should include clear success metrics to track whether communication efforts drive adoption. These include:

- **Awareness.** Measure the percentage of employees who received and opened communications. Awareness matters because it can indicate initial visibility.

- **Engagement.** Measure the percentage of employees who registered for a training course. Engagement matters because it indicates interest and traction.
- **Completion rates.** Measure the percentage of employees who finished a training course. Completion rates matter because they demonstrate delivery effectiveness.
- **Application rates.** Measure the percentage of employees who applied their knowledge on the job. Application rates matter because they connect training to business results.
- **Manager endorsements.** Measure the percentage of managers actively promoting a training course. Manager endorsements matter because they predict long-term success.

By tracking these data points, L&D can continuously refine future GTM strategies to enhance learning adoption and effectiveness.

Even the most well-designed learning initiatives will fail to deliver if you don't communicate about them effectively. Simply making a training program available is not enough. Employees must see its value, managers must reinforce its importance, and the organization must integrate it into daily workflows. A structured GTM approach ensures that training initiatives are actively promoted, adopted, and reinforced across the business.

Successful learning adoption comes from meeting employees where they are, using the right channels, and positioning training as a business priority. When employees understand why a training initiative matters, how it benefits them, and how it supports company goals, they are far more likely to engage.

Pause to Reflect

When business priorities shift, how does your L&D team reassess and adjust its learning initiatives to stay aligned? What processes could improve your responsiveness?

The Bottom Line

Change is constant in business, and we must structure our L&D functions to keep pace. Developing an adaptable, business-aligned learning strategy makes training relevant, effective, and powerful, no matter how often priorities shift. The ability to pivot learning initiatives based on real-time data, changing business needs, and workforce capabilities is not just a competitive advantage but an operational necessity.

Agility does not mean sacrificing structure. The most successful L&D teams blend adaptability with discipline, combining proactive stakeholder engagement, data-informed prioritization, and just-in-time learning deployment. By embedding mechanisms for continuous alignment, L&D can move from a reactive function to a strategic business driver, helping organizations stay ahead of change rather than struggling to catch up. And the final challenge is deploying learning solutions quickly and ensuring they are embraced, applied, and sustained across the organization.

How to Take Action for Strategic Agility

Strategic agility requires more than rapid pivots and fast turnarounds. It depends on building systems that help your team anticipate change, adjust priorities, and stay aligned with shifting business needs. Consider these actions as a starting point for your journey:

- **Take a critical look at how your L&D team prioritizes learning initiatives.** Are you using real-time business data or operating with outdated training plans? Set up a quarterly (or even monthly) review process with key stakeholders to ensure training remains connected with shifting business needs.
- **Replace rigid annual learning calendars with a dynamic backlog of training initiatives.** Use a simple framework to categorize training needs as urgent, emerging, or long-term so your team can rapidly shift focus when business needs change.
- **Even the best learning solutions won't drive results if employees and managers don't see their value.** Choose one upcoming training program and develop a GTM plan. Outline key messaging, communication channels, and ways to reinforce learning beyond the initial rollout.

Chapter 8
Change Management in L&D

At a nationwide retail healthcare company, business leaders launched a new operating model designed to improve margins in underperforming offices. The changes were sweeping: Support roles were consolidated, new scheduling protocols were introduced, and clinic managers were expected to take on broader operational responsibilities, often with little warning.

The L&D team moved fast. Within weeks, they rolled out a well-produced training package that covered the new scheduling system, refreshed expectations for customer service, and offered a time management module for frontline leaders. The content was clean, accessible, and well-received in early feedback.

But just a few weeks after launch, performance metrics had begun to trend in the wrong direction. Escalations from regional leaders poured in. Several high-volume clinics missed targets. Turnover spiked. Despite the training initiative, managers and staff were confused, overwhelmed, and unsure of how to navigate the new expectations.

The problem wasn't poor execution; it was poor alignment. The business had initiated a structural change, but L&D responded with a skills solution. What managers needed wasn't another training module. They needed support leading through disruption, guidance on communicating trade-offs, and clarity on what success looked like in the new model.

When L&D tackles change as a learning problem rather than a business problem, even the best-designed solutions fall flat. In this chapter, we'll explore how L&D teams can drive adoption by aligning with the business from the start, anticipating resistance, and designing learning experiences that help leaders and teams move successfully through change.

Overcoming Resistance to Change

Change is inevitable but resistance to change remains one of the biggest barriers to successful L&D initiatives. Whether it's business leaders who question the value of learning programs, employees who are reluctant to embrace new skills, or L&D teams that struggle with internal shifts, resistance can stall progress and reduce the effectiveness of your learning efforts. To drive meaningful adoption, we must shift learning from a mandated activity to a business-driven investment that employees and stakeholders actively embrace. We do that by getting stakeholder buy-in and creating a culture of continuous learning through good communication and collaboration across our organizations.

Get Buy-In From Stakeholders and Change Champions

Early stakeholder engagement is one of the most effective ways to overcome resistance. Too often, L&D teams develop learning programs in isolation and only involve business leaders and employees at the rollout stage, which results in last-minute pushback. A *co-creation model*—in which business leaders, department heads, and even select employees help shape learning programs—can significantly increase buy-in and ensure the programs align with business goals.

Another powerful tool is leveraging *change champions*—influential employees or managers who advocate for learning initiatives within their teams. Change champions help bridge the gap between corporate L&D messaging and frontline employee adoption, reinforcing the value of learning through peer influence.

When you're seeking support from people beyond L&D, framing training as a business enabler rather than a compliance requirement is critical. Employees and business leaders alike need to understand how learning initiatives directly affect their success. Instead of generic messaging about "upskilling" or "professional development," you should connect learning programs to specific business goals, career growth opportunities, and performance improvements.

Proactively identifying resistance points is also essential. Conduct pulse surveys, stakeholder interviews, and small-scale pilot programs before full rollouts to uncover potential objections early so your L&D team has time to adjust its approach before encountering major pushback. Resistance is often a sign of uncertainty, not unwillingness, and by addressing concerns early, you can transform skeptics into advocates.

Create a Culture of Continuous Learning

While individual learning programs are important, they are only as effective as the learning culture that surrounds them. Engagement is often low in organizations that see learning as a one-time event or an obligation. In organizations that embed learning into daily operations, however, employees actively seek development opportunities and view change as an opportunity rather than a disruption.

Here are several steps you can take to create a culture of continuous learning:

- **Start at the top.** A strong learning culture starts at the leadership level. When executives and managers consistently participate in training, discuss professional growth, and recognize employees who invest in skills development, it sends a clear message that learning is a priority. Without leadership modeling, even the most well-designed programs struggle to gain traction.
- **Integrate learning into workflows.** Embedding learning into existing workflows is as important as leadership modeling. Employees often resist training because they see it as a distraction from their daily work. Instead of requiring them to step away for lengthy training sessions, organizations should integrate microlearning, AI-enabled content recommendations, and on-the-job learning tools within workflows to provide value in the moment of need. By making learning a natural part of the workday, you will remove barriers to engagement.
- **Collaborate!** Collaboration also plays a key role in driving a culture of learning. When employees learn from one another through peer coaching, cross-functional knowledge, sharing, and internal communities of practice, knowledge growth becomes a shared responsibility rather than a top-down directive. Collaborative approaches create an environment of continuous knowledge exchange, reinforcing innovation and adaptability.

Overcome Resistance With a Culture of Continuous Learning

Ultimately, a culture of continuous learning will lead to a culture of innovation. Organizations that prioritize skills development outperform their competitors, adapt more quickly to change, and maintain stronger employee engagement. By making learning a core organizational value, you can ensure that change efforts are implemented, sustained, reinforced, and embraced over time.

When you, as an L&D leader, take the time to discover and address concerns early, you will reduce friction, sharpen learning solutions, and build the credibility required to become a true business partner.

Proactively engaging stakeholders, co-creating solutions, and linking learning initiatives directly to measurable outcomes isn't optional. It's the cost of entry. Skipping these steps often leads to stalled programs and wasted resources. However, when you treat resistance as useful data, you can increase your odds of success. Find where expectations are unclear, priorities conflict, and your strategy needs adjustment before you waste time and budget. Help make it easy for the business to adopt new ways of working. That means ensuring learning is tied to business goals, delivered in the flow of work, and supported by leaders who model the change themselves.

The takeaway here is simple: Resistance is inevitable. How you handle it is the differentiator. If you address resistance early and align learning to business drivers, you'll turn potential blockers into advocates, scaling adoption and results at the speed your business requires.

Pause to Reflect

Consider your current learning initiatives. Are you reacting to resistance instead of using it as an early signal to adjust your approach and strengthen alignment with business priorities?

Conducting a Change Readiness Assessment

One of the most common mistakes learning teams make when managing change is assuming that readiness will take care of itself. We push ahead with new initiatives—whether that's a shift in learning strategy, a new platform rollout, or organization-wide capability building—without understanding whether the conditions for successful adoption exist. The results? Leaders lose confidence, employees disengage, and momentum stalls.

Change readiness isn't a gut feeling. It's something you measure.

Assessing readiness precisely allows you to identify strengths you can leverage and gaps you need to address before launching new initiatives. It also gives the business confidence that your L&D team is approaching change with rigor, discipline, and clear-eyed pragmatism, which is critical when positioning yourselves as a strategic partner.

Why Readiness Matters

Readiness is often the difference between programs that stick and those that fade into the background. It's not about whether people like the new approach or your team is ready to execute the plan. You need to know if the organization has the infrastructure, leadership buy-in, communication mechanisms, and cultural conditions required to adopt and sustain the change.

Before you launch any significant L&D initiative—whether it's a new learning platform, a shift to skills-based learning, or a broader role in supporting enterprise transformation—assessing readiness across a few key dimensions is critical.

The Change Readiness Framework

A structured readiness assessment will help you uncover potential roadblocks early and create an actionable mitigation plan. The six dimensions in this framework each include a set of questions to answer after consulting with other leaders in the organization.

1. **Strategic alignment:**
    - Do you have clarity on the business case for this change?
    - Are the initiative's goals tied directly to the organization's strategic priorities?
    - Have key leaders signed off on the objectives and outcomes?
2. **Leadership sponsorship:**
    - Are executive sponsors visible and actively involved?
    - Are mid-level and frontline managers prepared to reinforce and model the new behaviors?
    - Do leaders have the tools and messaging to advocate for this change in their teams?
3. **Organizational culture and willingness:**
    - Does the current culture support learning, experimentation, and change?
    - Have employees successfully navigated similar changes in the past?
    - Is there a baseline level of trust in leadership and communication channels?

4. **Capability and capacity:**
   - Does the organization have the skills and capabilities required to implement and sustain the change?
   - Do teams have the capacity to support this initiative alongside other priorities?
   - Does the L&D function have the resources (both people and budget) to execute effectively?
5. **Communication and engagement:**
   - Is there a communication strategy that addresses both the why and the how of the change?
   - Are communication channels available to gather feedback and adjust messaging in real time?
   - Have stakeholders been segmented so messages are relevant and actionable at every level of the organization?
6. **Measurement and feedback loops:**
   - Are success metrics clearly defined and tied to business outcomes?
   - Is there a plan for capturing feedback throughout implementation, not just post-launch?
   - Will there be opportunities to adjust the approach based on what the data tells you?

An effective readiness assessment doesn't have to be complicated. Start by creating a simple diagnostic survey or interview guide that follows the six dimensions. Then, engage executive sponsors, managers, and frontline employees to gather their perspectives on each area. If you find gaps, build action plans to address them before you proceed.

For example:
- If leadership sponsorship is weak, you may need to delay the rollout until you've secured a more visible commitment.
- If capacity is an issue, adjust timelines to avoid overwhelming teams.
- If the culture isn't ready, introduce pilot programs or proof-of-concept initiatives to build momentum and credibility.

The assessment isn't a pass/fail exercise. It's a tool for gaining clarity so you and your stakeholders can make informed decisions about timing, resource allocation, and scope.

Demonstrating Business Rigor and Discipline

Conducting a formal readiness assessment reinforces L&D's role as a disciplined, business-minded function. It shows you aren't rushing to deliver a program without ensuring the conditions for success are in place. In fact, readiness assessments often reveal areas where business partners need to step up, whether that's assigning sponsors, freeing up capacity, or supporting other initiatives.

Readiness is about lowering the risk involved in change and making sure you've done the work upfront to build momentum, secure engagement, and create an environment in which people are ready to adopt new ways of working. When you lead with this kind of discipline, a learning initiative isn't just another program to complete. It becomes business-critical enabler of change.

Too often, L&D teams are eager to launch initiatives without confirming whether the organization is ready to adopt them. That's a gamble most L&D functions can't afford, especially when they're positioning themselves as strategic partners to the business.

Using a structured change readiness framework doesn't mean slowing things down. The framework can help you limit the risks of your work and set yourself (and your stakeholders) up for success. It provides a clear-eyed view of the landscape, including where leadership is aligned, where gaps exist, and whether the conditions are right for full-scale adoption. When you uncover challenges early, you give yourself time to address them before they become major obstacles.

You can't always wait for perfect conditions, but you can make sure you have a realistic plan that's grounded in data and positions your learning initiatives as business-critical solutions. When you lead with readiness, you are saying, "This isn't training for the sake of training. It's a disciplined, business-driven approach to enabling change."

Pause to Reflect
What would a structured readiness assessment reveal about your organization's ability to adopt and sustain your next major learning initiative? Have you asked the right questions to find out?

L&D's Role in Enterprise-Wide Change

Change is a constant in today's business environment. Organizations are always in flux, whether driven by digital transformation, mergers and acquisitions, evolving customer expectations, or regulatory shifts. While strategies and technologies often take center stage in these change initiatives, their success hinges on people. Without a prepared, capable, and confident workforce, even the most well-intentioned change efforts can falter. This is why L&D needs to step forward, not just as a function that supports isolated training initiatives but as a critical driver and enabler of enterprise-wide change.

In its most effective form, your L&D team can act as the bridge between strategy and execution. You can translate business priorities into the behaviors, mindsets, and skills needed for transformation. By embedding learning into change efforts from the outset, you'll equip leaders and employees to navigate complexity, adopt new ways of working, and deliver measurable business outcomes.

From Project Participant to Change Partner

Too often, our L&D teams are engaged *after* major decisions have been made. We are handed a directive to train employees on a new system, process, or policy. In this scenario, learning is an afterthought—a necessary but secondary step in the implementation plan. Your L&D function is reduced to a task owner responsible for delivering content but with little influence over the broader change strategy.

High-performing L&D teams take a different approach. They secure a seat at the table early, partnering with business leaders as change is being designed, not just deployed. They collaborate with HR, operations, IT, and strategy teams to understand the organization's priorities, identify capability gaps, and co-create solutions that promote behavior change at scale. When you can position your L&D team as a change partner, it becomes a force multiplier, accelerating adoption, reducing resistance, and ensuring that people, processes, and technology evolve in concert.

The shift from participant to partner means moving beyond traditional training delivery. It requires a deep understanding of the business strategy and an ability to diagnose where skills and mindset gaps will impede execution. It also means designing learning solutions that are integrated into change initiatives rather than bolted on after decisions are made.

Change Without Learning Is a Risky Business

Organizational change is inherently risky. Even with a clear vision and robust strategy, many change initiatives fail to deliver their intended outcomes. Up to 70 percent of transformation efforts fall short of their goals—often because people weren't adequately prepared to work differently (Brassey, Christensen, and van Dam 2019). New technologies go underused. New processes are ignored or circumvented. Culture initiatives stall.

You can mitigate this risk by helping employees make the transition from the old way of working to the new. Without targeted learning programs that build their capability and confidence, your organization will leave transformation plans vulnerable to delays, disengagement, and underperformance.

Consider the example of a typical large-scale digital transformation. Companies invest millions in new technologies such as HR systems, cloud platforms, and AI-enabled tools. All that investment is wasted, however, if employees aren't trained to use these tools effectively and don't understand how they support new workflows and decision-making processes. L&D can help people get ready to adopt and optimize these technologies, closing the gap between strategy and execution.

L&D's Role in Cultural Change

Many transformations require employees to adopt new mindsets as well as learning new skills. A digital-first strategy may demand agility and experimentation. A customer-centric pivot may require deeper empathy and active listening. These cultural shifts are often the hardest changes to achieve and the most essential to long-term success.

Your L&D team plays a pivotal role in driving cultural change by designing programs that foster desired behaviors and values, building awareness and understanding, and providing opportunities for practice and reinforcement. Leadership development programs, peer coaching, and communities of practice all help embed new cultural norms into the fabric of daily operations.

For example, an organization aiming to foster a more innovative culture might implement learning experiences that focus on design thinking, rapid prototyping, and psychological safety. These programs don't just teach concepts; they build the behaviors and mindsets that support innovation as an ongoing practice.

Your Responsibilities as a Learning Leader

For your organization's L&D function to fulfill its role as an enabler of enterprise-wide change, it must be integrated into the broader change strategy from the beginning. This requires a shift in both mindset and practice. As a learning leader, you must:

- Engage early in strategy discussions by building relationships with key stakeholders across the business.
- Understand the business's goals and challenges and identify where learning can have the greatest impact.
- Use data and insights to anticipate future skills needs and design proactive initiatives.

In short, you need to become a strategic partner in the organization. This model positions L&D as a co-architect of change, not just a downstream executor. When learning is part of the plan from day 1, it accelerates adoption, reduces resistance, and drives better business outcomes.

L&D as a Strategic Lever for Business Transformation

L&D doesn't just support change—L&D enables it. In the best organizations, learning is woven into the fabric of transformation efforts, accelerating the shift from strategy to execution. By focusing on building capability as a core component of change, you can equip employees to deliver on the business's most critical priorities. Organizations that get learning right during periods of change have a competitive advantage. In fact, companies that focus on skills building as part of their transformation efforts are more than four times as likely to outperform their peers (Brassey, Christensen, and van Dam 2019).

An expanded role for your L&D function during times of change requires you to move beyond content creation and course delivery. You must think strategically, engage in cross-functional collaboration, and adopt a relentless focus on business results. When your team operates as a strategic lever for transformation, you help the organization navigate complexity, build resilience, and accelerate growth.

Practical Considerations in Times of Change

As an L&D leader taking on an expanded role during periods of organizational transformation, you can take these steps to become more effective:

- **Understand the business's priorities.** Engage with senior leaders to identify the organization's most pressing challenges and opportunities.
- **Conduct capability assessments.** Map current skills against future needs to identify gaps that could impede progress.
- **Design content as a change enabler.** Develop learning solutions that directly support behaviors and capabilities required for change.
- **Measure what matters.** Shift from tracking participation to measuring how learning drives results, performance, adoption, and business outcomes.
- **Partner across the business.** Build alliances with HR, IT, and other functions to ensure learning is integrated into broader change efforts.

Enterprise-wide change doesn't just succeed because executives announce a new strategy or IT launches a new system. It succeeds when people at every level adopt new behaviors, build new capabilities, and have the confidence to operate in new ways. This is how L&D earns its seat at the table as a critical driver of execution.

A Global Software Company's Agile Transformation

L&D was instrumental in a global software company's shift toward Agile practices. Rather than delivering standalone training on Agile frameworks, the learning team collaborated with product and engineering leaders to embed learning into sprints.

Employees engaged in real-time learning experiences, applying new practices immediately within their workflows. This approach accelerated adoption and helped the organization build a flexible mindset that continues to support innovation.

When your L&D function steps up as a true change partner, it closes the gap between strategy and results (equipping people to deliver on business priorities), accelerates adoption, and makes sure everyone in the organization has the skills and mindset needed to sustain change over time.

This only happens when you and your team operate with business rigor, embedding learning into the change process from the start, connecting programs with measurable outcomes, and holding yourselves accountable for driving business results.

Change without learning is risky. In any enterprise, if L&D isn't proactively leading the charge to prepare the workforce for what's next, the business is flying blind. High-performing learning teams don't wait to be asked. They position themselves as essential to enterprise transformation. They become indispensable.

Pause to Reflect

How are you ensuring that your learning strategy directly supports the behaviors and capabilities your organization needs to execute its most critical changes?

Scalable Change Management and Learning Operations

Change management is often viewed as a standalone discipline—something applied to initiatives in the final phases of implementation. But in a well-run learning organization, change isn't a one-time project or an afterthought. It's a consistent, disciplined capability embedded into the daily operations of L&D. This is where learning operations come in.

Earlier in this book, I introduced the Learning Operations Blueprint as the foundation for running L&D like a business. The blueprint provides the governance, systems, and processes that bring order and predictability to your work in L&D. It's also a powerful enabler of scalable, sustainable change management.

Organizations that struggle to manage change typically lack the operational rigor to support it. They rely on heroics, ad-hoc efforts, or fragmented processes that make every initiative feel like a reinvention. In contrast, organizations that have invested in learning operations create the conditions for change to be repeatable, measurable, and scalable, whether they're rolling out a new learning platform, launching a skills-based learning strategy, or supporting an enterprise transformation.

Your Blueprint for Change

At its core, the Learning Operations Blueprint is a change management engine. It formalizes how L&D governs decisions, engages the business through intake processes, prioritizes initiatives, manages resources, and measures outcomes. Each of these operational elements plays a critical role in making change stick. For example:

- **Governance ensures that learning initiatives align with business priorities and have the necessary sponsorship to drive adoption.** When governance is clear, decisions are made faster, risks are mitigated earlier, and accountability is shared.
- **Intake processes bring clarity to what gets done and why.** They prevent L&D teams from being pulled in different directions by ad-hoc requests, allowing team members to focus on initiatives that are business critical and needed for change.
- **Prioritization frameworks help L&D leaders make trade-offs.** Not every change can or should happen at once. Prioritization helps the organization focus on changes that will deliver the greatest business value supported by the right resources and timing.
- **Resource management makes it possible to deliver on commitments.** Without visibility into capacity and workload, even the most important change initiatives risk underdelivering and team burnout. Learning operations provides this visibility, ensuring L&D teams can scale without compromising quality.
- **Measurement and reporting close the loop.** Learning operations supplies the data infrastructure to track adoption, measure results, and course correct when necessary. This data isn't just about employee satisfaction. It also demonstrates the business value of change.

Scaling Change, Not Just Projects

Change management that relies on individual efforts or project heroics doesn't scale. Learning operations allows L&D to move beyond tactical execution to systemic enablement. It turns change management into a repeatable capability, not a one-off deliverable.

For example, following a standardized intake and governance process means that every new learning initiative includes early stakeholder engagement, business alignment checks, and an executive sponsor before resources are allocated. This isn't a custom step added during a change initiative; it's simply how work gets done. As a result, resistance is lower, buy-in is stronger, and your L&D function builds a track record of delivering complex, highly effective programs.

Similarly, a prioritization model ensures that the most critical initiatives—whether it's skills acceleration, leadership development, or technology adoption—receive the attention they need, while lower priority efforts are either delayed or declined. This helps manage change fatigue by pacing initiatives based on organizational readiness and capacity.

Learning Operations for Organizational Agility

Perhaps most important, learning operations makes it possible for your L&D team to respond to business pivots and strategic shifts with speed and precision. Priorities can change rapidly, and if your L&D team relies on manual processes and informal decision making, it will struggle to keep up. Teams grounded in learning operations principles can adjust quickly because they have clear methods for prioritizing work, reallocating resources, and supporting new business objectives.

In short, a well-designed Learning Operations Blueprint provides the agility and stability necessary to lead change rather than react to it.

Pause to Reflect
How well does your L&D team anticipate and support the speed, scale, and complexity of the changes your business is navigating today?

First Alignment, and Then Engagement

One of the most common mistakes L&D teams make when implementing change is focusing too much on employee engagement before securing buy-in from business leaders. Learning programs that are engaging but lack direct business relevance will struggle to gain leadership support, leading to budget cuts and limited long-term effectiveness. To ensure your learning efforts drive real business outcomes, try to prioritize alignment with strategic goals before launching engagement initiatives.

Business-Driven (Not Learning-Driven) Change

If you want your L&D function to be taken seriously, your learning initiatives must be directly tied to business priorities, KPIs, and measurable outcomes. Before rolling out any training program, engage in business impact assessments to answer a few questions:

- **What business problem are you solving?** (Closing a skills gap, improving compliance, or increasing productivity)
- **How will success be measured?** (Revenue growth, efficiency improvements, or cost reduction)
- **Which stakeholders must be involved?** (Senior leadership, department heads, or frontline managers)

Don't ever operate on assumptions about what employees need. Instead, collaborate with other business units to make sure that you're developing learning initiatives based on real operational challenges rather than generic skills development goals.

Positioning your L&D function as a revenue enabler rather than a cost center is also crucial. Business leaders too often perceive training as an expense rather than an investment. By using data-informed reporting and ROI measurement, you can demonstrate how training initiatives contribute to financial and operational success.

Business Leaders and Learning

After securing buy-in from business leaders, you'll find that employee engagement becomes significantly easier. Employees are more likely to participate in training when they see its direct influence on their work and career growth. The connection is strengthened when business leaders actively participate in learning efforts.

As an L&D leader, you should equip managers with tools and strategies to support learning adoption within their teams. And instead of treating a training program as a standalone initiative, managers should integrate learning discussions into team meetings, performance reviews, and one-to-one coaching sessions.

Another critical shift to initiate as a learning leader is moving from traditional training completion metrics to business impact indicators. Rather than focusing on participation rates or course satisfaction scores, make sure to measure:

- Improvements in employee performance metrics
- Reductions in skill-related errors
- Time-to-productivity for new hires
- Revenue or cost savings resulting from training programs

By shifting the focus from engagement for engagement's sake to engagement tied to measurable business outcomes, your training efforts won't just be perceived as valuable; they'll become indispensable.

Employee engagement matters, but only when it serves a clear business objective. Even the most engaging learning experiences risk becoming irrelevant distractions if they don't align to strategic priorities. Your L&D team's role isn't to create programs that people like; it's to deliver learning content that equips people to do what the business needs them to do.

When learning initiatives are connected to measurable outcomes, engagement becomes easier to achieve because the learning content is so clearly relevant and visibly valuable. When leaders see that connection, they're more likely to advocate for the programs, model the desired behaviors, and reinforce learning in the flow of work.

The takeaway is simple: Prioritize business alignment early and often to guarantee that employee engagement drives real adoption and that adoption drives business results.

 Pause to Reflect

Are your learning initiatives designed to solve a business problem first? Or are they focused on driving engagement without a clear link to measurable outcomes?

The Bottom Line

Leading change isn't about checking a box or delivering a program. It's about building the capabilities that allow the business to move faster, scale smarter, and sustain results over time. For your L&D team, this will require more than great content or high engagement scores. It will require business rigor, operational discipline, and a seat at the table from the start.

In this chapter, we've explored the ways that learning leaders can step up and lead enterprise change with confidence and positive influence:

- **Overcome resistance to change.** Engage stakeholders early, co-create solutions, and use resistance as an early warning system to refine your approach.
- **Conduct a change readiness assessment.** Identify where the conditions for adoption exist and where gaps need to be closed before launch.
- **Drive enterprise-wide change as a strategic partner.** Bridge the gap between vision and execution
- **Promote scalable change management through standardized processes, governance, and workflows.** Allow L&D to scale and sustain change without relying on heroic effort.
- **Prioritize business alignment before focusing on employee engagement.** Engagement without alignment risks wasted time and missed outcomes.

The organizations that thrive are the ones that treat change as a core business capability. Your L&D function is uniquely positioned to build that capability, but that can only happen when your team leads change with business alignment, scalable operations, and a clear focus on measurable outcomes.

In the next chapter, we'll shift from leading change to proving effectiveness. We'll discuss how to move past participation metrics and satisfaction scores to see how learning initiatives drive the business outcomes your organization cares about most so your L&D function can secure its role as a strategic partner in driving enterprise performance.

How to Take Action to Drive Change Management

Change management in L&D starts with sharpening how we connect learning to business momentum through clarity alignment and repeatable actions. Take these steps to get started:

- **Select an in-progress or upcoming initiative and assess its readiness across three dimensions: leadership sponsorship, organizational capacity, and stakeholder alignment.** Use a simple 1–5 scale for each and identify one concrete action you can take to strengthen your weakest area. This quick pulse check can help prevent downstream resistance or delays.
- **Take one of your active learning programs and articulate, in one sentence, how it directly supports a specific business change or transformation initiative.** If you can't do it clearly and succinctly, schedule a discussion with your business partner to clarify how the learning program can better support their priorities. This exercise builds the muscle you need to align programs to business priorities in the context of change.
- **Choose one process—such stakeholder communication, pilot testing, or reinforcing behavior change after a rollout—and document it as a repeatable workflow.** Focus on a process that supports sustained adoption, not just program delivery. Even a one-page checklist creates operational consistency that enables you to scale.

PART 5
Demonstrating Value and Continuous Improvement

Chapter 9
The Impact of L&D

In 2023, a multinational technology company invested more than $50 million in learning initiatives. When the CFO asked what they got for that investment, the L&D team pointed to course completion rates and participant satisfaction scores. Not sales growth or employee retention or productivity gains—just Level 1 data. Two months later, a quarter of the team was let go in a reduction in force.

Only 20 percent of organizations say they effectively measure the business impact of their learning programs (BCG 2020). Yet those that do are more likely to see higher levels of executive support, sustained investment, and demonstrable performance gains across the workforce.

So, why do many L&D teams struggle to move beyond activity-based metrics? And more important, what would it take to start measuring what actually matters?

Proving ROI and Business Impact

L&D's role as a strategic partner depends on demonstrating how learning initiatives support business outcomes. Measurement provides the proof by connecting L&D directly to priorities like revenue growth, customer retention, and operational efficiency. Without accurate measurement, L&D may be seen as expendable. With solid data, however, it becomes a driver of business value.

Proving L&D's influence on business outcomes elevates it from an internal service provider to an integral part of the business. As we move into measuring L&D's effectiveness, remember that measurement is the proof of alignment in action.

A Data-Informed Approach to Track a Learning Initiative's Success

For decades, L&D has struggled to consistently answer one question: Does learning drive business results? Many teams rely on traditional metrics, such as course completions, employee satisfaction scores, or hours spent in training courses. While these numbers provide operational insights, they do little to demonstrate how learning supports the business. A data-informed approach to measuring L&D success starts with shifting from activity-based metrics to business-aligned metrics. Instead of measuring what L&D produces, you should focus on what the business achieves as a result.

A robust, data-informed framework for evaluating a learning initiative's success begins by connecting learning outcomes with business goals. As an L&D leader, you'll need to partner with business executives to define success, ensuring that training initiatives directly contribute to critical objectives, such as sales productivity, customer retention, or efficiency improvements. Defining both leading and lagging indicators is also crucial. *Leading indicators* track immediate effects (such as skill acquisition and behavioral changes), while *lagging indicators* measure long-term business results (including revenue growth and employee retention). Integrating learning data with business performance data (by linking LMS analytics with your CRM, HRIS, or customer satisfaction scores, for example) provides a more comprehensive understanding of your L&D team's effectiveness.

Beyond Traditional Learning Evaluation Models

Traditional learning evaluation models (such as the Kirkpatrick Model) have long been used to assess a training program's effectiveness, but they often fail to connect learning to broader business metrics. The Phillips ROI Methodology, quantifies financial return by converting learning benefits into monetary values. This model, which was developed by Jack Phillips, offers a structured approach to proving L&D's financial effect on the business. In addition to these traditional models, we can now leverage advanced learning analytics and AI to help identify correlations between training and performance, enabling predictive insights that drive business decisions.

While the Kirkpatrick Model is used in many organizations, it's often applied in a limited way, focusing primarily on Level 1 (Reaction) and Level

2 (Learning). These levels provide insight into employee satisfaction and knowledge acquisition, but they do not measure how learning translates into workplace performance and business success. Level 3 (Behavior) and Level 4 (Results) are more challenging to assess; however, they are the keys to demonstrating a learning initiative's effectiveness. Organizations that focus only on completion rates and participant feedback risk missing the bigger picture: whether employees are actually applying new skills (Level 3) and whether those skills are improving key business outcomes (Level 4).

The Phillips ROI Methodology expands on the Kirkpatrick Model by adding a fifth level, ROI, which explicitly ties learning initiatives to financial performance. This model considers the tangible and intangible benefits of training, allowing organizations to make informed decisions about future L&D investments. A crucial aspect of this methodology is isolating the impact of a training program from other factors (such as market trends or operational changes) to ensure that improvements in performance can be attributed to learning initiatives.

Incorporating learning analytics into evaluation strategies further enhances measurement accuracy. With xAPI, organizations can capture learning data wherever it happens (rather than being limited to the LMS), connecting formal training to real work experiences for a more complete view of performance. Together, AI tools and xAPI technology enable your L&D team to track learning interactions beyond the LMS by capturing data from various sources, including job performance systems, collaboration tools, and real-time workflow applications. By integrating learning data with operational metrics, your organization can move beyond theoretical models and establish clear cause-and-effect relationships between training programs and business results.

Evaluating L&D's Contribution to Business Success

To truly evolve beyond traditional evaluation models, as an L&D leader, you must collaborate with business stakeholders to define meaningful success metrics. This requires focusing on performance-based KPIs that align with organizational priorities. By adopting a comprehensive approach that includes financial analysis, predictive modeling, and real-world application tracking, your team can be perceived as a critical driver of business success.

To effectively evaluate L&D's contribution to business success, you must track three key types of metrics:

- **Business impact metrics measure how L&D contributes to overall business success.** These metrics include revenue growth, customer satisfaction, cost reduction, and improvements in employee retention. For example, tracking how a leadership development program affects internal promotion rates or how a sales training initiative leads to increased deal closure rates provides tangible proof of L&D's effectiveness.
- **Behavioral and performance metrics assess whether employees are applying the skills learned in training to their roles.** Measuring improvements in productivity, gathering peer and manager feedback, and reviewing performance assessments can help link L&D's efforts to measurable improvements in workplace behaviors. Try leveraging competency frameworks to track employees' skill progression over time.
- **Efficiency and effectiveness metrics focus on optimizing L&D's operations.** These metrics include cost per employee, time to proficiency, engagement with learning programs, and content use rates. Organizations should evaluate how efficiently learning programs are delivered and whether they are scalable and cost-effective while maintaining high-quality outcomes.

L&D Metrics and Business Intelligence Systems

A modern approach to KPI tracking involves integrating L&D metrics with business intelligence systems, which allows organizations to continuously monitor the relationship between training investments and business outcomes. AI-enabled learning analytics can further refine KPI tracking by identifying patterns in employee engagement and correlating them with key business results.

Measuring L&D's influence on business outcomes is a journey, not a one-off task. As your organization matures, your expectations and capabilities for measurement will evolve as well. Some L&D teams are just beginning to track basic employee engagement, while others are using predictive analytics to forecast business performance improvements tied directly to learning initiatives.

Demonstrating ROI and business results is fundamental to building trust and influence with business leaders. Without clear evidence that learning initiatives drive measurable outcomes, your L&D team risks being sidelined as a support function rather than recognized as a strategic partner.

By adopting a business-first measurement approach, you can focus on what matters most to stakeholders. Advanced analytics, integrated KPIs, and frameworks like the Phillips ROI Methodology provide ways to connect learning directly to business performance.

Credibility in L&D comes from showing the connection between learning investments and business results. Measurement is no longer just about reporting; it's about guiding decisions, securing future investment, and shaping strategy. In the next section, we'll explore how to build a maturity model that moves your measurement strategy from basic tracking to predictive insights and proactive decision making.

 Pause to Reflect
How confident are you that your current measurement approach demonstrates clear, measurable value to the business?

The Learning Impact Maturity Model

The Learning Impact Maturity Model™ provides a structured framework to help you assess where your team currently stands and plot your path forward. The model draws on widely used evaluation concepts across both performance and learning disciplines, including foundational practices like measuring behavior change and business results. However, it goes a step further by positioning measurement as a tool for strategic decision making and continuous improvement, ultimately enabling L&D functions to operate as a value-driving business partner.

Five Levels of Measurement Maturity

The Learning Impact Maturity Model defines five progressive levels of measurement maturity:

- **Level 1, activity and efficiency tracking,** focuses on basic learning activity data, typically from your LMS. Level 1 measurement is often driven by compliance requirements or simple reporting requests.
- **Level 2, employee reaction and satisfaction,** measures how employees feel about training, usually through surveys. Level 2 measurement is about engagement and experience, not outcomes.
- **Level 3, behavior change and application,** begins measuring whether employees apply what they've learned on the job. Level 3 measurement signals early alignment with performance outcomes.
- **Level 4, business outcome measurement,** ties learning outcomes to key business metrics. Co-owned success measures with stakeholders begin to emerge in Level 4.
- **Level 5, predictive and prescriptive analytics,** uses data to predict future learning impact on business outcomes. Level 5 insights drive proactive strategies and targeted initiatives.

Each stage builds on the one before it as metrics and required capabilities become more focused on enhancing value for your organization's business strategy. Table 9-1 provides more details about the primary focus, example metrics, and the capabilities required at each level.

Table 9-1. Five Levels of Learning Impact Maturity

Maturity Level	Primary Focus	Example Metrics	Capabilities Required
Level 1: Activity and efficiency tracking	Tracking and efficiency	• Number of completed courses • Employee enrollments • Hours of learning	• Basic LMS reporting • Minimal stakeholder involvement
Level 2: Employee reaction and satisfaction	Satisfaction and engagement	• NPS • Satisfaction ratings • Instructor evaluations	• Survey tools • Postsession feedback loops

Table 9-1. *(Continued)*

Maturity Level	Primary Focus	Example Metrics	Capabilities Required
Level 3: Behavior change and application	Application and adoption	• Application rate • Manager observations • 360-degree assessments	• Observation tools • Behavior tracking surveys • Manager feedback loops
Level 4: Business outcome measurement	Business results	• Increased sales • Reduced error rates • Customer satisfaction • Reduced time-to-proficiency	• Cross-functional data integration • Business partnership • KPI alignment
Level 5: Predictive and prescriptive analytics	Forecasting and optimization	• Predictive models on turnover risk • Future sales performance based on learning data	• Advanced analytics platforms • AI tools • Data science partnerships • Automated dashboards

Using the Learning Impact Maturity Model

The Learning Impact Maturity Model can help you assess where your team stands today in terms of real influence on your organization's success and where you need to go next. Maturity, for its own sake, is not the goal. You must create a measurement strategy that builds credibility with business leaders.

To use the model effectively, you'll need to ask yourself (if you are a team of one) or the L&D team leader some essential questions:

- **To assess your organization's current level of maturity,** ask, "Which level describes your L&D function's current measurement practices?"
- **To identify important gaps or your biggest challenges,** ask, "What prevents you from moving to the next level? Technology, skills, stakeholder buy-in, or something else?"

- **To develop a progression plan,** ask, "How will you establish a road map to advance your team's capabilities over the next 12 to 24 months?"

Whether your team is focused on activity metrics or is already exploring predictive analytics, your journey to reaching the next level of maturity should be guided by one question: How does this metric help you demonstrate and increase a learning initiative's tangible influence on business outcomes?

Leveling Up Your Organization's Learning Maturity Gives L&D a Seat at the Table

For several years, the L&D team at a midsize home furnishings company focused heavily on employee satisfaction surveys that didn't resonate with the executive team. When the chief learning officer (CLO) realized their organization was stuck at Level 2, they put the Learning Impact Maturity Model to work.

The L&D team systematically and efficiently worked through Level 3, focusing on employee behavior change and the application of learning on the job. The team then adopted Level 4 practices and integrated learning data into their CRM. For example, they demonstrated how sales training drove a 15 percent increase in sales conversion rates, which elevated L&D's role in strategic planning discussions.

Ultimately, tracking the right KPIs enables L&D leaders to make informed decisions, secure executive buy-in, and optimize learning programs for maximum value. Maturity alone doesn't guarantee credibility, however. To maintain business trust and secure future investment, L&D must continually demonstrate its value beyond efficiency metrics and in ways that resonate with the business.

As you progress through the model, moving from reporting data to providing insights, you'll inevitably align more closely with what the business cares about. Your team will earn trust by showing that L&D is not just tracking learning metrics but also contributing to the success of the organization.

Pause to Reflect
At what level of measurement maturity is your L&D team operating today? What would it take to move to the next level?

Proving Value to Your Customer

As we've discussed, L&D exists to serve employees and the business. When it comes to proving value, however, business leaders (your customers) need more than engagement metrics and training completion rates. They are primarily concerned with whether learning initiatives help drive business objectives, improve efficiency, and affect KPIs such as revenue, retention, and customer satisfaction.

To gain continued investment and influence, your L&D team must align metrics reporting with the expectations of your primary customer, the business. While engagement metrics may satisfy your consumers (the employees), decision makers in the organization need to see how learning initiatives accelerate business performance. Proving value to your customer means collecting data that demonstrates clear, measurable contributions to their goals.

Metrics Business Leaders Really Care About

A common pitfall in the way L&D teams measure their influence is relying too much on employee feedback. While satisfaction surveys offer insights into engagement and experience, they do not indicate whether a learning initiative has improved business performance. Executives are not interested in how much employees enjoyed your training course; they care about whether it solved a business problem.

Your L&D team must present metrics business leaders really care about, such as how training reduced time to proficiency for new hires or improved sales conversion rates. Ideally, business leaders should co-own these metrics so learning initiatives are embedded in performance reviews and operational dashboards. To achieve this integration, L&D must establish clear success metrics that align with the organization's strategic objectives. Business leaders prioritize outcomes such as increased revenue, reduced costs, improved employee retention, and enhanced customer satisfaction; therefore, L&D teams should focus on metrics that demonstrate real business results, such as improved productivity, higher sales performance, or decreased error rates.

By leveraging tools such as HR analytics platforms, CRM software, and financial performance dashboards, L&D can directly correlate training programs with business outcomes. For example, a company implementing a leadership development program should track internal promotion rates and leadership effectiveness post-training. Similarly, a customer service training initiative should be evaluated based on changes in customer satisfaction scores, resolution times, and customer retention rates.

The Power of Collaboration

Stakeholder collaboration is essential for establishing the right success measures. As an L&D leader, you must engage with executives, department heads, and frontline managers to define meaningful KPIs. For instance, if you conduct business impact assessments before and after training initiatives, you can provide tangible proof of effectiveness and demonstrate that learning solutions directly contribute to organizational goals. Structured feedback loops—such as regular meetings with business leaders to review L&D performance data—can also help refine metrics over time and ensure continued alignment with evolving business priorities.

L&D's ability to prove its value depends on its capacity to speak the language of the business and work in concert with other functions. By prioritizing metrics that business leaders care about, leveraging integrated analytics, and collaborating closely with stakeholders, L&D teams can shift the conversation from training participation to measurable business success, securing their role as strategic partners in driving organizational performance.

Proving your team's value to the business starts by understanding what your stakeholders expect from L&D. They want clear evidence that learning initiatives are helping them achieve their goals, whether that is increasing revenue, improving customer satisfaction, or reducing turnover—period. When your L&D team demonstrates its contribution to the outcomes that your customer (the business) cares about, it shifts their perception of L&D from a cost center to a strategic partner.

Proving your value is also about building trust. When business leaders see that L&D delivers measurable outcomes tied to their priorities, they are more likely to invest in learning initiatives, collaborate with L&D, and view learning as critical to the organization's success.

Pause to Reflect
If your business leaders were asked to explain the value L&D brings to their priorities, what would they say?

Speaking the Language of the Business

Measurement without insight is a missed opportunity. One of the most common frustrations I hear from L&D leaders is that despite their efforts to collect and share data, stakeholders still don't see the value of learning. More often than not, the problem isn't in the data; it's in the story the data is telling.

You can shift from being perceived as a cost center to being acknowledged as a credible business partner, but to do that, you have to speak the language of the business, not the language of learning. In this section, we'll discuss a structured process for reporting learning outcomes in new ways that resonate with business leaders, influence strategy, and ensure that every piece of information you share reinforces the value L&D brings to the business.

Why Impact Reporting Matters

Effective impact reporting answers two critical questions that are always on the minds of business leaders:
- What is the measurable business value of our investment in learning?
- What decisions should we make based on these insights?

Executives don't have time to sift through data that isn't immediately relevant to their priorities. They want to know how L&D is driving revenue, reducing risk, improving customer experience, or increasing efficiency. A well-constructed impact report does exactly that by highlighting outcomes, not activities, and making clear recommendations based on what the data shows.

Design Principles of Impact Reporting

Let's examine the design principles we should be using to present information:
- **Clarity.** Always focus on the insights and outcomes that matter. Avoid data dumps.
- **Relevance.** Align every metric to a business priority or decision point.
- **Actionability.** Your reports should prompt decisions. Include clear calls to action or recommendations.

- **Consistency.** Use consistent formats and visuals. Over time, stakeholders will become familiar with interpreting your reports.
- **Accessibility.** Prioritize readability. Executive summaries should offer the most essential, meaningful parts of the story at a glance.
- **Visual hierarchy.** Use layout and design to emphasize what matters most. Key takeaways should be impossible to miss.

These six principles apply whether you're delivering a one-page executive summary, a detailed slide deck, or an interactive dashboard.

The Learning Impact Reporting Blueprint

The Learning Impact Reporting Blueprint can help you design and deliver reports in business language. It consists of just four steps:

1. Define your audience.
2. Identify your audience's key questions.
3. Select the right KPIs.
4. Choose the right format and visual design.

Each step is designed to help you build reports that inform, engage, and drive action. Let's discuss them in more detail.

Step 1. Define Your Audience

Who is the report for? Different stakeholders care about different metrics, and they interpret value differently. Executives want a high-level overview. Managers want to know how their teams are performing. L&D teams need operational data to inform future learning designs. Tailor your report to the audience; for example:

- **For executives,** focus on business results, ROI, and alignment with strategic goals.
- **For managers,** focus on team performance, skills application, and productivity.
- **For L&D teams,** focus on engagement, employee satisfaction, and operational efficiency.

Step 2. Identify Your Audience's Key Questions

What decision is your audience trying to make? Build your reports around answering the stakeholders' most pressing questions. For example:

- Did this program reduce customer churn?

- Are new hires reaching proficiency faster after onboarding?
- What effects did leadership development have on employee retention?

Step 3. Select the Right KPIs
Choose metrics that directly address those business questions you identified in step 2. Avoid the temptation to include everything you've measured and just focus on what matters most. Examples of KPIs you might choose include:
- An increase in sales following product training
- A reduction in compliance violations after mandatory training
- Improvements in time-to-proficiency for new hires
- Rising employee retention rates linked to leadership programs

Step 4. Choose the Right Format and Visual Design
Reports should be formatted based on your audience's preferences and the decisions they need to make. Executives often prefer concise dashboards or one-page summaries; managers may prefer detailed reports with more statistics and action plans. Here are three formats you can adapt to your customers' needs:
- **Executive dashboards** include summarized KPIs, high-level trends, and clear calls to action.
- **Program reviews** present detailed data on participant engagement, learning effectiveness, and recommendations.
- **Success stories or case studies** show a learning initiative's direct influence on an employee, a team, or a customer outcome in narrative form.

Talk the Business Talk
The Learning Impact Reporting Blueprint is a clear, practical approach to demonstrating L&D's contribution to business outcomes. By focusing on what matters most to stakeholders—such as aligned metrics, relevant insights, and decision-ready data—you will position the L&D function as a credible partner in producing business results.

However, showing alignment and contributions is only part of the job. To influence how your organization invests in learning, you also need to talk about financial outcomes.

When executives review budgets and allocate resources, they want to know whether their investment in learning programs increased revenue, improved productivity, reduced turnover, or mitigated risk—and by how much. In other words, they want proof that L&D delivers measurable value to the business.

That's why your learning impact reporting needs to go further than just proving business outcomes. By translating outcomes into financial terms, your L&D team can make the case for learning as a strategic investment. Whether through increased sales, operational efficiencies, or reduced risk, your L&D team's contribution should be positioned in the same way as any other business investment—in the language of clear, quantifiable returns.

I hope you'll agree that the Learning Impact Reporting Blueprint isn't just a communication exercise. It can help your L&D function earn trust, secure investment, and prove its role in business performance. When used properly, the blueprint shifts the conversation from what we deliver to why it matters and what's next.

Learning Impact Reporting in Action

A global retail organization transitioned from reporting learning completions to demonstrating the direct business outcomes of its leadership development program. Its quarterly executive dashboard highlighted a 12 percent increase in store manager retention and a 7 percent increase in same-store sales within six months of program completion.

The result? The company increased the L&D budget by 25 percent for the following year. The learning team was also invited to partner on workforce planning initiatives at the executive level.

A Few Common Pitfalls to Avoid

Even well-intentioned learning impact reports can fall flat if you fail to focus on what matters. Here are a few common mistakes to avoid as you write your report:

- **Data dumping.** Don't present too much data without prioritization or context.

- **Prioritizing activity over results.** Don't spend time reporting on completions and satisfaction scores instead of behavior change and business results.
- **Using overcomplicated visuals.** Don't include complex charts or dashboards that require explanation to understand.
- **Lacking stakeholder input.** Don't build reports without talking to stakeholders about what they actually care about.
- **Offering no actionable insight.** Don't just report data without also providing clear recommendations.

Speaking the language of business is not about simplifying what L&D does. You need to clearly demonstrate how learning affects outcomes that matter. Business leaders want to understand how learning improves productivity, increases customer retention, or enables growth. They make decisions based on measurable results, not activities.

This shift requires more than new metrics or reports. It calls for L&D to adopt a mindset focused on creating value the business can see and measure. When learning initiatives are positioned as drivers of business priorities, L&D earns its place as a trusted partner in the success of the organization.

 Pause to Reflect
How well does your L&D team demonstrate its influence in terms that business leaders value and understand?

The Bottom Line

The future of L&D depends on our ability to demonstrate measurable, meaningful results for the business customers we serve. Traditional metrics (such as completion rates and employee satisfaction) no longer justify investment or secure L&D's place at the strategy table. Business leaders expect clear evidence that learning is driving valuable outcomes like revenue growth, operational efficiency, and workforce capability.

To meet this expectation, your L&D team must adopt a data-informed approach that connects learning initiatives directly to organizational performance. This requires integrating learning data with enterprise analytics, linking training outcomes to business KPIs, and delivering insights that guide decision making. When learning measurement is embedded in the broader data landscape of sales, operations, and customer insights, your L&D function can shift from defending its relevance to influencing strategy.

Measurement, however, is not an end in itself, but a feedback loop that enables continuous improvement. Your L&D team must adopt an ongoing evaluation mindset that allows for real-time iteration and refinement. As business priorities evolve, so must your measurement strategy, ensuring that learning remains a lever for growth and competitive advantage.

Organizations that embrace this shift will position L&D as a driver of performance rather than a support function. The question is no longer whether L&D should prove its value but how effectively it can do so by building a measurement approach that tracks and drives outcomes.

How to Take Action to Measure the Impact of L&D

If you're not ready for advanced analytics or dashboards, there are still some practical ways to begin demonstrating value right now. You start to shift how the business perceives L&D by taking these actions:

- **Pick a program already in motion, like onboarding or sales enablement, and connect it to a metric the business cares about.** For onboarding, that might be time-to-productivity; for sales, it could be deal-closing rates. You don't need a complex dashboard to start, just a clear line of sight between learning and a real business outcome. Even a directional link is more powerful than activity metrics alone.
- **Shift postprogram evaluations beyond satisfaction by adding a single question: How will this training initiative improve your work or business results?** This question invites employees to reflect on real-world applications and gives you qualitative data that reflects results. Over time, patterns in responses will uncover themes worth exploring further. This small change

will help move your conversations from the learning experience to business outcomes.
- **After your next key initiative, skip the lengthy reports.** Instead, write a one-page summary that highlights the business problem, what was delivered, and what's changing as a result. Include participation data, early indicators of behavior change, and next steps. Share the one-page report with stakeholders to show how L&D connects to their priorities. Simple, clear communication builds trust and reinforces L&D's value.

In the next chapter, we will move beyond measurement as proof of value and explore how to create a culture of continuous improvement. We'll discuss how your L&D function will need to shift from tracking outcomes to actively driving value through informed iteration and innovation.

Tool 9-1.
Learning Impact Reporting at a Glance

Not all reports serve the same purpose, so you should deliver reports that meet your audience's needs and decision-making timelines. Use this table as a guide.

Report Type	Audience	Purpose	Frequency
Executive impact report	CEO, CFO, CHRO	Demonstrate a learning initiative's ROI and business contribution.	Quarterly
Operational dashboards	Managers	Show program progress, team performance, and actions.	Monthly
Program review reports	L&D teams	Evaluate learning effectiveness and areas for improvement.	Ongoing

Tool 9-2.
A Learning Impact Reporting Blueprint Outline

To make the Learning Impact Reporting Blueprint more actionable, try this simple process to plan your next impact report:

1. **Audience.** To whom are you reporting?
2. **Key business questions.** What problem are they trying to solve or what question are they trying to answer?
3. **Relevant KPIs.** What metrics demonstrate results?
4. **Data sources.** Where is the data coming from?
5. **Report format.** Should you use a dashboard, one-page summary, or narrative?
6. **Recommended actions.** What decisions or next steps should they take?

Here's a sample structure you can use or adapt:

- **Executive summary:**
    - Key outcomes
    - Business impact highlights
    - ROI (if applicable)
- **Learning objectives and alignment:**
    - Program goals
    - Links to business priorities
- **KPIs:**
    - Metrics that demonstrate a learning initiative's effectiveness (e.g., time-to-proficiency or cost savings)
- **Insights and analysis:**
    - What does the data show?
    - Why does it matter to the business?
- **Recommendations or next steps:**
    - Proposed actions based on findings
    - Opportunities for scaling, improving, or pivoting programs
- **Supporting data (optional appendix):**
    - Detailed charts and data points for validation
    - Methodology and data sources

Chapter 10
A Culture of Continuous Improvement

A national retail chain was piloting a new learning initiative designed to improve frontline customer interactions. The program launched with high hopes and included engaging microlearning modules, upbeat facilitation, and a clever mnemonic that employees could use to remember how to greet and serve customers. Corporate leaders celebrated the rollout, citing strong early completion rates.

But then, a curious executive did two unannounced site visits. The first store greeted them with energy, eye contact, and personalized service. Employees were clearly applying what they'd learned. At the second store, however, the contrast was stark. No greeting. No product guidance. The training program had been completed on paper but hadn't been translated to the floor.

The question wasn't whether the training program had been delivered, but whether the information stuck. More important, the company needed to determine if the learning content was being reinforced, adapted, and improved as business needs evolved.

Many companies fall short at this stage of learning. A successful program should create the kind of learning culture that sustains and improves employees' behavior over time. In this chapter, we'll look at what it takes to build a culture of continuous improvement inside your L&D function and across the organization.

Building a Learning Culture

A strong learning culture is a strategic lever that drives business performance. As we outlined in chapter 1, running L&D like a business begins with aligning learning initiatives to business objectives. Continuous improvement is a business imperative. A learning culture should ensure that development efforts produce measurable outcomes for your customer (the business) and your consumers (the learners).

In chapter 2, I emphasized the importance of developing a Learning Operations Business Model. Without a commitment to ongoing learning and iteration, however, even the best-aligned learning strategies can become stagnant and lose relevance. We'll now discuss how to keep that model dynamic and responsive in a culture of continuous improvement.

What a Learning Culture Is and What It Isn't

When people talk about fostering a learning culture, they often focus on surface-level actions like launching new training programs, rolling out an LMS, or increasing the number of courses available to employees. But a real learning culture embeds learning into how your organization operates.

A *learning culture* is a set of values, behaviors, and practices that encourage individuals and teams to continuously acquire, apply, and share knowledge in ways that advance their development and the organization's goals. An effective learning culture enables learning to happen everywhere, not just in formal programs. In organizations with a strong learning culture:

- Employees are curious and take ownership of their development.
- Leaders champion learning as a business priority.
- Psychological safety allows people to experiment, fail, and learn from their mistakes.
- Knowledge sharing is a norm, not an exception.
- Learning becomes a habit woven into everyday decisions, workflows, and conversations, not a one-off event.

A learning culture is also:

- Not accomplished with a large library of courses or the latest learning technology
- Not compliance-driven training that employees complete because they have to
- Not a quarterly leadership off-site meeting labeled "development"

These activities may be components of a learning strategy, but they don't constitute a learning culture unless they are integrated into how people work and how decisions are made.

Learning Culture vs. Learning Organization vs. Continuous Improvement

The terms *learning culture*, *learning organization*, and *continuous improvement* are often used interchangeably, but they represent different concepts. Understanding the distinctions will help you design your L&D strategy more intentionally.

- **The focus of a learning culture is organizational values and behaviors that promote continuous learning.** Some of its key characteristics are curiosity, knowledge sharing, psychological safety, and leadership modeling.
- **The focus of a learning organization is using systems thinking to adapt and transform as an organization (Senge 2006).** Some key characteristics of this kind of organization are shared vision, team learning, personal mastery, and mental models.
- **The focus of continuous improvement in an organization is incremental improvement of processes and performance based on customer feedback and data (Imai 2012).** Some key characteristics associated with continuous improvement are iterative cycles, data-driven decision making, process optimization, and a customer-centric approach.

Many organizations say they want a learning culture but end up focusing exclusively on improving processes or deploying learning technologies. Without leadership commitment, embedded practices, and psychological safety, these efforts rarely result in a sustainable learning culture.

In this chapter, we're focusing on creating a learning culture because it serves as the foundation for agility and continuous improvement of a learning organization. Without it, your L&D team's efforts could be perceived as transactional rather than transformational.

Fostering a culture of continuous learning is one of the most effective ways to future-proof your organization. A strong learning culture promotes curiosity, encourages employees to develop new skills, and ensures adaptability in a rapidly evolving business landscape. Organizations that prioritize learning create environments in which employees are engaged, motivated, and empowered to contribute innovative ideas. Cultivating this culture requires deliberate strategies, leadership commitment, and an infrastructure that supports seamless, ongoing development.

Pause to Reflect
Which elements of your current learning strategy reflect a learning culture? Which are more about delivering content?

Fostering Curiosity, Growth, and Development

We've established that building a learning culture requires embedding learning into the daily rhythm of work. When learning is part of how work gets done, employees are more likely to engage, adapt, and grow. Here are some suggestions for fostering curiosity, growth, and development at your organization:

- **Make learning accessible and integrated.** Just-in-time learning solutions, microlearning modules, and AI-driven personalization can support development without pulling people out of their workflow. Embedding knowledge resources directly into tools employees already use (such as CRM systems, scheduling platforms, or messaging tools) ensures learning happens in the moment of need.
- **Create space for peer learning.** Leverage lunch & learns, discussion forums, SME-led sessions, and internal showcases to normalize knowledge sharing. Don't think of these as add-ons. They are cultural cues that reinforce curiosity and collective growth.
- **Encourage leaders to set the tone.** When executives model learning behaviors, ask better questions, and engage in development themselves, it signals that learning is expected, not remedial. Managers should be equipped to coach, explore lessons in team discussions, and reinforce the link between development and business outcomes.
- **Link learning to what matters.** Employees need to see how learning connects to career mobility, project opportunities, and measurable business results. When L&D systems are structured for

agility, governed by clear processes, resourced effectively, and built for scale, teams can pivot quickly without sacrificing quality.

Creating this kind of environment doesn't happen by chance. It requires a clear operational model that defines what to build, how to build it, and how to sustain it. The next section introduces a framework designed to help your L&D team make learning an essential part of how your organization runs.

The Learning Culture Operational Model

Creating a learning culture is about operations, not enthusiasm. L&D leaders often talk about building a culture of continuous learning, but they rarely define it in operational terms. Without clear structure and accountability, *culture* is a vague aspiration (something you hope happens if people like the content enough). A strong learning culture is always the result of deliberate design that shows up in daily behaviors, decisions, systems, and workflows. It's observable, and most important, it's manageable.

The Learning Culture Operational Model™ provides a structured way to design and scale a learning culture that delivers real business value. It consists of four interconnected domains—infrastructure, behavioral norms, systems of enablement, and cultural analytics—that together form an operational foundation to make learning a visible, repeatable part of how the organization runs. Let's discuss each domain in detail.

Infrastructure: Make Learning Inescapable

A learning culture starts with infrastructure. If development isn't embedded in how work gets done, it becomes an additional thing to do, or something employees may want but can't realistically prioritize. In organizations that embed learning into the flow of work, it shows up in the systems and tools people already use. Just-in-time guidance can be baked into CRM systems, EHR tools, scheduling software, and messaging platforms. Microlearning modules, checklists, and AI-enabled nudges are available in an e-learning module at the moment decisions are made (not weeks later).

Embedding learning also requires standardizing core L&D processes, including how you scope your programs, engage SMEs, and move projects from intake to execution. These same operational principles (which we covered in chapters 3 and 4) promote scalability, speed, and consistency.

When learning is part of your organization's infrastructure, it's not a separate initiative—it supports how work gets done.

Behavioral Norms: Reinforce Learning Through Leadership and Safety

While infrastructure makes learning accessible, behavior change makes it acceptable. A culture of learning requires leadership to model curiosity, vulnerability, and continuous improvement.

Everything starts at the top. When executives ask better questions, discuss what they're learning, or attend development programs, they signal that learning isn't remedial; it's expected. People managers must reinforce learning through daily interactions, including coaching during one-on-ones, discussing lessons in team huddles, and recognizing growth, not just output.

Psychological safety is also critical, but you must go beyond the buzzword. Teams need structured rituals, such as retrospectives, premortems, or innovation sprints (which create space for experimentation and reflection). These aren't HR initiatives. They're operational tools that reinforce the message: In this organization, it's safe to try, fail, and learn.

Behavioral norms never emerge by accident. They're shaped by what leaders do, how teams are managed, and how failure and growth are treated inside the business.

Systems of Enablement: Scale Learning Through Peer Sharing and Growth Pathways

You can't scale a learning culture through content alone. You must let people share what they know, learn from one another, and see how growth connects to opportunity.

Peer learning mechanisms are essential and could include brown bag lunch & learns, SME-created videos, internal knowledge hubs, or cross-functional showcases. In high-performing cultures, sharing knowledge is a habit built into how teams operate.

Equally important are visible growth pathways. Employees are more likely to engage in development when they understand how it connects to advancement, mobility, and project opportunities. Your L&D team will need to collaborate with HR and other business functions to ensure skills frameworks, internal job postings, and talent reviews are aligned with development priorities.

Finally, enablement also includes feedback systems. Structured input before, during, and after delivery helps your L&D team and business partners change course in real time, not just during postmortems. When feedback loops are operationalized, they serve both business alignment and learner relevance. Enablement doesn't require more content; instead, you must offer better access, better pathways, and better support for learning to happen naturally at scale.

Cultural Analytics: Measure What Matters, Not What's Easy

A culture is real when it's visible, and what's visible can be measured. A learning culture is no exception.

The first level of measurement is usage. You are not just counting who completed a course but also those who engaged with learning content embedded into the tools they already use. For example, are people opening guidance in the CRM system? Are team leaders actually using coaching prompts? These signals tell you whether learning is showing up in the workflow.

What about outcomes? Strong learning cultures often appear in lagging metrics like faster onboarding, higher internal mobility, and reduced turnover in growth roles. If development is working, those signals will become measurable over time.

Finally, look for business-level results. In a service organization, this could be improved customer satisfaction or NPS numbers tied to customer training. In sales, you might see faster ramp up times or improved close rates after targeted enablement. These aren't always easy to isolate, but they're critical for securing investment and sustaining learning as a strategic capability.

If you want a business to value a learning culture, treat it like a business capability. Track the leading and lagging indicators that show it's working.

Apply the Model

The Learning Culture Operational Model can help you assess, design, and scale your efforts. Use it as:

- **A diagnostic.** Which domains are well-established in your organization? Which are missing or underinvested?

- **A design guide.** What initiatives do you need to strengthen weak areas? Are you focusing heavily on infrastructure but ignoring behavior or analytics?
- **A communication tool.** Use the framework to define *learning culture* in terms your business partners will understand (such as operational components, not aspirational language).

By now, I hope it's clear that building a learning culture isn't about increasing content or adding new platforms, but about embedding curiosity, growth, and development into the actual systems, behaviors, and decisions that move the business forward. Done well, this approach should allow your L&D team to help your organization learn faster, adapt quicker, and execute better. That's the real opportunity and the real measure of learning culture.

A strong learning culture creates the conditions for growth, but conditions alone are not enough. Culture must be reinforced through structure, specifically through the decisions leaders make, the behaviors they model, and the systems they oversee. Without clear accountability and governance, even well-intentioned learning efforts can drift, lose relevance, or fail to scale. The next section explores how leadership and governance anchor a learning culture and ensure it produces measurable business value.

 Pause to Reflect
What if someone observed how work gets done in your organization today? What visible evidence would they see of a learning culture in action?

Maintaining Leadership Accountability and Governance

Establishing a learning culture is one thing. Sustaining it over time and ensuring it continues to drive measurable business outcomes requires more than enthusiasm or leadership modeling. It demands governance, co-ownership, and clear accountability. We introduced these concepts in chapter 4 when we explored the learning governance framework as a foundational element for running L&D like a business. You may recall that:

- **Executive sponsors** set the tone for learning as a strategic business priority.
- **Steering committees** create governance structures that align learning investments with enterprise objectives and provide decision-making discipline.
- **Business unit co-ownership** ensures that learning priorities and accountability for outcomes are shared between L&D and operational leaders.

These structures are the foundation that makes sure the L&D function supports the business strategy. Without them, L&D risks becoming fragmented, reactive, or disconnected from enterprise goals.

An Engine for Continuous Improvement

Governance involves creating clarity, discipline, and accountability, and it's the mechanism that drives continuous improvement at scale. Through governance:

- Learning priorities stay connected to shifting business needs.
- Leaders are accountable for participation and performance outcomes, not just course completions.
- Data-informed feedback loops inform decisions about when to iterate and when to scale.

Some practical steps for implementing governance include:

- Engaging executive sponsors to champion and allocate resources for learning initiatives
- Establishing steering committees that provide ongoing governance and portfolio oversight
- Structuring co-ownership models that make business leaders directly accountable for capability-building outcomes

If your team hasn't formalized these governance roles or decision-making processes, it's a good idea to revisit chapter 4. There, you'll find actionable frameworks including decision rights, investment criteria, and review cadences.

Listen to the Business (Operationalize!)

Listening to the business doesn't mean engaging in a one-time intake conversation. Listening is a discipline. In high-performing L&D teams, leaders build this discipline into their operating models through regular check-ins, decision-making routines, and feedback channels that keep learning priorities aligned with business needs as they evolve.

Too often, L&D functions rely on sporadic leader input or passive intake forms that result in a backlog of disconnected requests, reactive programming, and missed opportunities to influence strategy. To stay relevant, adopt a structured approach to listening, one that keeps your team close to the work and responsive to change. Start by taking these steps:

- **Match the existing business cadence.** Start with the rhythms that already drive the business. Quarterly business reviews, monthly operational checkpoints, and annual planning sessions are moments when priorities are clarified and trade-offs are made. Your L&D team should be part of those discussions as a strategic partner that observes, asks smart questions, and identifies where capability building supports execution.
- **Build stakeholder checkpoints into the workflow.** Establish recurring conversations with business leaders—not to ask for project requests, but to understand their goals, pressures, and plans. These checkpoints allow you to get clarity on what success looks like for them and where your team can have the most influence. Think of them as customer interviews, not internal meetings.
- **Create feedback loops before, during, and after delivery.** Business conditions change quickly. What was relevant in January may be outdated by March. Build in mechanisms to revisit assumptions midproject, and use short feedback cycles, not just retrospectives. Ask yourself, "Is learning still aligned with what the business needs right now? If not, what needs to shift?"
- **Use governance to recalibrate, not just report.** As I described in chapter 4, governance should be designed to uncover trade-offs, not just track status. Use steering committees, portfolio reviews, and investment reviews to validate priorities and adjust course

when needed. When you use governance to guide decisions, not just justify them, you stay connected to the work that matters most.
- **Let data drive the conversation, not just the retrospective.** Listening isn't limited to conversations. Business performance data, workforce trends, skills gaps, and learner behavior can speak louder than words by revealing unmet needs and capability risks. Use data to open conversations with leaders, validate assumptions, and shape what gets built next. This is especially useful when the business isn't always sure what to ask for.

From Governance to Culture

Governance is the infrastructure that sustains your learning culture. Without it, your organization will struggle to maintain focus, measure results, and continuously improve its learning programs. Building a culture of continuous learning requires leadership alignment, operational rigor, and shared accountability, which is exactly the infrastructure your governance framework delivers.

Let's now focus on how to foster curiosity, growth, and continuous learning within that framework to ensure learning becomes an everyday behavior and not just another initiative.

Build Capabilities Inside Your Team

Continuous improvement begins at home. If you expect the broader organization to develop, adapt, and reskill, your L&D function must first model that behavior internally. Too often, L&D teams focus entirely on delivering learning content to others while neglecting their own capability development. The result is a function that struggles to keep up with the changing needs of the business—not because of a lack of effort, but because of outdated skills, limited exposure to new methods, or a narrow view of what capabilities the team actually needs to succeed.

Running L&D like a business requires new capabilities that go beyond instructional design or facilitation. Your L&D team should become agile, credible, and future-ready in four areas:

- **Data fluency and analytical thinking.** Teams must be able to interpret business data, identify trends, and use learning analytics to make informed decisions. This includes understanding performance metrics, drawing connections between learning and

business outcomes, and making the case for investment with data that speaks the language of the business.
- **Internal consulting and stakeholder management.** Your L&D team must operate like a business partner, not an order taker, which means developing the ability to ask the right questions, uncover root causes, and define success in terms that matter to the business. Skills in influence, negotiation, and problem solving are critical for this shift.
- **Agile design and iterative delivery.** Traditional waterfall learning development cycles often can't keep up with changing business priorities. Your L&D team must become comfortable with iterative approaches, rapid prototyping, testing, and refining based on feedback. This requires capabilities in Agile project management, minimal viable product (MVP) thinking, and flexibility in content creation.
- **Systems thinking and operational awareness.** High-performing L&D teams understand how their work connects to the broader system, customer experience, compliance, talent strategy, and operational KPIs. Developing systems thinking will help you and your team see the upstream and downstream effects of programs and design solutions that complement how work actually gets done.

Make It Practical

Upskilling doesn't require a formal program or a large budget. It starts with intention and a clear view of what capabilities your team needs to deliver to support your operating model. A simple team capability map can help identify the roles on your team, assess your current strengths, and highlight which priority gaps to close over the next six to 12 months.

A great starting point is ATD's Talent Development Capability Model, which outlines the knowledge and skills required across three broad areas: personal, professional, and organizational. I recommend using it as a reference to benchmark your team's strengths, inform development plans, and prioritize learning investments. This model is particularly useful if you lead a team with varied roles or levels of experience, or if you're trying to connect individual development goals to the function's broader strategic goals.

Focus first on the capabilities that directly support your organization's current business priorities, whether that's consulting with stakeholders, improving agility in delivery, or building data fluency. You can't scale results if your team is running on legacy skill sets.

Agility and Foresight in a Competitive Market

Agility doesn't just mean reacting quickly. It's about structuring your L&D team to adapt confidently to shifting priorities, emerging skills needs, and evolving business strategies. In a competitive market, adaptability helps L&D deliver value at the pace the business demands.

Building agility starts with assessing how your team plans and prioritizes work. Flexible planning cycles (such as rolling quarterly road maps or dynamic backlogs) allow you to adjust without derailing core priorities. Business needs rarely align perfectly with annual learning calendars, so having the ability to shift focus based on current goals is important.

Team structure also plays a role. Cross-functional teams, embedded learning partners, and shared services models let your L&D team stay close to the business and respond to changes quickly. Agile L&D teams often invest in internal upskilling cross-functionally so learning designers can work with data, facilitators can coach, and program leads can shift between initiatives as priorities evolve.

Forward-thinking teams also build in time for scanning the horizon. This includes trend analysis, skills forecasting, and technology evaluations that inform long-term planning. In other words, don't wait to be told what the business needs. Bring insights to the table and help shape the conversation early. Agility and foresight are not optional. For L&D to remain relevant and valuable in a market defined by change, teams must be designed to flex, evolve, and lead with confidence.

Remember: You'll sustain a strong learning culture with strong infrastructure, so prioritize governance systems, leadership alignment, and shared accountability to keep learning initiatives tied to business priorities and performance outcomes. When you operationalize listening, embed regular stakeholder checkpoints, and use governance to drive decisions, you'll move from a reactive function to a strategic partner.

Culture also depends on the capabilities of the people on your L&D team to execute, adapt, and lead. In the next section, we'll look at how to build those capabilities to support transformation.

Pause to Reflect

How well does your current governance structure support a culture of continuous improvement? Where might it be reinforcing the status quo instead of enabling change?

Driving Continuous Innovation Based on Customer Needs

Continuous innovation helps you solve real business problems in new ways. It requires your L&D team to stay tightly connected to the evolving priorities of internal customers. Innovation becomes possible through structured listening, rapid iteration, and operational discipline.

The details about what your customer needs won't always arrive as a formal request. Often, needs appear through shifts in strategic direction, changes in workforce performance data, or feedback gathered during program delivery. High-performing L&D teams build routines to listen for these points. They participate in quarterly business reviews, look at customer satisfaction and sales performance metrics, and hold project debriefs with business stakeholders after key initiatives. These moments allow for insight into what's working, what's shifting, and where learning solutions can accelerate outcomes.

This kind of responsiveness can't happen without structure. Your governance processes need to allow for thoughtful pivots, and your intake systems should be flexible enough to accommodate emerging needs without derailing all your planned work. Most important, portfolio reviews should include space to retire outdated programs and reinvest in experiments that address high-priority gaps.

To sustain innovation over time, L&D teams need a way to evaluate whether a new idea, process, or technology meets a true business need. A simple set of questions like these can help:

- What business problem does this solve?

- How do you know whether this problem matters to your customer?
- What outcome will you measure?
- What are you replacing or improving?

When innovation is grounded in business priorities, it stops being a side project and becomes part of how your L&D team delivers value. You aren't necessarily doing more; you're working smarter. And that starts with treating business needs as the engine, not the afterthought.

Iteration Based on Business Requirements, Not New Trends

The best L&D teams treat iteration as a business practice, not a creative refresh. They adjust learning solutions based on evolving performance goals, organizational shifts, or changes in customer expectations—not because of a new trend in the L&D industry.

Effective iteration starts with listening and staying plugged into the rhythms of the business through quarterly planning, off-site team activities, talent reviews, and performance reporting. Capture what sales leaders, operations managers, and HR business partners are saying about what's not working and what's next. With that information in hand, iteration can become a tool to make L&D more relevant and efficient.

You may need to sunset a program that no longer maps to a business priority or revise a leadership course based on gaps that were uncovered during promotion cycles. You might have to shift delivery methods from full-day workshops to workflow-embedded nudges, based on feedback from time-strapped teams. Whatever form iteration takes, the goal is the same: Learning solutions should evolve in step with business needs.

Iterating in this way also builds trust. When business leaders see that L&D is willing to update, adapt, and occasionally let go of outdated work, they're more likely to bring you into the next round of planning. This partnership separates an L&D team that delivers content from one that drives value.

Remember that you don't need to chase every trend. You need to run an iterative process that keeps your learning portfolio responsive and high performing. That starts with relevance, not novelty.

Continuous improvement isn't a value statement; it's a way of operating. High-performing L&D teams build it into the way they run, applying the same standards—relevance, rigor, and repeatability—to innovation efforts as they do to core delivery.

Your team will need to stay close to the business through regular participation in the cadences that shape decisions, including attending quarterly reviews, workforce planning sessions, postmortems, and performance check-ins. These touchpoints can create a feedback loop that reveals new business needs before they become urgent. Treat innovation like the rest of your learning portfolio and as a strategic investment with clear criteria for success.

Learning only matters if it solves something that matters to the business. When L&D leaders adopt this mindset, we can stop asking what's new in the L&D industry and start asking what's needed in the business. That shift transforms L&D from a service provider into a strategic operator.

Pause to Reflect

What mechanisms does your L&D team have in place to consistently identify unmet business needs before they show up as formal requests?

The Bottom Line

Your learning culture doesn't sit on the sidelines of your L&D strategy. It is the operating environment that makes your business model work. Without it, even the most sophisticated systems (such as intake, governance, and resource management) risk becoming performative or ignored. When your learning culture is active and intentional, those systems have the conditions they need to function as designed.

Shared accountability makes governance real, and transparency ensures that your prioritization is understood, not questioned. A culture of continuous learning will turn retrospectives into improvement cycles instead of status updates. Behavioral norms—including leadership modeling, psychological safety, and peer feedback—make operational tools usable and sustainable.

Good infrastructure embeds learning within the systems, workflows, and tools employees already use, which makes it easy for people to access, share, and apply knowledge without disruption. Cultural analytics provide the visibility needed to change course and prove whether your learning investments are shifting behaviors and not just meeting deadlines. Each domain of learning culture reinforces the four pillars of your L&D business model:

- **Business alignment** is sustained when leadership values learning and teams are encouraged to ask better questions, reflect on outcomes, and improve together.
- **Operational efficiency** depends on cultural habits that support consistency, feedback, and adaptability, not just process compliance.
- **Consumer experience** is shaped by how learning content shows up as relevant, timely, and trusted in real workflows.
- **Customer value** is defined by the business and cultural outcomes that emerge, such as internal mobility, performance improvement, or speed to readiness.

Finally, when learning culture is treated as a business enabler, not a byproduct, you will find it easier to scale learning initiatives, adapt to change, and measure results. This will allow you to close the loop between intention and execution.

Culture is not what happens after you build the model. It is what ensures the model works—day after day, decision after decision.

How to Take Action to Create a Culture of Continuous Improvement

Putting continuous improvement into practice doesn't require a full transformation overnight. Start simple, stay consistent, and scale as you go. Here are three steps you can take immediately to build momentum and embed the habits outlined in this chapter:

- **Set aside one hour each month to review stakeholder feedback, intake trends, and shifting business priorities.** Even if it's informal, this creates a predictable feedback loop and reinforces that L&D decisions are grounded in current business needs.
- **Choose a single metric that reflects how efficiently your team is operating.** For example, record the average turnaround time for a learning request or the percentage of prioritized projects

delivered on time. Use that metric to spark team discussions and identify improvement opportunities.
- **Create protected time for your team to build their skills.** Whether you do so through internal knowledge sharing, peer reviews, or self-paced development, consistency matters more than format; start small but keep it regular.

Tool 10-1.
Checklist: Is Your L&D Team Listening Like a Business Partner?

Use this checklist to assess whether your team has operationalized strategic listening practices.

Aligning to the business cadence:
- ❏ We regularly attend planning or business review meetings to stay informed about shifting priorities.
- ❏ We review quarterly goals and key metrics across major business units.

Structuring stakeholder touchpoints:
- ❏ We have recurring check-ins with department leaders to understand their goals and pain points.
- ❏ We record and document business needs in a consistent format (e.g., intake forms or briefing templates).

Building feedback loops:
- ❏ We gather midinitiative feedback from sponsors and learners to adapt in real time.
- ❏ We conduct postlaunch reviews tied to business outcomes, not just learner satisfaction.

Making governance-informed adjustments:
- ❏ We use governance forums (e.g., steering committees and investment reviews) to recalibrate priorities, not just report on progress.
- ❏ We review learning programs quarterly to assess continued relevance and performance.

Engaging in data-informed listening:
- ❏ We use business performance data and workforce insights to identify skills gaps and capability risks.
- ❏ We initiate learning conversations based on trends in KPIs, turnover, or customer metrics.

How many boxes did you check? If you checked fewer than eight, consider where your listening practices may be reactive or inconsistent. A structured approach to business listening strengthens alignment, reduces waste, and keeps your team positioned to lead without chasing the wrong problems.

Conclusion
L&D at a Crossroads

In a global 2023 survey by RedThread Research, only 23 percent of business leaders viewed L&D functions as strategic partners. The rest were seen as reactive service providers or worse—disconnected from the business entirely. Meanwhile, organizations continued to invest heavily in learning platforms, content, and headcount, with no consistent method for proving whether any of it worked.

This disconnect raises an uncomfortable but important question. If learning is meant to prepare employees for the future, why are so many L&D teams still operating with outdated mindsets and structures? What's preventing us from making the shift from cost center to growth engine?

Throughout this book, we've examined what it looks like to operationalize L&D with the same discipline, strategy, and accountability found in other business functions. Now, as we close, it's worth asking a more personal question. If your current approach isn't driving the outcomes your business expects, what are you willing to do differently?

Across industries, L&D leaders are facing a defining moment. Budgets are under scrutiny, expectations from businesses are rising, and the pressure to demonstrate measurable value is intensifying. At the same time, organizations are navigating shifting workforce expectations, accelerating digital transformations, and new business model disruptions. The question is no longer whether L&D needs to change but how quickly we can adapt to remain relevant.

In this environment, L&D can no longer rely on legacy practices or position itself as a reactive support function. The path forward requires a new kind of clarity. L&D must operate with business intent, not just instructional expertise. We must make decisions that are grounded in customer needs, backed by operational rigor, and measured in terms all businesses recognize.

That is what it means to run L&D like a business.

This book has laid out frameworks, questions, and practices to help you, as an L&D leader, scale your team's influence without scaling headcount. Now, it is time for you to connect the dots.

The good news? You're not starting from scratch. The tools, frameworks, and mindset to reposition L&D already exist, and many have been outlined here. What you need now is the courage to move forward differently.

From Service Provider to Strategic Function

For too long, L&D has been viewed as the team that builds courses, delivers training, and checks boxes. That reputation didn't come out of nowhere. It reflects how L&D teams have historically positioned themselves, measuring their value by volume, responsiveness, and completion rates rather than business outcomes.

But that story can change.

L&D's real mandate isn't to produce content; it's to build the workforce capabilities that businesses need to execute their strategies. This means shifting from activity-based planning to outcome-based accountability. Our success is not defined by how much content we produce or how many employees log in, but by whether people are better at their jobs, faster to ramp up, more adaptable, and more likely to stay at their organizations.

Throughout this book, you have seen how L&D can adopt the same rigor your business brings to other strategic functions. Finance aligns spending with revenue goals. Product teams prioritize features based on customer value. L&D can and should operate in the same way by aligning learning investments to performance, productivity, and growth.

We can begin to shift the way we operate by asking better questions:
- What performance gap are we solving for?
- What does success look like in business terms?
- What happens if we do nothing?

None of these questions are abstract. Your answers will change how projects are scoped, how resources are allocated, and how L&D earns its seat at the table. With clear frameworks, stronger intake processes, and tighter business alignment, L&D teams can become effective enablers of business success.

Becoming a Strategic Partner

Once you understand that your true mandate is building capabilities to serve business strategy, the next step is showing up as a strategic partner. It is not enough to align learning initiatives with business priorities in theory. You have to operationalize your mandate every day in the ways your team engages with the business.

Strategic L&D teams do not wait for a request to land in their inbox. They show up early. They bring insights, analyze data, and identify capability gaps before they appear in performance reviews or business results. More important, they collaborate with stakeholders to address root causes rather than simply responding with training solutions.

This kind of partnership is built on proximity. It requires L&D professionals to become embedded in the business, involved in planning conversations, and trusted enough to be invited in before decisions are made. The most effective L&D teams participate in business reviews and strategic planning, not just when learning is the topic, but as part of the regular operating rhythm.

Strategic partnership also requires a tolerance for ambiguity. Business leaders don't always know what they need. Often, what sounds like a training request is actually a symptom of a broader issue related to processes, leadership, or culture. Strategic L&D teams help unpack problems by asking thoughtful questions and guiding stakeholders through discovery and design. They can clearly communicate what L&D can deliver, when, and why.

This shift in perspective is less about saying yes to everything and more about showing up differently. When your L&D team brings a point of view, works consultatively, and focuses on business outcomes, the conversation improves. Your function is no longer seen as only a responder. You become a partner in how the business executes and grows.

Managing Two Audiences

As your L&D team's work becomes more strategic, it's easy to lose sight of the people you are serving. Remember that every L&D team supports two audiences: the business (the customer) and the employees (the consumers). However, the business is what defines the mandate, funds the work, and sets the performance expectations.

Put the Business Audience First

L&D's primary responsibility is to serve the business. That means aligning learning initiatives to strategic priorities, building capabilities that drive performance, and delivering measurable value. When that clarity exists, your L&D team can operate with purpose and direction. Without it, the function risks becoming a content provider focused on engagement rather than outcomes.

Employees are our consumers—our second audience. They interact with the learning experience, and their engagement is critical to our success—but only when it serves a business goal. If a program is relevant, timely, and easy to access, it is more likely to stick. But the experience should always be grounded in the question, "What capability are we building, and why does the business need it?"

The most effective L&D teams don't try to serve both audiences equally. They design by putting the business problem first, and then translating that need into a meaningful experience for the employee. When that translation is done well, the work delivers both results and engagement, but the order of events matters. Without a clear customer-first mindset, even the most beautifully designed programs can miss the mark.

Understanding your true customer clarifies your mandate. Designing for the employees ensures the learning sticks.

However, to function as a true business partner, your L&D function must go one step further. You must make smart, disciplined choices about where to invest time and resources.

The Payoff: The Right to Prioritize

When your L&D function operates as a strategic partner, you earn something more valuable than recognition. You earn the right to prioritize. That is not a privilege reserved for large teams or mature organizations; it is a capability any L&D function can build by leading with clarity and purpose. At this point, everything you have built so far starts to pay off.

Earlier in the book, we explored how to establish an L&D business model that defines who you serve, how you deliver value, and what success looks like. You developed intake processes and governance structures to bring consistency and visibility to how work is scoped. You learned how to shift from volume-based activities to outcome-based planning. All of these actions make up the groundwork for your payoff moment. Without prioritization, even the best strategy falls apart.

When Everything Is Urgent, Nothing Is Strategic

When every request is treated equally, quality suffers and results get diluted. Teams burn out, stakeholders lose confidence, and learning starts to look like noise.

Strategic L&D teams change that pattern. They use structured decision-making criteria to evaluate requests based not just on who asked, but on what the business needs most. They ask pointed questions: Is this aligned with one of our top business priorities? Does it address a defined capability gap? Is the problem clearly scoped? Is the solution likely to deliver measurable outcomes?

This stage is not about bureaucracy. It's how L&D demonstrates accountability, resourcefulness, and leadership.

When you and your team can clearly articulate why you've prioritized one project over another, using shared business language and logic, you build trust. Stakeholders begin to see L&D as a function that operates with the same discipline they apply to product road maps, financial plans, and go-to-market strategies. You, in turn, are no longer reacting to noise. You are curating a portfolio of initiatives that advances the organization's goals.

This approach also creates space for smarter tradeoffs. Not every request deserves a fully built course. Sometimes, a curated resource, a coaching conversation, or a shift in workflow is a better solution. The power to prioritize gives you the clarity and confidence to make those calls. It also gives your team the bandwidth to execute with excellence.

Here is where L&D steps fully into its role as a strategic function. Not just through vision, but through everyday decisions about where to focus, how to deliver, and when to say no. These decisions are the difference between being busy and being effective.

Prioritization is a powerful shift, but it is only part of the equation. To deliver sustained value, L&D cannot sit on the sidelines waiting to react, even with a strong filter in place. The most effective learning teams don't just align learning initiatives with strategy. They help enable that strategy by embedding their work in the rhythm of how the business plans, measures, and evolves.

Link L&D and Business Strategy

L&D teams often talk about wanting a seat at the table, but that seat will never be granted because we build more content or respond faster to requests. We earn our seat when learning becomes a tool the business can use to solve real problems. That opportunity is now in front of us.

We have defined a strategic L&D function as one that aligns learning objectives with business priorities, operates with efficiency, and delivers measurable value. A successful L&D function is part of how the organization plans, makes decisions, and moves forward because we are embedded in the business strategy.

Connect to Real Business Problems

Strategic L&D teams connect learning investments to specific business goals. They participate in planning sessions, review operating plans, and stay close to the metrics that matter most to business leaders. When L&D understands what is driving growth, where risk is emerging, and which teams are struggling to execute, you can start prioritizing learning in a way that adds value.

To gain that understanding, you'll need to ask better questions. Instead of asking, "What course do you need?" you should ask, "What capability is missing?" Instead of "How many employees do you expect to attend?" ask, "What does success look like in business terms?" These questions anchor your team in performance, not activity. They also create space to determine whether learning is the right lever or whether a process change, leadership action, or tool redesign is a better solution.

Bringing about this kind of alignment is not a one-time exercise. It's an ongoing discipline that requires listening to the business, validating assumptions, and adjusting plans as priorities shift.

Design Your Learning Portfolio Around Strategic Goals

Once your alignment is clear, you will need to make sure it is reflected in how your L&D team allocates its time and resources. This is why managing your learning portfolio is essential.

The portfolio approach allows L&D to operate like other investment functions in the business. Finance doesn't fund every idea. The product team doesn't build every feature. L&D should not deliver on every request.

Managing L&D as a learning portfolio helps you understand what is in flight, what it supports, and what it is worth.

Without a portfolio view, your L&D team will quickly become reactive and overextended. You'll chase too many disconnected requests, quality will suffer, and your value will be unclear. With a disciplined approach, you can review your function's full body of work and ask:
- What are we doing?
- Why are we doing it?
- Does it map to the outcomes we said mattered most?

Answering these questions will bring a clarity that allows you to make better decisions. You'll meet some needs with light, quick-turnaround solutions. Others will warrant deeper investment. The choice you make should not be based on who made the request or how loud they were, but on business value and the strategic relevance of that request.

Portfolio management is about making space for you to be responsive without losing focus, not about slowing down the work with bureaucracy. It gives your team room to adjust as the business evolves while still delivering with intention.

Communicate in Business Language

Embedding L&D in business strategy also requires a shift in how we communicate. As we discussed in chapter 9, business leaders won't be persuaded by satisfaction scores or attendance numbers. They want to know if learning programs improved performance, reduced errors, accelerated readiness, and supported talent retention. They expect the same level of reporting and accountability as they get from any other function.

You do not need perfect data to start having these conversations. What you need is a consistent practice of translating learning outcomes into business terms. That often means partnering with finance, HR, and operations teams to track performance indicators and validate a learning initiative's effectiveness over time. Simply put, it means telling the story of the learning experience in the language of the business.

When you adopt the native language of the business, the perception of L&D changes. It becomes part of the strategy-execution engine—no longer just something nice to have, but a lever for performance and growth.

Make Tradeoffs Transparently

The final hallmark of being embedded in business strategy is making decisions with intention and doing so openly. Every L&D team has a finite capacity. Saying yes to every request is not a sign of partnership, but it is a fast track to diluted value and team burnout. Strategic teams make tradeoffs based on business priorities, and they communicate those tradeoffs clearly.

Clarity builds trust, showing the business that your L&D team is managing its resources with discipline. You are also setting expectations and creating an opportunity for better partnerships. When business leaders understand how L&D makes decisions, they are more likely to collaborate early and adjust expectations when priorities shift. A business-driven approach to L&D brings this reality into focus. Not everything will get done, but what does get done will matter more.

Leverage Technology With Purpose

Modern L&D teams are bombarded with tools, platforms, and promises of dramatic transformations. But technology is not a strategy—technology is a lever, and like any lever, its value depends on what you are trying to move.

We've emphasized the importance of prioritizing business alignment over trends, managing the learning portfolio with discipline, and designing solutions that serve the customer first and the consumer second. These same principles apply here. Technology can scale results, improve access, and increase speed, but only if it's selected and deployed with intention.

Use Tech as a Tool, Not a Strategy

Too often, L&D teams invest in new platforms out of excitement, internal pressure, or the fear of being left behind. The result? A cluttered ecosystem full of disconnected tools, low adoption, and minimal ROI. Activity increases, but outcomes do not improve.

Running L&D like a business means that your technology decisions start with a defined business need. Whether you are closing a capability gap, improving access to learning in the flow of work, or enabling more precise measurement, your use case needs to come first. The tool comes second. For example, a content curation platform makes sense if frontline managers are spending too much time searching for answers or if a decentralized workforce needs fast access to reliable resources. On the other hand, if those problems are not real or clearly defined, the platform won't deliver value, no matter how impressive the interface.

This mindset reframes technology adoption from chasing "what's new" to prioritizing "what works." It also shifts L&D's role from tech implementer to business enabler.

Integrate With Business Operations

Technology does not create value on its own. It must be integrated with how work gets done. Just as we explored in the chapters on operational agility and employee experience, the most effective L&D functions embed learning content into the business, not beside it. That means enabling access within existing tools like CRM systems, project management platforms, or messaging apps. It also means aligning learning content delivery with broader workflows, milestones, and moments that matter.

When technology is embedded in this way, it stops being something that employees just go to. Instead, it becomes part of how they perform, and that changes how the business perceives the function behind it.

Your strategic L&D team can make intentional decisions about how technology is configured, where it shows up, and how success is measured. You can eliminate redundancy, streamline access, and enable the business—not just your L&D team—to use the tools in meaningful ways.

Measure Impact, Not Just Usage

Technology makes data easier to collect; however, the presence of data does not mean it is being used well. A common mistake is stopping at usage metrics. Logins, clicks, and completion rates are easy to track, but they rarely tell a compelling story. The business wants to know if a platform helped reduce onboarding time, improved customer interactions, and supported talent development in measurable ways.

As we discussed in chapter 9, measurement must be tied to business goals. That principle also applies fully to your tech stack. Your team needs to collaborate with partners in operations, HR, and finance to connect platform usage to achieve outcomes the business already cares about. That might mean tracking a reduction in error rates, an increase in sales productivity, or a measurable improvement in manager effectiveness. When learning technology is evaluated based on value, not just volume, it becomes part of the performance infrastructure, not just a tool for content delivery.

Stay Grounded

Understand that the pace of innovation will not slow down. AI, adaptive platforms, and immersive learning environments offer exciting potential, but our job as L&D professionals is to build solutions that work, not chase trends.

Remain curious but grounded. Test new technologies when there is a clear problem to solve. Run pilot tests with purpose. Measure results before scaling. Use the same prioritization filters for tech that you apply to every other part of your portfolio. This is not hesitation; it is discipline. These actions signal to business leaders that you and your team are not there to accumulate tools, but to solve problems.

By putting purpose ahead of any platform, you can strengthen L&D's credibility and create space for innovation that lasts. Technology becomes an accelerator, not a distraction, and the business begins to see learning systems as an asset instead of an expense.

Sustain a Culture of Continuous Improvement

By now, it should be clear that running L&D like a business is not a one-time pivot. It requires ongoing discipline and intentionality, not just in how programs are designed and delivered, but in how the function evolves over time.

A strategic L&D function stays in sync with the business by staying in motion. Priorities shift. Capabilities mature. Operating models evolve. To remain relevant and valuable, L&D leaders must create the conditions for continuous improvement—starting with their teams.

Listen to the Business

As I outlined in chapter 10, operationalizing your feedback loops is one of the simplest and most powerful ways to stay aligned with business priorities. This goes far beyond postcourse surveys. It includes formal and informal touchpoints that help you stay connected to what's working, what's shifting, and what the business is worried about next. That might look like quarterly reviews with business sponsors, usage analytics from your learning tech stack, or structured retrospectives after high-stakes programs. It could also mean identifying signals in workforce data, attrition rates, performance gaps, and hiring delays that indicate an opportunity to add value.

Listening signals accountability. It shows stakeholders that L&D is not just pushing content but actively measuring whether its work is solving the right problems. And over time, it builds the kind of trust that earns repeat engagement and earlier involvement in strategic conversations.

Develop Your Team's Capabilities

If your organization's L&D function is going to increase its value, your team must grow, too. We've talked about the skills your L&D team needs to operate more like a business, such as data literacy, agile workflows, governance, stakeholder engagement, and portfolio management. These are core competencies that elevate the entire function.

Investing in your team's development reinforces the operating model you've been building, chapter by chapter. It ensures that your team can interpret data with confidence, respond with agility, and communicate in the language of the business. It also signals that the L&D team holds itself to the same standards of growth and accountability that it promotes across the organization.

Just as important, a well-developed and skilled L&D team sets the tone for the culture you are helping to shape. If your team is not experimenting, upskilling, or evolving its ways of working, it is hard to model those expectations for others. A learning culture cannot be something L&D delivers; it has to be something L&D lives.

Recognize Continuous Improvement as a Strategic Discipline

Continuous improvement means staying open to change while staying focused on value. It means running the L&D function with the same clarity and cadences other business units apply to their operations.

High-performing L&D teams apply retrospectives to how they take requests, prioritize them, develop solutions, and measure their effectiveness. They examine whether systems are enabling scaling or creating friction. They test and refine their processes regularly as standard practice.

A continuous improvement mindset turns your capability into maturity. It creates room for innovation because it eliminates waste. It creates better stakeholder partnerships because it builds credibility. And it allows your L&D function to keep pace with the business, not just react to it.

You do not need a full transformation to begin. However, you do need the willingness to step back, ask sharper questions, and adapt based on what you learn. That is what it means to operate with continuous improvement, and that is what will keep L&D positioned as a strategic function in the business for the long term.

Serve the Business, Support Employees

If there is one mindset shift to carry forward from this book, it is this: L&D does not exist to deliver content. It exists to solve business problems through learning. That is the throughline of every framework, every operating principle, and every example you have seen in these pages. The business is your customer; the employee is your consumer. Both matter, but the customer sets your direction.

We've explored how this distinction shapes your team's priorities, resource allocation processes, measurement strategies, and design decisions. It affects how you manage your learning portfolio. It influences how you select technologies, how you report results, and how you say no. This clarity is the backbone of a strategic L&D function.

When business goals shape your road map, your metrics reflect business outcomes, and your partnerships are grounded in trust and accountability, you are no longer chasing relevance; you are driving it. And when that happens, something powerful shifts. The business begins seeing L&D not as a service but as a partner. Employees begin engaging not just because learning is required but because it is useful. And your team begins operating in pursuit of outcomes rather than responding to demands.

None of this requires more headcount. It only requires more clarity.

Reframe Your Approach

As you reengage with your organization, use some of the questions you've seen throughout this book to reframe how you approach each new project:
- Who is the customer for this request?
- What business problems are you solving?
- How will you know your solution made a difference?

These are operational questions, not hypothetical ones. When these questions shape your intake process, your conversations, and your priorities, they build trust, create consistency, and position L&D as an effective, business-aligned team.

Running L&D like a business means running your team with more focus, not more complexity. It means going forward with greater purpose, not more activity. You have the tools. You have the mindset. Now, you get to decide how you will lead.

The Final Bottom Line

I hope you've learned that L&D doesn't need to wait for permission to operate differently. You already have what it takes to lead with more clarity, deliver with more purpose, and create value that actually matters to the business.

The mindset shift from content provider to business partner unlocks everything. With that shift in place, your decisions change, and so do your conversations, your priorities, and the way your team shows up. You stop measuring effort and start measuring value. You stop reacting to requests and start driving outcomes. You stop fighting for relevance and start owning your seat at the table.

This is not a theoretical model; it is a practical way forward. Whether you lead a global L&D function or a team of one, the same principles apply. You now have the tools to:

- Align your work with the business strategy, not just employee needs.
- Prioritize based on value, not volume.
- Operate with repeatable processes that scale.
- Leverage technology with purpose, not pressure.
- Measure results in business terms, not just learning activity.
- Evolve your team to match the ambition of your mandate.

Take Action

Start with one decision. One request. One conversation.

Ask sharper questions. Redefine what success looks like. Push back when needed, with purpose and clarity. Run a retrospective. Realign your portfolio. Share your wins in business language. None of this requires permission. It requires leadership, and you already have that within reach.

Running L&D like a business is about building something that works—that earns trust, delivers results, and scales your results over time. You are not just supporting the business. You are shaping how it performs and grows.

Now, go lead like it.

References

ATD (Association for Talent Development). 2015. "Needs Analysis and Assessment." *TD at Work*, October. ATD Press.

ATD. 2024. *Learning Technology Ecosystems: The Tools, Strategies, and Skills Needed for Success*. ATD Press.

BCG Henderson Institute. 2020. "Three Steps to Turn Your Company Into a Learning Powerhouse." BCG Global, November 17. bcg.com/publications/2020/turn-your-company-into-a-learning-powerhouse.

Ben-Hur, S., B. Jaworski, and D. Gray. 2015. "Aligning Corporate Learning With Strategy." *MITSloan Management Review* 57(1).

Bersin, J. 2022. "The Definitive Guide to Learning: Growth in the Flow of Work." The Josh Bersin Company, October 12. joshbersin.com/definitive-guide-to-learning.

Bersin, J., and M. Zao-Sanders. 2019. "Making Learning a Part of Everyday Work." *Harvard Business Review*, February 19. hbr.org/2019/02/making-learning-a-part-of-everyday-work.

Biech, E., ed. 2022. *ATD's Handbook for Training and Talent Development*. ATD Press.

Bingham, T. 2007. "Communicating the Value of Learning." *TD*, April 7. td.org/content/td-magazine/communicating-the-value-of-learning.

Boulter, M. 2021. "Malcolm Knowles' Five Assumptions of Learners and Why They Matter." Maestro. maestrolearning.com/blogs/malcolm-knowles-five-assumptions-of-learners-and-why-they-matter.

Brassey, J., L. Christensen, and N. van Dam. 2019. "Essential Components of a Learning and Development Strategy." McKinsey, February 13. mckinsey.com/capabilities/people-and-organizational-performance/our-insights/the-essential-components-of-a-successful-l-and-d-strategy.

Burns, S. 2019. "Do You Have Customers or Consumers?" *Forbes*, July 30. forbes.com/sites/stephanieburns/2019/07/30/do-you-have-customers-or-consumers.

Cantu, T. 2024. "The Blueprint for Developing a Learning Operations Blueprint." *TD*, April. td.org/content/td-magazine/the-blueprint-for-developing-a-learning-operations-blueprint.

Chopra-McGown, A. 2025. "Connect Your Learning Programs to Your Company's Strategy." *Harvard Business Review*, January 10. hbr.org/2025/01/connect-your-learning-programs-to-your-companys-strategy.

Chutivongse, N., and N. Gerdsri. 2020. "Creating an Innovative Organization." *Journal of Modelling in Management* 15(1): 50–88. doi.org/10.1108/jm2-05-2018-0067.

Cloke, H. 2024. "Learning in the Flow of Work: The Ultimate Guide." Growth Engineering, February 21. growthengineering.co.uk/learning-in-the-flow-of-work.

Collings, D., and J. McMackin. 2021. "The Practices That Set Learning Organizations Apart." *MIT Sloan Management Review* (62)4. sloanreview.mit.edu/article/the-practices-that-set-learning-organizations-apart.

Cook, D.A., and A.R. Artino. 2016. "Motivation to Learn: An Overview of Contemporary Theories." *Medical Education* 50(10): 997–1014. doi.org/10.1111/medu.13074.

D'Silva, L. 2024. "L&D Strategy: Understanding Employees' Needs and Aligning With Their Interest are Crucial." HR.com, February 6. hr.com/en/magazines/all_articles/l-d-strategy-understanding-employees-needs-and-ali_lsabax0x.html.

Defelice, R. 2021. "How Long Does It Take to Develop Training? New Question, New Answers." ATD Blog, January 13. td.org/insights/how-long-does-it-take-to-develop-training-new-question-new-answers.

Garavan, T., C. Hogan, A. Cahir-O'Donnell, and C. Gubbins. 2020. *Learning and Development in Organisations: Strategy, Evidence and Practice*. Oak Tree Press.

Godin, S. 2024. "How to Avoid Strategy Myopia." *Harvard Business Review*, October 22. hbr.org/2024/10/how-to-avoid-strategy-myopia.

Gonsalves-Fersch, S. 2024. "The Future of Corporate Learning and Development in Technology Accelerating Organisations." Middlesex University Research Repository, March 21. repository.mdx.ac.uk/item/112z8q.

Imai, M. 2012. *Gemba Kaizen: A Commonsense Approach to a Continuous Improvement Strategy*, 2nd edition. McGraw Hill.

Josh Bersin Academy. 2020. *Adaptive Learning Organization.* Josh Bersin Academy, November 6. joshbersin.com/wp-content/uploads/2020/11/ALO-Research-Report-11032020-v2.pdf.

Kirkpatrick, J.D., and W.K. Kirkpatrick. 2016. *Kirkpatrick's Four Levels of Training Evaluation.* ATD Press.

Kirsi, E. 2010. "Strategic Roadmap Creating Process." Laurea University of Applied Sciences, May. theseus.fi/bitstream/10024/15751/1/Kirsi_Eetu.pdf.

Knowles, M.S., E.F. Holton, and R.A. Swanson. 2015. *The Adult Learner: The Definitive Classic in Adult Education and Human Resource Development*, 8th edition. Routledge.

Lake, K. 2024. "L&D Trends in 2024: Shaping Future Workforces and Optimizing Learning as a Business." Training Industry, February 15. trainingindustry.com/articles/strategy-alignment-and-planning/ld-trends-in-2024-shaping-future-workforces-and-optimizing-learning-as-a-business-seo-ei.

LearningTechnologies. 2024. "L&D in 2024: What the AI Noise Tells Us About L&D." YouTube video, April 4. youtube.com/watch?v=hzluFeSfJr4.

Lin, B., Z.-H. Lee, and R. Peterson. 2006. "An Analytical Approach for Making Management Decisions Concerning Corporate Restructuring." *Managerial and Decision Economics* 27(8): 655–666. doi.org/10.1002/mde.1302.

LinkedIn. 2024. *Workplace Learning Report 2024.* LinkedIn Learning. learning.linkedin.com/content/dam/me/business/en-us/amp/learning-solutions/images/wlr-2024/LinkedIn-Workplace-Learning-Report-2024.pdf.

Lockstone, T. 2023. "Does Your Corporate L&D Plan Align With Your Business Strategy?" HR Future, February 27. hrfuture.net/talent-management/training-development/does-your-corporate-ld-plan-align-with-your-business-strategy.

Macon, D. 2021. "Successfully Build an Essential L&D Department." *TD at Work*, August. ATD Press.

Merriam, S.B., and L. Baumgartner, L. 2020. *Learning in Adulthood: A Comprehensive Guide*, 4th edition. Jossey-Bass.

Moore, C. n.d. "Action Mapping: A Visual Approach to Training Design." Action@work Blog. blog.cathy-moore.com/action-mapping-a-visual-approach-to-training-design.

Nathan, O. 2023. "The 'Secret Sauce' in Your Strategy for Success—Aligning Corporate, Talent and L&D Strategies." LinkedIn Pulse, July 5. linkedin.com/pulse/secret-sauce-your-strategy-success-aligning-corporate.

Nuriddin, H. 2024. *Quality Management in Learning and Development*. ATD Press.

Phaal, R., C. Farrukh, and D. Probert. 2005. "Developing a Technology Roadmapping System." Presented at *Technology Management: A Unifying Discipline for Melting the Boundaries Technology Management*, Portland, OR, July 31. doi.org/10.1109/PICMET.2005.1509680.

Phillips, J.J., and P.P. Phillips. 2019. *ROI Basics*, 2nd edition. ATD Press.

Porter, M. 1996. "What Is Strategy?" *Harvard Business Review*, November–December. hbr.org/1996/11/what-is-strategy.

Project Management Institute (PMI). 2013. *The Standard for Portfolio Management*, 3rd edition. Project Management Institute.

Rajeh, M.F. 2020. *5 Whys: One of the Simplest and Fastest Problem-Solving Ways to Get to the Root of the Problem*. Independently Published.

RedThread Research. 2021. "Learning Content—Embracing the Chaos." RedThread Research. members.redthreadresearch.com/posts/learning-skills-final-report-learning-content-embracing-the-chaos-53123538.

RedThread Research. 2023. "The Learning Technology Market: Growth, Optimism, and Innovation." RedThread Research. members.redthreadresearch.com/posts/learning-skills-final-report-the-learning-technology-market-growth-optimism-and-innovation-53104600.

RedThread Research. 2024. "Hope Isn't a Plan: Building a Progressive L&D Strategy." RedThread Research. members.redthreadresearch.com/posts/learning-skills-final-report-hope-isnt-a-plan-building-a-progressive-ld-strategy.

Richards, D. 2023. "Preparing Your Organization for New Technologies." *TD at Work*, September. ATD Press.

Sanders, L., and K. Keating. 2024. "Charting the Course for 2024: Embracing L&D Evolution in the Post-Pandemic Era." Training Industry, January 15. trainingindustry.com/articles/strategy-alignment-and-planning/charting-the-course-for-2024-embracing-ld-evolution-in-the-post-pandemic-era-cptm.

Schipperheijn, K. 2022. *Learning Ecosystems: Creating Innovative, Lean and Tech-Driven Learning Strategies*. Kogan Page.

Senge, P.M. 2006. *The Fifth Discipline: The Art and Practice of the Learning Organization*. Doubleday.

Serrat, O. 2017. *Knowledge Solutions: Tools, Methods, and Approaches to Drive Organizational Performance*. Springer.

SHRM (Society for Human Resource Management). 2024. "Aligning Workforce Strategies With Business Objectives." SHRM, April 2. shrm.org/topics-tools/tools/toolkits/aligning-workforce-strategies-business-objectives.

Sidhu, R. 2020. "The OI, IO & IA of an L&D Strategy: How Can L&D Function Stay Ahead of the Game." HR.com, November 5. hr.com/en/magazines/training_development_excellence_essentials/november_2020_training_development/the-oi-io-ia-of-an-l-d-strategy_kh4lk93y.html.

Slaughter, M. 2024. "Want Funding? Align Learning Initiatives With Business Needs." Reworked, March 6. reworked.co/learning-development/want-funding-align-learning-initiatives-with-business-needs.

Spoerl, C. 2016. "Handling Resistance to Technological Change in the Workforce." Unicorn HRO, June 7.

Tulsiani, R. 2024. "AI-Powered Personalized Learning: Transforming the Future of Employee Development." eLearning Industry, November 8. elearningindustry.com/ai-powered-personalized-learning-transforming-the-future-of-employee-development.

Udell, C., and G. Woodill. 2019. *Shock of the New: The Challenge and Promise of Emerging Technology*. ATD Press.

Van Vulpen, E. 2023. *Learning and Development: A Comprehensive Guide*. AIHR (Academy to Innovate HR), December 15. aihr.com/blog/learning-and-development.

Vance, D., and P. Parskey. 2020. *Measurement Demystified: Creating Your L&D Measurement, Analytics, and Reporting Strategy*. ATD Press.

Watershed. 2024. *Measuring the Business Impact of Learning 2024*. Watershed. watershedlrs.com/resources/research/measuring-the-business-impact-of-learning-2024-report.

Watkins, K.E., and V.J. Marsick. 2023. "Rethinking Workplace Learning and Development Catalyzed by Complexity." *Human Resource Development Review* 22(3): 333–344. doi.org/10.1177/15344843231186629.

Zukof, K. 2021. *The Hard and Soft Sides of Change Management: Tools for Managing Process and People*. ATD Press.

Index

A

Action Mapping visual design approach, 11
adaptive learning paths, 128–131, 144, 146, 161. *See also* strategic agility
adoption risks, 86, 109
agility. *See* strategic agility; workforce agility
analytical thinking, 221–222
artificial intelligence (AI), 15
　and adaptive learning, 129
　AI-enabled personalization, 97
　chatbots, 97
　and content development, 160
　ethical questions, 113–114
　workforce analytics, 155
assessment. *See also* data, use of
　audits of learning portfolios, 88–89
　business intelligence systems, 194–195
　and business success, 193–194
　change readiness, 174–176
　data-informed tracking, 192
　of impact, 239–240
　impact of learning technologies, 114
　learning dashboards, 98
　learning evaluation models, innovative, 192–193
　measurement of learning outcomes, 43–44, 142
　measurement of resource allocation, 75
　metrics, 168–169
　needs assessment for resource allocation, 72–73
　of technological innovation, 109

audits
　of learning portfolios, 88–89
　process audits, 63–64
augmented reality, 97
awareness
　awareness materials, 166
　and consumer adoption, 164
　measurement of, 168
　operational, 222

B

behavioral norms, 216, 226
budget limitations, 72
business alignment, 3, 86
business-critical training, 40, 91, 107
business "language," 237
business models for L&D
　action steps, 23–24
　balancing needs of leaders vs. employees, 9
　components of, 2–4
　customers vs. consumers, 6–9
　Learning Operations Blueprint, 16–22
　need for, 1–2
　reaction vs. strategy, 4–5
　reactivity vs. proactivity, 10–16
　value of, 22–23
buy-in. *See also* engagement
　for change management, 172
　executive, 49, 185
　for SOPs, 64

C

capability development, 91
capacity planning models, 73

case studies
    construction firm and knowledge retention, 154–155
    KPI approaches, 155–156
    pharmaceuticals manufacture and skills gaps, 155
    VR training for experiential learning, 134
centralized resource management systems, 73
certification programs, 159
change management, 20–21
    action steps, 188
    alignment and engagement, 184–186
    business rigor and discipline, 177
    change champions, 172
    change readiness assessment, 174–176
    enterprise-wide change, 178–182
    resistance, overcoming, 172–174
    scalability, 182–184
    value of, 187
chatbots, 97
Checklist: Is Your L&D Team Listening?, 229
co-creation models, 172
collaboration
    and culture of continuous learning, 173
    frameworks for, 38–39
    power of, 200
    using learning strategy to elevate, 36–38
committees, governance, 59–60
communication. *See also* listening
    business "language," 237
    for consumer adoption, 164–169
    gaps and disconnects, 29–30
    poor, 61
compliance incident scenarios, 131
consulting mindsets, 10–11
consumers
    communication to ensure adoption, 164–169
    consumer-driven priorities, 42
    consumer experience, 227
    customers vs. consumers, 8–9
    definitions, 6
    employees as L & D consumers, 7
    and learning methodologies, 136
content
    development bottlenecks, solutions for, 159–160
    relevance risks, 86
    repurposing, 73

continuous improvement, culture of, 63–64, 173–174, 240–242
    action steps, 227–228
    curiosity, growth, and development, 214–218
    innovation and customer needs, 224–226
    leadership accountability and governance, 218–224
    learning culture, building, 211–214
    Learning Culture Operational Model, 215–218
    value of, 226–227
cost and resource risks, 86
cost-benefit analysis, 93–94
cost reduction, 48
cross-functional teams, 69, 113, 156, 223
cultural analytics, 217
culture
    based on governance, 221–223
    culture change initiatives, 132
curiosity, 214–218
customers
    business as L & D customer, 6–7
    customer-centric learning, 42
    customer-centric processes, 58
    customer experience, 4
    customer needs and innovation, 224–226
    customers vs. consumers, 8–9
    customer value, 3–4, 227
    definitions, 5
    and learning methodologies, 136
    proving value to, 199–200
    shifting customer priorities, 161–163

D

data, use of
    data fluency, 221–222
    data-informed technology strategy, 45–46
    data-informed tracking and assessment, 192
    to identify learning gaps, 31–32
    learning portfolios, assessment of, 92–94
    metrics, 93
    real-time data and decision making, 154–156
    for resource allocation, 72
    use of for learning adjustments, 163

252 Index

decision-making
    business-first decision matrix, 139–140
    models of, 117–118
    and real-time data, 154–156
    risk assessment matrix, 140–141
    siloed processes, danger of, 143
digital workplace tools, 48, 160
disconnection
    symptoms of, 29, 46
    of technological innovation, 109

E

Employee Learning Experience Scorecard, 25
employees
    employee engagement, 94–95, 117
    Employee Learning Experience Scorecard, 25
    employee turnover, 90–91
    and ownership of learning portfolios, 85
    support of, 242–243
enablement, systems of, 216–217
engagement, 169
    with business strategy, 138–139
    with change management, 184–186
    employee, 94–95, 117
    leadership and managers, 95
evaluation. *See* assessment
executives, 35. *See also* stakeholders
    executive buy-in, 49–50
    as tech role models, 108–109
experiential learning, 128, 133–136, 145, 146
extended reality (XR), 112

F

finance leaders, 36. *See also* stakeholders
financial considerations
    budget limitations, 72
    cost and resource risks, 86
    cost-benefit analysis, 93–94
    cost reduction, 48
    iterative funding, 108
Five Whys technique, 11, 32

G

go-to-market (GTM) strategy, 164–168
governance models, 58–61, 98
    governance committees, 59–60
    and learning technologies, 110
    for organizational growth, 60–61

growth pathways, 216–217

H

HR (human resources). *See also* stakeholders
    HR partners, 35–36
    and learning portfolios, 84–85

I

impact reporting, 201–205
    design principles of, 201–202
    Learning Impact Reporting Blueprint, 202–203
individualized learning. *See* personalized learning
industry trends, 100
innovation
    and customer needs, 224–226
    investment in, 108
    with learning technologies, 106–111
intake forms, 64–68
iteration, effective, 225
iterative funding, 108
iterative learning sprints, 162

J

just-in-time learning, 160–161

K

Kirkpatrick Model, 192–193

L

lagging indicators, 192
leaders
    leadership development, 48
    and learning technologies, 113
    role of with technological innovation, 107–109
Leadership and Organizational Support Scorecard, 26
leading indicators, 192
learnability as core value, 153
learning and development (L&D)
    action steps, 206–207, 243–244
    business audience for, 234
    future directions, 231–244
    impact of, 191–207
    prioritization, right to, 234–235
    purpose, use of, 238–240
    strategic functions of, 232–235
Learning Culture Operational Model, 215–218

learning cultures, 95
learning dashboards, 98
learning experience platforms (LXPs), 19
learning fatigue risks, 86
learning gaps, 30–32. *See also* needs analysis
    contrasted with process problems, 32
    prioritization of, 33–34
Learning Impact Maturity Model, 195–198
Learning Impact Reporting at a Glance, 208
Learning Impact Reporting Blueprint, 203–204
    outline, 209
    pitfalls to avoid, 204–205
learning initiatives as business priority, 165–166
learning methodologies
    action steps, 147
    adaptive learning, 128–131
    and business priorities, alignment with, 128–136
    experiential learning, 128, 133–136
    portfolio-based learning strategies, 144–146
    selection of, 136–144
    social learning, 128, 131–133
    value of, 146–147
learning needs, business-focused
    action steps, 51–52
    learning plans, 39–43
    needs analysis, 30–34
    organizational alignment, 43–50
    stakeholder collaboration, 35–39
    value of, 51
learning objectives, 91
learning operations
    action steps, 76
    building the framework, 56–61
    pitfalls, avoiding, 61–62
    resource management and allocation, 71–75
    scalable processes, 62–71
    structured governance models, 58–61
    value of, 76
Learning Operations Blueprints, 16–22, 182–183
    change management, 20–21
    implementation, 19–20
    learning plans, 39–42
    teams, structuring of, 18
    technology, 19
    value of, 21–22
Learning Operations Decision-Making Model, 117–118
learning platforms, 97, 110
learning portfolios
    action steps, 101
    audits of, 88–89
    data, use of, 92–94
    employee engagement, 94–95
    future-proofing, 99–100
    learning objectives and strategic goals, 91
    management principles, 84–87
    return on investment (ROI), 90–91
    scalability and adaptation, 96–100
    strategic learning priorities, 91–92
    value of, 100–101
learning road maps, 39–42
    agility and adaptability, 41
    governance and accountability, 40–41
    phases of, 40
    prioritization, 41–42
learning strategy, alignment with business, 162–163
learning technologies, 105–122
    action steps, 122
    case study, 118–120
    and innovation, 106–111
    Pilot Program Framework for Learning Technology Adoption, 123–125
    pilot programs, 114–115
    problems, prioritization of, 116–120
    upskilling and experimentation, 112–116
    value of, 121
lifelong learning, 100
listening, 220–221. *See also* communication
    to the business, 240–241
    Checklist for L&D Team tool, 229

M

management, 35–36. *See also* stakeholders
market expansion, 48
metrics. *See* data, use of
microlearning modules, 158–159
minimal viable product (MVP) thinking, 222
modular learning design, 96
Moore, Cathy, 11

N

natural language processing (NLP), 161
needs analysis, 30–34
needs assessment, continuous, 96–97

O

objectives and key results (OKRs), 162
operational awareness, 222
operational efficiency, 3, 227
operations leaders, 36. *See also* stakeholders
organizational structures
    alignment with learning needs, 43–50
    and buy-in for standard operating procedures (SOPs), 64
    embedding L & D in, 14–15
    Leadership and Organizational Support Scorecard, 26

P

peer learning, 214
peer sharing, 216–217
performance-based learning frameworks, 92
personalized learning, 9, 137
    AI-enabled, 97, 129
Phased Approach to Scaling L & D Processes, 80–81
Phillips, Jack, 192
Phillips ROI Methodology, 192–193
Pilot Program Framework for Learning Technology Adoption, 123–125
pilot programs, 119
    for learning technology, 114–115
portfolio-based learning strategies, 144–146
prioritization
    conflicts, navigating, 70
    criteria for, 68
    right to, 234–235
    scoring systems, 69
    short-term vs. long-term, 70–71
    stakeholder input, 69
proactive approaches, 10
    to agility, 153
process audits, 63–64
productivity metrics, 94
product road maps, 162

Q

Quick-Start Learning Operations Blueprint Checklist, 27

R

reactive approaches, 10
    symptoms of, 29
RedThread Research, 231
resource management and allocation, 71–75
return on investment (ROI), 90–91, 191–193
revenue growth, 48
rigor, business, 177, 182, 187
risk assessment matrix, 140–141
risk management, 85–87
rolling learning backlog, 153
root cause analysis, 32

S

Sample Service Level Agreement, 77–79
scalability
    barriers to, 99
    of change management, 182–184
    intake forms, 64–68
    of learning portfolios, 96–100
    learning technologies for, 110–111
    Phased Approach to Scaling L&D, 80–81
    for pilot programs, 115
    prioritization, 68–71
    scalability risks, 86
    scalable processes, 62–71
    standard operating procedures (SOPs), 62–64
scenario-based training, 158–159
scenario planning, 74
self-service knowledge access, 158
service-level agreements (SLAs), 18
    and customer-centric processes, 58
    Sample Service Level Agreement, 77–79
skills-based approaches, 16, 44–45
    skills taxonomies, 100
skills gaps, 30–32. *See* learning gaps; needs analysis
    contrasted with process problems, 32
social learning, 128, 131–133, 145, 146
staffing models, 74
stakeholders
    business case for, 143–144
    collaboration, 35–39, 200
    input in prioritization process, 69
    relationships with, 12–13
    stakeholder management, 222

standard operating procedures (SOPs), 62–64
strategic agility
    action steps, 170
    agile design, 222
    communication for consumer adoption, 164–169
    in competitive markets, 223
    content development bottlenecks, 159–160
    cross-functional teams, 156
    just-in-time learning, 160–161
    of learning portfolios, 96–97
    model of, 152–153
    proactive agility, 153
    rapid deployment of training, 157–161
    real-time data, 154–156
    shifting customer priorities, 161–164
    shifts in business environment, 151–157
    tiered learning response model, 157–159
    value of, 170
strategic workforce enablement, 91
subject matter experts (SMEs), 36
    and content development, 160
    and rapid insight, 156, 158
systems of enablement, 216–217
systems thinking, 213, 222

T

Talent Development Capability Model, 222–223
talent management partners, 35–36. *See also* stakeholders
talent strategy and retention, 44, 48
teams
    structuring of, 18
    team capacity, 72
technology, 97. *See also* learning technologies
    efficiency, leveraging for, 74
    integrated with operations, 239
    role models, 108–109
    in standard operating procedures (SOPs), 64
    strategic use of, 57–58
    streamlining resource allocation, 72
    to support learning strategies, 19
    tech-enabled just-in-time learning, 160–161
    tech strategy, 45–46
    as tool, 238–239
tiered learning response model, 157–159
time constraints, 72
tools
    Checklist for Listening, 229
    Employee Learning Experience Scorecard, 25
    Leadership and Organizational Support Scorecard, 26
    Learning Impact Reporting, 208
    Learning Impact Reporting Blueprint Outline, 209
    Phased Approach to Scaling, 80–81
    Pilot Program Framework for Learning Technology Adoption, 123–125
    Quick-Start Learning Operations Blueprint Checklist, 27
    Sample Service Level Agreement, 77–79
transparency, 12, 226, 238

U

upskilling, 112–116, 222

V

value, drivers of, 47–48
virtual reality (VR), 97
    case study, 134

W

Web Content Accessibility Guidelines (WCAG), 130
workforce agility, 48

About the Author

Tracie Cantu is a recognized expert in learning operations and technology, with more than two decades of experience leading and transforming enterprise L&D functions at organizations like Meta, Atlassian, and Whole Foods Market. As chief learning strategist at Your CLO, she partners with companies to modernize learning operations, optimize technology ecosystems, and implement scalable processes that drive measurable business impact. Her expertise spans learning technology strategy, process automation, and ecosystem governance, enabling organizations to enhance efficiency without increasing headcount.

Tracie has a proven track record of delivering results, from achieving multimillion-dollar cost savings through technology consolidation to accelerating content development and improving learning experience design. She is a sought-after advisor and speaker, who regularly presents at industry conferences on running L&D like a business, learning operations, and learning technology. Passionate about operational excellence, she helps organizations rethink their approach to learning, ensuring L&D is not thought of as a support function but instead seen as a strategic enabler of business success.